1 e4 c6 2 d4 d5 3 e5

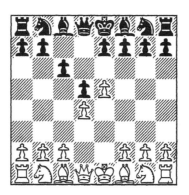

To Jay.

The Caro-Kann Advance

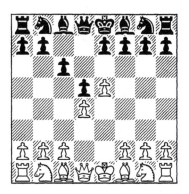

CHESS PRESS OPENING GUIDES

Other titles in this series include:

Chess Press Opening Guides

The Caro-Kann Advance

Byron Jacobs

The Chess Press, Brighton

First published in 1997 by Chess Press, a division of First Rank Publishing

Copyright © 1997 Byron Jacobs

Reprinted 2003

British Library Cataloguing-in-Publication Data
A catalogue record for this book is available from the British Library.

ISBN 1 901259 05 6

Distributed in North America by The Globe Pequot Press, P.O Box 480, 246 Goose Lane, Guilford, CT 06437-0480.

All other sales enquiries should be directed to Everyman Chess, Gloucester Publishers plc, Gloucester Mansions, 140A Shaftesbury Avenue, London WC2H 8HD
tel: 020 7539 7600 fax: 020 7379 4060
email: info@everymanchess.com
website: www.everymanchess.com

The author would like to thank Jon Tait for his substantial analytical contributions to Chapters 5-9 and John Elburg for database material

Cover design by Ray Shell Design.
Production by Navigator Guides.

Printed by Lightning Source

CONTENTS

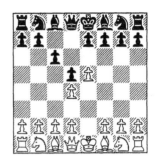

1 e4 c6 2 d4 d5 3 e5

BIBLIOGRAPHY

Books

Encyclopaedia of Chess Openings vol.B, (Sahovski Informator, 1984)

B12 Caro-Kann, Seirawan (Chess Informant, 1993)

Beating the Caro-Kann, Kotronias (Batsford, 1994)

New Ideas in the Caro-Kann Defence, Speelman (Batsford, 1992)

The Caro-Kann in Black and White, Karpov and Beliavsky (R & D Publishing, 1994)

Caro-Kann Defence Advance Variation, Tirabassi (s1 Editrice, 1994)

Caro-Kann Vorstossvariante Van der Wiel System, Siebenhaar (R. Dreier, 1992)

Trends in the Caro-Kann Advance, Jacobs (Tournament Chess, 1991)

Trends in the Caro-Kann Advance, Vol 2, Jacobs (Tournament Chess, 1994)

Periodicals

Informator

ChessBase MegaBase CD-ROM

New In Chess Yearbook

British Chess Magazine

Chess Monthly

INTRODUCTION

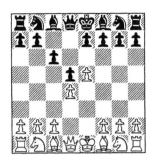

1 e4 c6 2 d4 d5 3 e5

We are all familiar with the kind of trick psychologists use to discern who are the optimists among us and who are the pessimists. The basic version goes something like this. Present your subject with half a pint of beer in a pint glass and the optimists will joyfully tell you it is half full. The pessimists, on the other hand, will ponder it mournfully and lament that it is half empty.

The position after 1 e4 c6 2 d4 d5 3 e5 ♗f5 in the Caro-Kann represents a similar test for chessplayers.

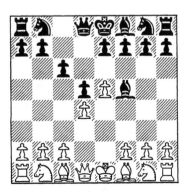

A pessimist will consider White's position and think. 'This is no good. Three moves gone and I haven't yet developed a piece. I have committed myself in the centre and allowed Black to play a French Defence where he has developed his bishop outside the pawn chain. I feel all exposed and vulnerable. This is not for me. I'm going to take up the Réti Opening.'

The optimist, however, will have a different perspective and think: 'This is wonderful. I have gained space, and now Black will have to waste further time to attack my centre with ...c6-c5. Not only that, but my opponent has offered up his bishop as a target for my kingside pawn advances. Now the only problem is whether to rush forward immediately on the kingside, or perhaps develop a piece or two first.'

Of course, the majority of chessplayers will take a view somewhere between these two extremes. Nevertheless, I would suggest that the Advance variation is a line best played with a positive frame of mind. A player who ventures 3 e5 and then tries to adopt a defensive posture is unlikely to be successful.

The basic concept of the Advance variation of the Caro-Kann Defence is a simple one. White gains space and has the added bonus of preventing the immediate development of the black king's knight on its most natural square, f6. Of course, there are also drawbacks. White is setting up an Advance French (1 e4 e6 2 d4 d5 3 e5) pawn structure where Black has the opportunity to develop his normally troublesome light-squared bishop outside the pawn chain (i.e. ...♗f5 or ...♗g4 and only then ...e7-e6).

It is for this reason that the Advance Caro-Kann was, for several decades, an infrequent guest in grandmaster tournaments. Over the years, the world's strongest players considered the position after 1 e4 c6 2 d4 d5 3 e5 ♗f5 and evidently did not like what they saw. Comparing the position to the Advance French, White will experience a slight plus in time (Black will almost certainly play ...c6-c5), but they have no doubt felt that this modest tempo gain is outweighed by the strategic pluses for Black that we have already discussed.

The following well-known game was probably critical in reinforcing this evaluation of 3 e5:

Nimzowitsch-Capablanca
New York 1927

1 e4 c6 2 d4 d5 3 e5 ♗f5 4 ♗d3 ♗xd3 5 ♕xd3 e6 6 ♘c3 ♕b6 7 ♘ge2 c5 8 dxc5 ♗xc5 9 0-0 ♘e7 10 ♘a4 ♕c6 11 ♘xc5 ♕xc5 12 ♗e3 ♕c7 13 f4 ♘f5 14 c3 ♘c6 15 ♖ad1 g6 16 g4 ♘xe3 17 ♕xe3 h5 18 g5 0-0 19 ♘d4 ♕b6

White's aggressive intentions have been stymied and now Capablanca skilfully demonstrates the strategic advantages of the black position.
20 ♖f2 ♖fc8 21 a3 ♖c7 22 ♖d3 ♘a5 23 ♖e2 ♖e8 24 ♔g2 ♘c6 25 ♖ed2 ♖ec8 26 ♖e2 ♘e7 27 ♖ed2 ♖c4 28 ♕h3 ♔g7 29 ♖f2 a5 30 ♖e2 ♘f5 31 ♘xf5+ gxf5 32 ♕f3 ♔g6 33 ♖ed2 ♖e4 34 ♖d4 ♖c4 35 ♕f2 ♕b5 36 ♔g3 ♖cxd4 37 cxd4 ♕c4 38 ♔g2 b5 39 ♔g1 b4 40 axb4 axb4 41 ♔g2 ♕c1 42 ♔g3 ♕h1 43 ♖d3 ♖e1 44 ♖f3 ♖d1 45 b3

45...♖c1

A wonderful conclusion, placing White in zugzwang.

46 ♖e3 ♖f1 0-1

For many years it was felt that the only way to press realistically for an advantage was to use the black light-squared bishop as target to mount an extremely swift kingside attack. Therefore variations such as 4 ♘c3 e6 5 g4 ♗g6 6 ♘ge2 c5 7 h4 (conventional opening theory tells us to meet a wing attack with a counter-thrust in the centre; here White meets a thrust in the centre by continuing his attack on the wing) 7...cxd4 8 ♘xd4 h5

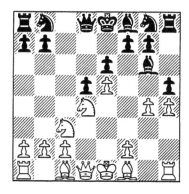

were regarded as the main lines. Such variations were frequently seen in club games where the priority is often to get the pieces out and initiate a tactical fight as soon as possible. However, at the rarified level of grandmaster chess, where slight inaccuracies are ruthlessly exploited, White's strategy was viewed with scepticism. The only top-class player who regularly gave the white strategy an outing was Jan Timman, a player notorious for his occasional lack of objectivity due to over-optimism!

Another player with a generally optimistic frame of mind was the great Latvian genius Mikhail Tal. However, his experiments with the Advance in his 1961 World Championship match against the great strategist Botvinnik were generally unsuccessful, the following being a typical example.

Tal-Botvinnik
World Championship, Moscow 1961

1 e4 c6 2 d4 d5 3 e5 ♗f5 4 h4 h6 5 g4 ♗d7 6 c3 c5 7 ♗g2 e6 8 ♘e2 ♗b5 9 ♘a3 ♗xe2 10 ♕xe2 cxd4 11 cxd4 ♗xa3 12 bxa3 ♘c6 13 ♗e3 ♕a5+ 14 ♔f1 ♘ge7 15 ♖b1 ♖b8 16 ♗h3 ♕a4 17 ♖d1 ♕xa3

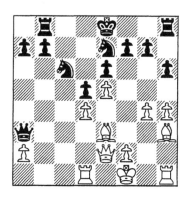

White's attempts to blast Black off the board have backfired badly.

18 ♔g2 ♕a6 19 ♕xa6 bxa6 20 h5 ♔d7 21 ♖b1 ♖b6 22 ♔g3 ♘a5 23 ♖xb6 axb6 24 f4 ♘c4 25 ♗c1 ♘c6 26 ♖d1 ♘b4 27 a3 ♘a2 28 f5 ♘xc1 29 ♖xc1 b5 30 ♖a1 ♔e7 31 ♔f4 ♖c8 32 g5 hxg5+ 33 ♔xg5 exf5 34 ♗xf5 ♖c6 35 ♔f4 ♖h6 36 ♗g4 ♖c6 37 ♖c1 f6 38 ♗f5 fxe5+ 39 dxe5 ♘xe5 40 ♖d1 ♔d6 41 ♗e4 ♖c5 0-1

The reason that the white players were so keen to try to score a quick knockout was the perception that Black, with his solid centre and well placed bishop, held all the long-term strategic trumps. However, in the early 1990s, all this changed. Following the lead of the English number one, Nigel Short, many grandmasters began to play White's position quietly (or at least relatively quietly). They took the view that, although Black's bishop on f5 could be regarded as a target, there was no need to go crazy trying to prove this immediately. White had a pleasant space advantage, plenty of time to develop his pieces and he could exploit the position of the black bishop at a later date. They simply mobilised their pieces with moves such as ♘f3, ♗e2, ♗e3 and 0-0 and awaited developments.

This proved to be much more to the taste of our leading exponents of the game and many of them have explored this new way to handle the white position. A few years ago, enthusiasts of the Advance variation who consulted the current *Informator* to examine the latest wrinkles in the opening, would be confronted by one or two obscure correspondence games. Now look up section B12 (the *Informator* code for the Advance) and you will find many references to games by players comfortably in the world's top twenty: Anand, Topalov, Short, Adams, Kamsky, Gelfand and Shirov.

This book explores both systems of playing: the strategic and positional themes arising from 4 ♘f3 are discussed in Chapters 1-4, while the violent tactics that often arise after 4 ♘c3 are explored in Chapters 5-7. Of course White has fourth move possibilities other than these two knight moves, and these are examined in Chapter 8. Likewise, Black is not obliged to develop his bishop on move 3. Alternatives such as 3...c5 or even the obscure 3...♘a6!? are quite playable and these are considered these in Chapter 9.

After a few years in the wilderness, the Advance Caro-Kann has regained full respectability and is now back at the forefront of top theoretical debate. This book will hopefully provide you with a good understanding of the intricacies of this fascinating variation and give you everything you need to play it confidently with either colour.

CHAPTER ONE

4 ♘f3 e6 5 ♗e2 c5 6 0-0 ♘c6 7 c3

1 e4 c6 2 d4 d5 3 e5 ♗f5 4 ♘f3 e6 5 ♗e2 c5 6 0-0 ♘c6 7 c3

Over the past few years, this has become an important position for the ♘f3 treatment of the Caro-Kann Advance. Both sides have developed their forces simply and logically and we have a typical French Defence position with Black's bishop outside the pawn chain on f5. Here Black usually takes the opportunity to capture on d4, eliminating the White options of d4xc5 or a quick central attack with c2-c4. However, this simplification also has a slight negative side – the pressure on White's centre is eased and he has more room to deploy his forces, for example he now has the option of ♘c3.

As is usual in these French Defence positions, White has a natural advantage on the kingside, but Black has good chances to manoeuvre for counterplay on the queenside. White's immediate decision is how to deal with this impending counterplay. He could either ignore it and charge ahead on the kingside, or opt for a more subtle strategy of attempting to limit Black's chances before initiating his own kingside expansion. There are various ways to carry out this limiting strategy, all of which are seen in the games in this chapter:

a) He can try to get a knight to the c5 square in favourable circumstances. This can be a nuisance for Black: if he kicks it out with ...b7-b6 (see Game 4), he has taken away the b6 square, often a useful square for his queen or knight, from his own pieces; if he trades it off for his dark-squared bishop, White can gain complete control of the queenside (see Game 10).

b) He can advance with a2-a3 and b2-b4, trying to clamp down on the queenside before Black can establish a hold there. This is double-edged – if Black counters with ...a7-a5 and meets White's b4-b5 with ...a5-a4, the white pawns on a3 and b5 can become serious weaknesses (see Game 6).

c) White can also try ♗b5, hoping to gain the advantage on the queen's wing by exchanging on c6 at a time when Black is obliged to recapture with the b-pawn. White then has a useful outpost on c5 and a target on c6 (see Game 5).

Black, in turn, has two main ways to develop his forces.

a) He can continue his development with ...♘c8, planning to use his knights to probe the queenside (see Games 1 and 7). In the first of these games Karpov gives an excellent demonstration of this strategy.

b) Black's position is slightly cramped and he can try to free himself with ...♗e4 and ...♘f5 (Games 2 and 3) which also puts pressure on White's d-pawn although, as we shall see, it is often very dangerous for Black to actually try to win this pawn. Also, his knight on f5 can sometimes provide a target for White's kingside ambitions with g2-g4 (see Game 2).

The final three games in this chapter (Games 8-10) deal with attempts by Black to delay ...c5xd4 or do without it altogether.

> ### Game 1
> ### Shirov-Karpov
> *Las Palmas 1994*

1 e4 c6 2 d4 d5 3 e5 ♗f5 4 ♘f3 e6 5 ♗e2 c5 6 0-0 ♘c6 7 c3 cxd4

Black's other possibilities here are discussed in Games 8-10.

8 cxd4 ♘ge7

see following diagram

9 a3

White's immediate decision in this position concerns how to deploy his queenside forces. Various possibilities come into consideration, all of which have been tried at some time:

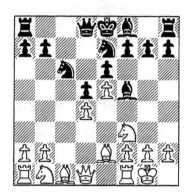

a) White can try leaving his a- and b-pawns unmoved so as not to provide targets for Black.

b) He can shuffle forwards with a2-a3 and b2-b3 with the same idea, but gaining a little more space and creating the option of developing the queen's bishop on b2.

c) He can advance with a2-a3 and b2-b4. This may signify the intention to play on the queenside or it may be simply to try to hamper Black's play in that sector. In this game we see Shirov choosing option 'b'. Systems with an early ♗e3 are seen in Games 4-7.

9...♘c8

Karpov plans queenside play with his knights. An alternative plan, seen in the next two games, involves 9...♗e4 followed by ...♘f5. There is probably not much to choose between these ideas but Karpov's choice here has the advantage of keeping more tension in the position.

10 ♘bd2

Shirov is planning the solid b2-b3, taking up a passive stance on the queenside, but hoping to gain a later initiative on the opposite wing. However, it is also possible to play actively on the queen's wing, e.g. 10 b4 ♘b6 11 ♘bd2 ♗e7 12 ♗b2 ♖c8 13 ♖c1 0-0

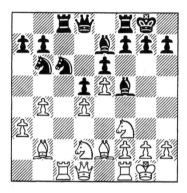

14 ♗c3 (14 ♘b3 encouraged Black to sacrifice a pawn with 14...♘c4 15 ♗xc4 dxc4 16 ♖xc4 ♕d5 in Hamdouchi-Adams, Cap d'Agde 1994. After 17 ♖c3 a5 18 bxa5 ♘xa5 19 ♘xa5 ♕xa5 Black has counterplay for his pawn but White could have maintained the better chances with 20 ♕c3.) 14...a6 15 ♕b3 ♖a8 16 a4 a5 17 bxa5 ♘xa5 18 ♕b5 ♘bc4 19 ♘xc4 ♘xc4 20 ♘d2 ♘xd2 21 ♗xd2 ♖a7 22 ♖c3 (White's active pieces give him an edge) 22...♕a8 23 ♖c7 ♗d8 24 ♖d7 ♗a5 25 ♗g5 ♗c3 26 ♗e7 ♖e8 27 ♗h5 ♗g6 28 ♗xg6 hxg6 29 ♗c5 ♖xa4 30 ♖xb7 ♗xd4? (After this the black king comes under too much pressure. Also losing was 30...♖d8 31 ♗e7 ♖c8 32 ♕d7 ♖a1 33 ♗a3!! ♖xf1+ 34 ♔xf1 ♕a6+ 35 ♔g1 ♖f8! 36 ♕e7! ♕a8 37 ♖a7 ♕b8 38 ♕xf8+ ♕xf8 39 ♗xf8 ♔xf8 40 ♖a4 winning, as given by Blatny. However, 30...♖a1 offered better chances for survival.) 31 ♕d7 ♗xe5 32 ♕xf7+ ♔h7 33 f4 ♗f6 34

♖b3 ♗h4 35 ♖h3 g5 36 fxg5 ♕c8 37 ♗f2 ♖f8 38 g6+ ♔h8 39 ♗xh4 1-0 Smirin-De Boer, Wijk aan Zee 1993

10...♗e7 11 b3 a5

Karpov takes advantage of Shirov's decision to omit b2-b4 to gain space on the queenside. Note that with White's pawn on b3, manoeuvring the knight to b6 would lose much of its point. Karpov intends a different role for this knight, seeing good opportunities to make use of it on a7.

12 ♗b2 ♘8a7 13 ♖e1

13 ♖c1!? was suggested by Karpov in *Informator 60*.

13...0-0 14 ♘f1 ♖c8

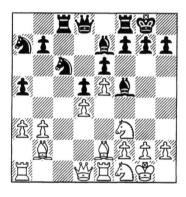

The battle lines are drawn for the forthcoming middlegame. White will try to expand on the kingside and hopes that the bishop on f5 may provide a target for his advances, either with f2-f4-f5 or h2-h4-h5. Meanwhile Black intends to pressurise the white queenside. This middlegame strongly resembles those which can arise from the Leningrad variation of the French Tarrasch (1 e4 e6 2 d4 d5 3 ♘d2 ♘f6 4 e5 ♘fd7 5 ♗d3 c5 6 c3 ♘c6 7 ♘gf3 cxd4 8 cxd4 ♘b6 9 a3 ♗d7 10 b3 a5 11 ♗b2 ♗e7) with the exception that

Black's bishop is placed outside the pawn chain.

15 ♘g3 ♗g6 16 ♕d2 ♕b6

Black's strategy in this position is to provoke weaknesses in the white queenside with piece play. Advancing with 16...b5 would thus be a mistake as it would take the important b5 square away from Black's pieces and would also make it easier for White to keep the position closed. For example, after 16...b5 White would always meet a subsequent ...a5-a4 with b3-b4 or, conversely, ...b5-b4 with a3-a4. Black's minor pieces would then lack squares to operate on the queen's wing.

17 ♗d1 ♖c7 18 h4 h6 19 ♖e2

White is trying to combine the twin ideas of mounting a kingside attack whilst keeping control of the queenside, in particular the vulnerable squares along the c-file.

19...♖fc8 20 ♕f4 ♘b8 21 ♖e3 ♘b5 22 ♘e2 ♘d7

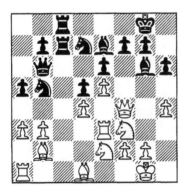

23 ♘h2

This knight manoeuvre does not generate much for White. His idea is to play h4-h5, ♖g3, ♘g4 and ♘xh6 but the problem is that the combination of h4-h5 and ♘g4 often runs into

...♗g5. Shirov may therefore have done better to play more solidly with 23 ♘e1 to keep an eye on the c-file. His kingside build-up looks promising but now Karpov finds an excellent way to regroup his pieces.

23...♖c6 24 ♘g4 ♕d8 25 ♖h3 ♕f8!

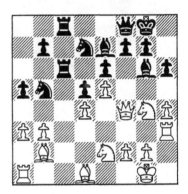

This geometric manoeuvre beautifully combines attack with defence. The black queen defends the kingside while simultaneously lending strength to the queenside attack by pressing against a3. Note that 25...♗xh4 would be disastrous on account of the simple combination 26 ♖xh4 ♕xh4 27 ♘f6+.

26 a4 ♘a3 27 ♗xa3

White may have been pinning his hopes on 27 h5 but after 27...♗c2! (not the compliant 27...♗f5 28 ♖g3 ♗xg4 29 ♗xa3 ♗xa3 30 ♖xg4 when White has a good position) 28 ♗xa3 ♗xa3 29 ♖g3 ♔h8 30 ♗xc2 ♖xc2 Black has invaded along the c-file while White's kingside attack has not achieved anything. White could now try 31 ♖xa3, hoping for 31...♕xa3 32 ♕xf7, but after the cold-blooded 31...♖xe2! Black keeps a clear advantage.

27...♗xa3 28 ♖g3

White has found a way to organise himself on the kingside but meanwhile Black's queenside play has made great progress.

28...h5 29 ♘e3 ♗b2! 30 ♖a2

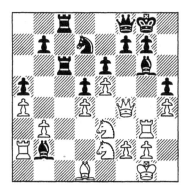

30...♗c1!

White's play has prevented the problem indicated earlier of ...♗g5 but now Karpov finds another way to irritate White on the c1-h6 diagonal.

31 ♕g5 ♕b4 32 ♘f4?

A better defence was offered by 32 ♔h2 but after 32...♗xe3 33 fxe3 ♘f8! Black holds everything together on the king's wing, as 34 ♘f4 ♘h7 leaves White's queen trapped. Now however, White simply loses a piece.

32...♗xe3 33 fxe3 ♖c1 34 ♘xg6 ♖xd1+ 35 ♔h2 fxg6 36 ♕xg6 ♕e7 37 ♖f2 ♕xh4+ 38 ♖h3 ♕xf2 0-1

Game 2
Shirov-Magem
Madrid 1994

1 e4 c6 2 d4 d5 3 e5 ♗f5 4 ♗e2 e6 5 ♘f3 c5 6 0-0 ♘c6 7 c3 cxd4 8 cxd4 ♘ge7 9 a3 ♗e4 10 ♘bd2 ♘f5

Black is now threatening to capture the d-pawn. However, as we shall see

here and in other games, the precarious situation of his bishop on e4 makes it difficult for him to carry out this threat. A capture on e4 will inevitably lead to an exchange of minor pieces in the centre after which White's lead in development can assume dangerous proportions.

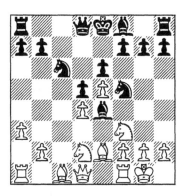

11 b4 a5?!

This is an obvious way for Black to try to undermine White's queenside but it fails dramatically thanks to some powerful play from Shirov. 11...♘cxd4 is a very dangerous capture, e.g. 12 ♘xd4 ♘xd4 13 ♘xe4 dxe4 14 ♕a4+ ♘c6 (14...♔e7!?) 15 ♗b5 and White has more than enough for the pawn. The solid 11...♕b6 is considered in the next game.

12 g4!?

This is a better try than 12 bxa5 which fizzled out to equality after 12...♕xa5 13 g4 ♘fxd4 14 ♘xd4 ♘xd4 15 ♘xe4 ♘xe2+ 16 ♕xe2 dxe4 17 ♕xe4 ♗c5 18 ♕xb7 0-0 19 ♕e4 ♕c3 20 ♖a2 ♕b3 in Yermolinsky-Seirawan, USA Championship 1992. White's extra pawn on a3 is far too sickly for him to have any chance of keeping the advantage.

12...♗xf3

This is dangerous for Black as, after the following forced variation, he finds himself dangerously behind in development. He would have done better to play 12...♘fxd4 13 ♘xd4 ♘xd4 14 ♘xe4 dxe4

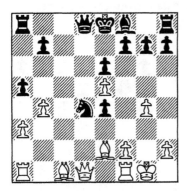

15 ♗e3 (15 ♕a4+? ♔e7 16 ♖d1 backfired in Prie-Hauchard, Nantes 1993, as after 16...♘xe2+ 17 ♔f1 ♕c8 18 ♗e3 f6 19 ♗c5+ ♔f7 20 ♔xe2 axb4 21 ♕d7+ ♕xd7 22 ♖xd7+ ♔g6 Black had survived the white attack and went on to win. Note that 16 ♖e1 is well met by 16...b5!) 15...♘xe2+ (this leaves Black with a miserable position so I am surprised that he did not try 15...♘c6, e.g. 16 ♕c2 ♕d5 with an unclear position) 16 ♕xe2 ♕d3 17 ♕b2 ♗e7 18 bxa5 0-0 19 ♖fd1 ♕a6 20 ♖d7 ♗h4 21 ♖xb7 ♕xa5 22 a4 ♕d8 23 ♕d4 ♕xd4 24 ♗xd4 and White's active pieces gave him a good endgame in Bologan-Khalifman, German Bundesliga 1993/94.

13 ♘xf3 ♘h4 14 ♘xh4 ♕xh4 15 b5 ♘b8

This is very regressive, but after 15...♘e7 16 ♗f4! White develops a straightforward initiative based on the

uncomfortable placement of the black queen and his lead in development, e.g. 16...h5 17 ♗g3 ♕g5 18 f4 ♕h6 (18...♕g6 19 gxh5 is strong) 19 g5 ♕g6 20 ♗d3 ♘f5 21 h4 and White is completely in control.

16 f4

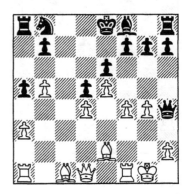

16...♗e7

Black must try to get his pieces out before White steamrollers him with f4-f5. After 16...♕d8, continuing the theme of retreating all his pieces to their original squares, 17 f5 ♗e7 18 fxe6 fxe6 19 ♗e3 ♘d7 20 b6! leaves the black king in desperate trouble thanks to White's control of the f-file and the a4-e8 diagonal. The theme of the pawn sacrifice with b5-b6 to free the b5 square for the bishop is a recurring one in this game.

17 ♗e3?

Even the strongest players are not immune from the danger of relaxing in a good position. With this natural developing move, Shirov misses the most dynamic continuation of 17 ♔g2!, intending to severely embarrass the black queen with ♖f3 and ♖h3. After 17 ♔g2 Black is in serious trouble, e.g. 17...♘d7 18 ♖f3! ♗d8 (capturing the g-pawn costs Black his queen: 18...♕xg4+ 19 ♖g3 ♕f5 20 ♗d3) 19 a4! and the threats of ♗a3 and ♖h3 leave Black in big trouble as 19...♕xg4+? allows an amusing queen trap after 20 ♖g3 ♕h4 21 ♖h3 ♕e7 22 ♗a3. After Shirov's lethargic 17 ♗e3 Black is able to complete his development, but White still retains a good position thanks to his bishop pair and space advantage.

17...♘d7 18 ♔g2 ♗d8 19 f5 ♕e7

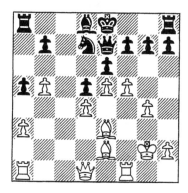

20 fxe6 fxe6?

Now Black will never get his king safe. He had to play 20...♕xe6, when he is only a little worse after 21 g5 ♘b6 22 ♗g4 ♕e7 23 ♕f3 0-0 24 h4. Black may now have been dreaming of blockading the queenside by placing a minor piece on b6, when he could face the future with some confidence. If so, Shirov's next must have come as an unpleasant surprise.

21 b6!

Now the b5 square is freed for the white bishop and Black will never be able to untangle himself.

21...♖f8

After 21...♗xb6 22 ♗b5 one immediate point is that 22...0-0-0? fails to 23

♕c1+ ♔b8 24 ♗g5 winning the exchange.

22 ♕c2 ♖xf1 23 ♖xf1 ♗xb6 24 ♗b5

With a fantastically active bishop pair and control of the open c- and f-files, White has a winning position.

24...g6 25 ♕c1! ♕h4

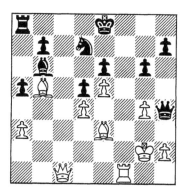

26 h3

Black has had endless trouble with his queen in this game. Now White again threatens to trap it with ♗g5.

26...♗d8 27 a4

Introducing the further possibility of ♕a3 but, for the second time in this game, Shirov relaxes at an important moment. Immediately terminal here was 27 ♗xd7+ ♔xd7 28 ♖f7+ ♔e8 29 ♖xb7 and ♕c6+ follows. However, Shirov's position is by now so overwhelming that it makes little difference.

27...♗e7

A better try was 27...♖b8 but White still wins with 28 ♗h6 ♗e7 29 ♕c7 ♖d8 30 ♗d2! ♗b4 31 ♕b6 ♕e7 32 ♗g5!

28 ♕c7 ♖d8 29 ♕b6 1-0

The pawn on e6 will drop after which the white pieces will soon run riot.

Game 3
Short-Karpov
Candidates (4), Linares 1992

1 e4 c6 2 d4 d5 3 e5 ♗f5 4 ♘f3 e6
5 ♗e2 c5 6 0-0 ♘c6 7 c3 cxd4 8
cxd4 ♘ge7 9 a3 ♗e4 10 ♘bd2 ♘f5
11 b4 ♕b6 12 ♗b2

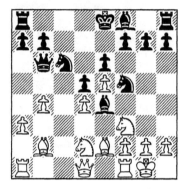

12...♗e7

12...♘cxd4 13 ♘xd4 ♘xd4 14 ♗xd4
♕xd4 15 ♘xe4 ♕xe4 (not 15...♕xd1
16 ♖fxd1 dxe4 17 ♗b5+ winning) and
now either 16 ♖e1 or 16 ♕a4+ with
dangerous play in either case.

13 ♖e1!

White does not need to defend his
d-pawn since, as we have seen previously, it is often very dangerous for
Black to capture this pawn while his
development lags. In Yermolinsky-
Adianto, St Martin 1993, White tried a
more solid continuation than Short's
energetic 13 ♖e1: 13 ♗c3 0-0
(13...♘cxd4 14 ♘xd4 ♘xd4 is unattractive, e.g. 15 ♘xe4 ♘xe2+ 16 ♕xe2
dxe4 17 ♕xe4 or 15 ♗xd4 ♕xd4 16
♘xe4 ♕xe4 17 ♗b5+ with a good
game in both cases. However, Black
should try 13...a5 when after 14 b5!?

♘cxd4 the above variations become
more attractive for Black as White can
longer check on the a4-e8 diagonal,
Black has obtained the c5 square for
his pieces and the white a-pawn has
become exposed.) 14 ♘b3 (White has
created the sneaky threat of b4-b5 and
♗a5, trapping the black queen)
14...♖fc8 15 ♖c1 (15 b5 runs into
15...♘xe5 16 ♗a5 ♘xf3+ 17 gxf3 ♗c2)
15...a5!? 16 bxa5 ♕a7 17 g4 ♗xf3 18
gxf5 ♗e4 19 fxe6 fxe6 20 ♗g4 and
White has a good position, as 20...♗f5
allows 21 ♗xf5 exf5 22 ♕f3 and
20...♘d8 21 ♗b4 is also good for
White

13...♖d8

Taking the bait is again not good,
e.g. 13...♘cxd4? 14 ♘xd4 ♘xd4 15
♗xd4 ♕xd4 16 ♘xe4 ♕xd1 17 ♖axd1
dxe4 18 ♗b5+ and Black has a miserable position.

14 ♗f1

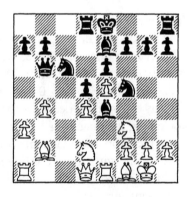

14...a5!

This is a good combative try from
Karpov. The alternatives 14...♗xf3 15
♘xf3 and 14...♘cxd4 15 ♘xd4 ♘xd4
16 ♘xe4 dxe4 17 ♖xe4 both leave
White with a very pleasant position.

15 ♘xe4 dxe4 16 ♖xe4 axb4 17

axb4 ♗xb4 18 ♖b1 ♕a5 19 h4

With the bishop pair and a potential attack on the kingside, White stands well.

19...0-0 20 ♗d3 ♖d7 21 ♖f4 g6 22 h5

22...♗e7

Remarkably, this position occurred in a later game, Short-Adianto, Jakarta 1996. Adianto came up with a new move 22...♖fd8, but White still maintained a promising attack on the kingside: 23 hxg6 hxg6 24 ♗xf5 exf5 25 ♖h4 ♗e7 26 ♖h3 ♗f8 27 e6 fxe6 28 d5 ♗g7? (28...♕xd5!, with an unclear position, was better according to Short) 29 ♗xg7 ♖xg7 30 ♕c1 ♕xd5 31 ♕h6 ♔f7 32 ♘g5+ ♔f6 33 ♕h4 b5 34 ♘h7+ ♔f7 35 ♕f6+ ♔g8 36 ♘g5 ♘e5! 37 ♕xe6+ ♕xe6 38 ♘xe6 ♖d2 39 ♘xg7 ♔xg7 and White, the exchange up, went on to win the endgame

23 hxg6 hxg6 24 ♗e4 ♘g7 25 ♖g4 ♖fd8 26 ♕c1 ♘f5 27 ♗c3 ♕c7 28 ♕b2

After this move Black feels obligated to give up the exchange but a better way for White to engineer this might have been 28 d5 ♖xd5 (not 28...exd5 29 ♗xf5) 29 ♗xd5 ♖xd5.

28...♘fxd4

29 ♘xd4 ♖xd4!

This exchange sacrifice is forced as 29...♘xd4? loses to 30 ♗xg6 ♕xc3 (30...fxg6 31 ♗xd4) 31 ♗d3+!

30 ♗xd4 ♖xd4 31 ♗f3 ♖xg4 32 ♗xg4 ♘xe5 33 ♕xb7 ♕c2 34 ♗d1 ♕d3 35 ♗f3 ♗f6 36 ♕e4 ♕c3

As the time control approaches, Karpov begins to lose his way. The easiest way was 36...♘xf3+ with a simple draw.

37 ♗e2 ♔g7 38 g3 ♕c5 39 ♔g2 ♘c6 40 ♖b7 ♘d4 41 ♗d3

41...♕h5??

Karpov blunders away a pawn after which Short is a clear exchange ahead.

42 ♖d7 ♘f5 43 ♕xe6 ♘h6 44 ♗c4

♕e5

45 ♕xe5?

Short, in turn, misses a simple win, e.g. 45 ♖xf7+ ♘xf7 46 ♕xf7+ ♔h6 47 ♗d3 ♕g5 48 f4 ♕h5 49 ♕xf6 ♕d5+ 50 ♔h2 ♕xd3 51 ♕h8 mate.

45...♗xe5

Now it is hard work for White but Short eventually manoeuvres his way into the black position.

46 ♔f3 ♔f8 47 ♔e4 ♗f6 48 ♖d5 ♗e7 49 f4 ♘g4 50 ♖a5 ♘h6 51 ♔f3 f5 52 ♖a7 ♘g4 53 ♗e6 ♘h6 54 ♖c7 ♘g4 55 ♖b7 ♘h6 56 ♔e3 ♘g4+ 57 ♔d4 ♘f6 58 ♖b8+ ♔g7 59 ♖b7 ♔f8 60 ♗d5 ♘h5 61 ♔e5 ♗f6+ 62 ♔e6 ♗d4 63 ♗f3 ♘xg3 64 ♖d7 ♗c3 65 ♖d3 ♗b2 66 ♖d2! ♗c1 67 ♖d1 ♗xf4 68 ♔f6 ♗c7 69 ♖d7 ♗a5 70 ♗c6! ♘h5+ 71 ♔xg6 ♘f4+ 72 ♔xf5 ♘e2 73 ♗f3 ♔e8 74 ♖d5 ♘g3+ 75 ♔e6 ♗c7 76 ♖d7 1-0

> *Game 4*
> **Hübner-Brunner**
> *Moscow Olympiad 1994*

1 e4 c6 2 d4 d5 3 e5 ♗f5 4 ♘f3 e6 5 ♗e2 c5 6 c3 ♘c6 7 0-0 cxd4 8 cxd4 ♘ge7 9 ♗e3 ♘c8 10 ♘bd2

White's main idea with this deployment of his pieces is to gain access to the c5 square as quickly as possible, in order to limit Black's play on the queenside. If this is combined with ♗b5xc6 then White can end up with a large structural advantage on the queenside. The alternative 10 ♘c3 is discussed in Games 6 and 7.

10...♗e7

10...♘b6 is considered in the next game.

11 ♘b3

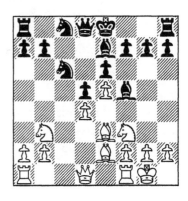

11...a5

After 11...♘b6 possible is 12 ♘c5 (12 ♗b5 is also promising) when 12...♗xc5 13 dxc5 ♘d7 14 ♘d4 ♘xd4 15 ♕xd4 is good for White.

12 ♖c1 ♘8a7 13 ♘c5 b6 14 ♘a4 0-0 15 ♘d2

Having taken time out to restrain Black on the queenside, White now resorts to his other plan of expansion on the kingside.

15...♖b8 16 f4 ♗g6 17 a3 ♕d7 18 ♖f2

see following diagram

18...♖fc8

After 18...f6 19 exf6 ♗xf6 20 ♘f3

White keeps control and will be able to expand further on the kingside with g2-g4.

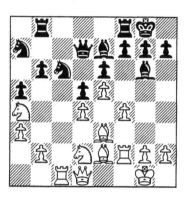

19 ♘f1 ♘d8 20 g4 ♖xc1 21 ♗xc1 f6 22 ♗e3 ♕c8 23 ♘c3 fxe5

Black could get his queenside counterplay going with 23...b5, but then 24 f5 ♗f7 25 exf6 ♗xf6 26 ♗f3 ♕d7 27 fxe6 ♗xe6 28 ♗f4 ♖c8 29 g5 ♗e7 30 ♘e3, as given by Hübner, is good for White. This emphasises an important aspect of White's plan – the advance with f4-f5 undermines Black's d-pawn as well as generating attacking chance on the kingside.

24 dxe5 ♗c5 25 f5 exf5

This opening of the position favours the active white pieces. Black would have done better to sit tight with 25...♗f7.

26 ♘xd5 ♘dc6 27 b4 axb4 28 axb4

see following diagram

28...♗xe3

All the action is now in the centre and on the kingside, whilst Black's pieces are huddled together on the queen's wing. Black is also suffering from the weakness of the a2-g8 diagonal as is shown by the variation

28...♘xb4 29 ♘xb4 ♗xb4 30 ♕b3+.

29 ♘fxe3 f4 30 ♘xf4 ♗e4 31 ♕b3+ ♔h8 32 ♕c4 ♗b1 33 ♖f1 b5 34 ♕d5 ♘e7 35 ♕f7 ♕c3 36 ♘fd5 1-0

Game 5
Lutz-Peelen
Groningen 1995

1 e4 c6 2 d4 d5 3 e5 ♗f5 4 ♘f3 e6 5 ♗e2 c5 6 0-0 ♘c6 7 c3 cxd4 8 cxd4 ♘ge7 9 ♗e3 ♘c8 10 ♘bd2 ♘b6 11 ♖c1 ♗e7 12 ♗b5 0-0

Or 12...♖c8 13 ♘b3 a6 14 ♗xc6+ bxc6 15 ♘c5 with a small but clear advantage for White.

13 ♗xc6 bxc6

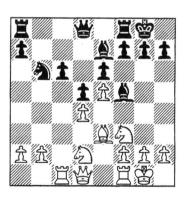

14 ♕e2

Black is trying to lure White into complications with 14 ♖xc6, when after 14...♗d3 15 ♖e1 ♘c4 the position has become messy as the white rook on c6 will prove difficult to extricate. Although this may nevertheless be good for White (he is, after all, a pawn up), Lutz has a clear strategic plan in mind and does not want to be distracted.

14...♕c8 15 ♗g5 ♗xg5 16 ♘xg5 h6 17 ♘gf3 a5 18 ♘h4 ♗h7

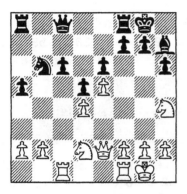

19 f4

By simple play White has obtained a very good position, holding the advantage on both sides of the board.

19...♖b8 20 b3 a4 21 ♖c3 axb3 22 axb3 ♘d7

After this Black loses more or less by force as he cannot cope with the transfer of White's major pieces to the kingside. A better try was 22...♕d7, but the position remains very good for White.

23 ♖g3

---

see following diagram

23...f5

Now Black loses a pawn. However, the counterattack 23...♖b4 is also

unsuccessful after 24 ♕g4 g6 25 ♕h5! ♖xd4 (25...♔g7 26 f5 is crushing) 26 ♘xg6! fxg6 27 ♖xg6+ ♗xg6 28 ♕xg6+ ♔h8 29 ♕xh6+ ♔g8 30 ♕g6+ ♔h8 31 ♖f3! ♖fxf4 32 ♖g3 ♖g4 33 ♕h6+ ♔g8 34 ♕xe6+ and White wins.

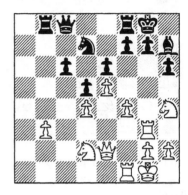

24 ♕h5 ♔h8

Black has no other way to protect his h-pawn.

25 ♘g6+ ♗xg6 26 ♕xg6 ♖g8 27 ♕xe6

White, a pawn ahead with a good position, is winning easily.

27...♘f8 28 ♕f7 ♖b4 29 ♘f3 ♖xb3 30 ♘h4 ♖xg3 31 hxg3 g6 32 ♖c1 ♕e6 33 ♕b7 ♖g7 34 ♕a8 g5 35 ♕xf8+ ♖g8 36 ♕xf5 1-0

1 e4 c6 2 d4 d5 3 e5 ♗f5 4 ♗e2 e6 5 ♘f3 c5 6 0-0 ♘c6 7 c3 cxd4 8 cxd4 ♘ge7 9 ♘c3 ♘c8 10 ♗e3 ♘b6 11 ♘a4 ♗e7 12 ♖c1 ♘xa4

Black wisely takes the opportunity to remove the white knight before it arrives on c5 from where, as we have already seen, it can seriously inhibit

Black's queenside play. 12...0-0 13 ♘c5 ♗xc5 14 ♖xc5, as in Anand-Seirawan, Roquebrune 1992, gives White the usual small plus.

13 ♕xa4 0-0 14 a3 a6 15 b4

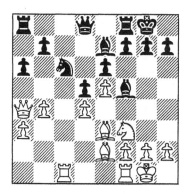

15...a5!

15...♕e8, with the unsubtle threat of 16...♘xd4 or 16...♘xe5, led to an equal game after 16 ♕d1 ♖c8 17 ♘e1 ♘a7 18 ♘d3 ♖xc1 19 ♕xc1 ♕c6 20 ♕xc6 ♘xc6 21 ♖c1 ♗xd3 22 ♗xd3 ♖a8 23 g3 f5 24 f4 ♖c8 in Grosar-Lobron, Graz Zonal 1993. Epishin's move is more interesting as it allows White to gain control of the c-file but, in return, Black has forced weaknesses in White's queenside.

16 b5 ♘b8 17 ♖c3 ♘d7 18 ♖fc1 ♘b6 19 ♕d1 a4 20 ♘d2

Black was threatening ...♘c4 here, exploiting the exposed position of the white a-pawn.

20...♕b8

If Black can now counter White's control of the c-file with ...♖c8, followed by exchanges, he will have a very good game thanks to the weakness of White's a- and b-pawns. White therefore now hurries to create play on the kingside.

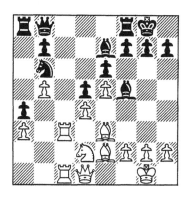

21 ♕f1 ♗g6 22 f4 f6

The kingside activity has temporarily distracted Black from his plan as 22...♖c8 is well met by 23 g4.

23 ♗g4!?

This is a very interesting decision. White does away with his own attacking chances on the kingside but, in return, he shuts the black light-squared bishop out of the game. However, he must have had his 25th move in mind when he took this decision.

23...f5 24 ♗e2 ♖c8 25 ♖c5!

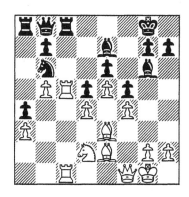

This is forced as 25 ♖xc8+? ♘xc8 leaves White with a miserable position due to his weakness on a3. The idea of blockading the queenside in this manner is known from the Leningrad

variation of the French Tarrasch, e.g.
1 e4 e6 2 d4 d5 3 ♘d2 ♘f6 4 e5 ♘fd7 5
♘gf3 c5 6 c3 ♘c6 7 ♗d3 cxd4 8 cxd4
♘b6 9 a3 ♗d7 10 b3 a5 11 ♗b2 ♗e7
12 h4 a4 13 b4 ♘a7 14 ♕e2 ♖c8 15 h5
h6 16 0-0 0-0 17 ♖ac1 ♕e8

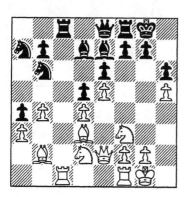

and now 18 ♖c5! as in Nunn-Hecht,
European Team Championship, Moscow 1977.

25...♕a7

Black should probably not make
the capture 25...♗xc5 26 dxc5 without
good reason, either now or later. The
clamp on the queenside and control of
the d4 square would leave White in
little danger in such a position.

**26 ♖1c2 ♗e8 27 ♕c1 ♗d7 28 ♕b2
♕a5 29 ♔f2 ♔f8**

Black has found a plan. He intends
to continue ...♔e8-d8, ...♗e8 and
...♘d7, regaining control of the c-file.
White must act quickly to keep the
balance.

30 h3 ♔e8 31 ♕b1 ♔d8 32 g4

White tries to distract Black by creating play on the kingside.

32...g6 33 ♕b2 ♗e8 34 ♕c1

This prevents Black from completing his plan with ...♘d7, but allows
another possibility.

**34...♗xc5!? 35 dxc5 ♗xb5 36 cxb6
♗xe2 37 ♔xe2 ♕b5+ 38 ♔f2 ♖xc2
39 ♕xc2 ♖c8 40 ♕d1 ♖c3**

41 ♗d4!

Black may have overlooked this
very important resource when he entered these complications. Now White
is able to hold the balance as 41...♖xa3
is well met by 42 ♕c1, and the white
queen invades the black position.

41...♖c6

Having struggled for so long to gain
control of the c-file, Black is reluctant
to let go. However, it may have been
better to play 41...♖xh3 42 ♕c1 ♕d7
43 gxf5 gxf5 44 ♘f3 with a balanced
position.

42 ♘f3 ♔d7

This does not do much to improve
Black's position. The immediate
42...♕b3! would have been an improvement.

43 ♕d2 ♖c4 44 ♔g3 ♕b3?

Black seems to have completely lost
track of the position over the last few
moves. This move is a disaster which
allows the white queen to enter into
the black position with decisive consequences.

45 ♕a5!

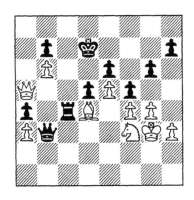

45...♔c6

Presumably Black overlooked that after 45...♖xd4 46 ♕c5 the white queen will wreak havoc, e.g. 46...♖c4 47 ♕d6+ ♔e8 48 ♕xe6+ ♔f8 49 ♕d6+ ♔g7 50 e6.

46 ♗f2 fxg4

After 46...♖c3 the sly retreat 47 ♔g2! leaves Black in terrible trouble.

47 hxg4 ♕xa3 48 ♕a8 ♔b5 49 ♕xb7 ♖c3 50 ♕d7+ ♔c4 51 ♔g2 ♖xf3 52 ♕c6+ ♔d3 53 ♔xf3 ♕b3 54 b7 a3 55 b8♕ ♕xb8 56 ♕a6+ ♔c2 57 ♕xa3 ♕b7 58 ♕c5+ ♔d3 59 ♕b6 1-0

Game 7
Anand-Speelman
Linares 1992

1 e4 c6 2 d4 d5 3 e5 ♗f5 4 ♘f3 e6 5 ♗e2 c5 6 0-0 ♘c6 7 c3 cxd4 8 cxd4 ♘ge7 9 ♘c3

9 b3 is a little too passive to create trouble for Black, e.g. 9...♗e4 10 ♘bd2 ♘f5 11 ♗b2 ♗b4 12 g4!? (not 12 a3? ♗xd2 13 ♕xd2 ♗xf3 14 ♗xf3 ♕b6 winning a pawn) 12...♗xf3 (also possible is 12...♘h4 13 ♘xe4 dxe4 14 ♘xh4 ♕xh4 15 ♕c2 h5 16 ♕xe4 hxg4

17 ♕g2 0-0-0 18 ♗xg4 ♔b8 19 ♖fd1 with unclear play in Short-Seirawan, Amsterdam 1992) 13 ♘xf3 ♘fe7 14 ♘e1 h5 15 gxh5 ♘f5 16 ♘c2 ♕g5+ 17 ♔h1 ♗d2 with good play for the pawn in Short-Garcia Palermo, Manila Olympiad 1992.

9...♘c8 10 ♗e3 ♘b6 11 ♖c1 ♗e7 12 ♘a4 ♘xa4 13 ♕xa4 0-0

14 ♗b5?!

Surprisingly, this allows Black to take the initiative on the queenside. It would have been better to play the immediate 14 a3, preventing Black's following manoeuvre, as we saw in the previous game.

14...♘b4! 15 a3 ♘d3 16 ♗xd3 ♗xd3 17 ♖fe1 a5 18 ♕d1

This queen manoeuvre explains why White preferred to place his king's rook on e1. He now forces Black to commit his bishop slightly earlier than he would like.

18...♗g6 19 ♕b3 ♖a6 20 ♗d2

see following diagram

White has not coordinated his forces and the position is about equal.

20...♕d7 21 ♖c3 a4 22 ♕d1 ♕b5 23 ♗c1 ♖c6 24 ♖ee3 ♖fc8 25 ♖xc6

Xxc6 26 &d2 Wxb2 27 Wxa4 Wa1+
28 &e1 &f8 29 Wa8 Xa6

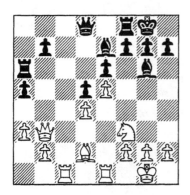

With both queens having broken through to undefended back ranks, the position has become complicated. Both players must be careful, e.g. 29...Xc1?? 30 h3 &e4 31 &h2 &xf3 32 &b4 and White wins. A fearsomely complex variation, pointed out by the always imaginative Speelman, is 29...&e4!? 30 h3 &xf3

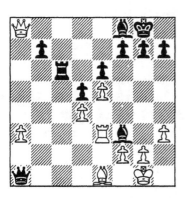

and now the remarkable continuation 31 &h2! &xg2!! (but not 31...Xa6 32 Wc8 Xxa3 33 Xxf3 Xxf3 34 &b4) 32 &xg2 Xa6 33 Wc8 Xxa3 34 Xf3 Xxf3 35 &b4 and now the point of Black's 31st move becomes clear: 35...Xxf2+ 36 &xf2 Wxd4+ and Black

wins.
30 Wxb7 Xxa3 31 Xxa3 Wxa3 32 Wc8 h6

Black has emerged from the complications with a small advantage thanks to the weakness of the white d-pawn.

33 Wc3 &e4 34 Wxa3 &xa3 35 &d2 &b2 36 f3! &xd4+?

This natural move is a surprising mistake. Better chances were offered by 36...&c2!, intending to bring the king into the game.

37 &f2 &c3

37...&xf2+? 38 &xf2 leaves Black without chances as White is in control of d4.

38 &xe4 dxe4 39 fxe4 &xe5 40 g4 &h7 41 &g2 &g6 42 &e3 &f6 43 h4 &c3 44 &f4 &e1 45 h5 &h4 46 &f3 &e7 47 &e3 &d6 48 &f4+ &c5 49 &e5 &f6 50 &b8 &d4 51 &d6 &g5 52 &f8 g6 53 &g7+ &d3 54 &f8 e5 55 &g7 gxh5 56 gxh5 f5 57 exf5 e4+ 58 &g2 e3 59 &e5 e2 60 &g3 &f6 61 &f3 &c3 62 &f2 &d2 63 &e4 &d1 64 &d3 &f6 65 &g3 &g5 66 &f2 e1W 67 &xe1 &xe1 68 &d4 &f2 69 &e5 &f3 70 f6 &g4 71 f7 &e7 72 &e4 ½-½

Game 8
Benjamin-Seirawan
USA Championship 1991

1 e4 c6 2 d4 d5 3 e5 &f5 4 &f3 e6 5 &e2 c5 6 0-0 &c6 7 c3 &ge7

Black wants to keep his options open by declining to capture on d4 immediately. However, this allows White a promising alternative strategy, as is swiftly demonstrated.

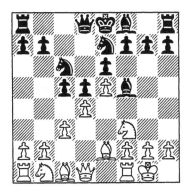 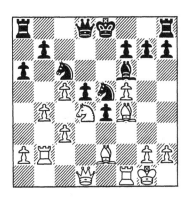

8 dxc5 ♘g6 9 b4

This plan generates a quick initiative for White as Black has to waste time recapturing his pawn.

9...♗e7

Black is in danger of being completely steamrollered after 9...a5, e.g. 10 ♘d4 ♗xb1 11 ♖xb1 ♘gxe5 12 b5 ♘xd4 13 cxd4 ♘g6 14 b6 ♘e7 15 ♗b5+ ♘c6 16 ♗xc6+ bxc6 17 b7 1-0 Nunn-Laplaza, Oviedo 1992. A frightening example of the dangers of not getting developed.

10 ♘d4 ♗xb1 11 ♖xb1 ♘gxe5 12 f4 ♘d7 13 f5 e5 14 ♘f3 e4 15 ♘d4 ♘de5

15...0-0 allows White to come into Black's queenside, e.g. 16 ♗f4 ♗f6 17 ♘b5 a6 18 ♘c7 ♗xc3 19 ♘xa8 ♗d4+ 20 ♔h1 ♕xa8 21 a4 ♘f6 22 b5 axb5 23 axb5 ♗xc5 24 bxc6 bxc6 25 ♖c1 ♗e7 26 ♗e3, as in Nunn-Drazic, Walsall 1992. If Black were only a piece down, his position would not be too bad, but a whole rook is far too much.

16 ♗f4 a6 17 ♖b2 ♗f6

Black has avoided immediate disaster by blockading solidly in the centre. However, the weaknesses in his position, particularly the d-pawn, remain.

18 ♖d2 ♕d7 19 b5!

This enables White to activate his knight and expose the black d-pawn.

19...axb5 20 ♘xb5 0-0 21 ♖xd5 ♕e7 22 a4 ♗g5 23 ♗xg5 ♕xg5 24 f6 g6 25 ♘d6 ♕e3+ 26 ♔h1 ♕xc3 27 ♘xe4 ♕b4 28 ♕c1

In his efforts to maintain a semblance of material parity Black has walked into a mating attack, e.g. 28 ♕c1 ♔h8 29 ♕h6 ♖g8 30 ♘g5.

28...♔h8 29 ♕h6 ♖g8 30 ♘g5 1-0

Game 9
Short-Karpov
Candidates (2), Linares 1992

---

1 e4 c6 2 d4 d5 3 e5 ♗f5 4 ♘f3 e6 5 ♗e2 c5 6 0-0 ♘c6 7 c3 ♗g4

Black is aiming for a simple development of his pieces with ...♘ge7 and ...♘f5. His plan is similar to that in the variations such as 7...cxd4 8 cxd4 ♘ge7 9 a3 ♗e4, but Black does not have to worry about his bishop becoming exposed on e4. This has the advantage that Black can complete his development easily. However, the drawback is that Black's play does not really challenge White's set-up, enabling him to obtain a pleasant game by playing very simple moves.

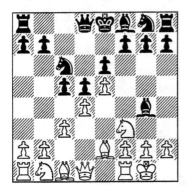

8 ♘bd2 cxd4 9 cxd4 ♘ge7 10 a3

10 h3 ♗xf3 11 ♘xf3 ♘f5 12 ♖b1 ♕b6 13 ♗e3 ♗e7 14 b4 0-0 15 ♗d3 ♘xe3 16 fxe3 gave White a small edge in Anand-Karpov, Reggio Emilia 1992.

10...♘f5 11 b4 ♗e7

It is difficult for Black to disturb the smooth flow of White's development, e.g. 11...♕b6 12 ♗b2 ♗e7 13 h3 ♗xf3 14 ♘xf3 0-0 15 ♕d2 ♘h4 16 ♘xh4 ♗xh4 17 ♗c3 a6 (or 17...♗d8 18 ♖ab1 ♖e8 19 a4 ♖c8 20 ♖fc1 ♕c7 21 b5 ♘e7 22 ♗b4 ♕d7 23 ♗d3 with a small edge, as in Sax-Schwarz, German Bundesliga 1994) 18 ♖ab1 ♗e7 19 f4 f5 20 ♔h2 ♔h8 21 g4 g6 22 gxf5 gxf5 23 ♗h5 ♗h4 24 ♖g1 ♕c7 25 ♖g2 ♖g8 26 ♖bg1 ♕e7 and again White has the better chances, although the simplified nature of the position means that Black should be able to hold, as in Fogarasi-Van Mil, Budapest 1993.

12 h3 ♗xf3 13 ♘xf3 0-0 14 ♗b2 a6 15 ♕d2 ♖c8 16 ♖ad1 ♘b8

This is a familiar manoeuvre. Black intends to relocate his knight via d7 to b6 and c4.

17 ♗d3 ♘h4 18 ♘e1

White is hoping for a kingside initiative and so keeps the pieces on.

18...♘d7 19 ♘c2 ♘b6 20 ♘e3 ♕d7

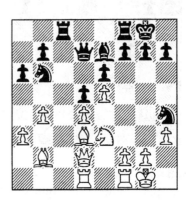

21 ♖de1

In *ChessBase Magazine*, Blatny, usually a very good analyst, suggests that 21 g3 is well met by 21...♘f5. I hope you do not need a Pentium-powered version of *Fritz* to spot the flaw with this reasoning!

21...♖c7 22 ♕d1 ♖fc8 23 g3 ♘f5 24 ♘xf5 exf5 25 ♕f3 g6 26 ♕f4 ♘a4 27 ♗c1

The position is balanced. Black's control of the c-file compensates for White's kingside play.

27...♖c3 28 ♗b1 ♖b3 29 ♗a2 ♖bc3 30 ♗b1 ♖b3 31 ♗a2 ♖bc3 32 ♗b1 ½-½

> ## Game 10
> ### Short-Seirawan
> *Manila Interzonal 1990*

1 e4 c6 2 d4 d5 3 e5 ♗f5 4 c3 e6 5 ♗e2 c5 6 ♘f3 ♘c6 7 0-0 h6

This move is not really in keeping with any of the black plans that we have seen in earlier games in this chapter, so the game is not theoretically important. However, it does provide a wonderful demonstration of how to exploit a space advantage.

8 ♗e3 cxd4 9 cxd4 ♘ge7 10 ♘c3 ♘c8 11 ♖c1 a6

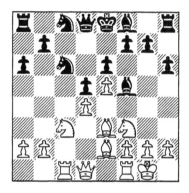

Seirawan is wasting time all over the place and he soon gets punished. However, this game was played in 1990, when Short had only just introduced his system into international play, and Caro-Kann players had not yet worked out coherent systems with which to counter it. It should be pointed out that Seirawan is usually a brilliant exponent of the Caro-Kann and has scored fine victories against Short, Nunn and Timman in the Advance variation.

12 ♘a4 ♘b6 13 ♘c5 ♗xc5 14 ♖xc5 0-0 15 ♕b3 ♘d7 16 ♖c3 ♕b6 17 ♖fc1

Not 17 ♕xb6 ♘xb6 18 ♖b3 ♘c4 19 ♖xb7 ♘6a5 20 ♖b4 ♘c6, when Black gains a perpetual attack against the white rook.

17...♕xb3 18 ♖xb3 ♖fb8 19 ♘d2 ♔f8 20 h4!

White has gained control on the queenside but needs to open another front in order to penetrate the black position.

20...♔e8 21 g4 ♗h7 22 h5 ♘d8 23 ♖bc3 ♘b6

Black is hoping to equalise by exchanging the rooks on the c-file, but White's next move cuts across this plan.

24 ♘b3 ♘a4

Or 24...♖c8 25 ♘c5 and if 25...♘d7 26 ♘xb7.

25 ♖c7 ♘xb2 26 ♘c5

Black has gained a pawn, but his position has been invaded and his rooks are asleep.

26...b5 27 g5! ♘c4 28 gxh6 gxh6 29 ♘d7

29 ♗xc4 bxc4 30 ♘d7 ♘b7 31 ♘f6+ ♔d8 32 ♖xf7 ♗f5 33 ♔h2, intending ♖g1, was another way to win.

29...♘xe3 30 fxe3 ♗f5 31 ♔f2 ♖b7 32 ♘f6+ ♔f8

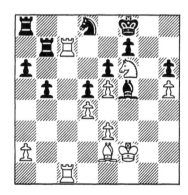

33 ♖g1 1-0

A very attractive finish. 33...♖xc7 is met by 34 ♖g8+ ♔e7 35 ♖e8 mate.

Summary

Based on recent evidence, this variation seems to be okay for Black. His two main plans of ...♗e4 and ...♘f5 or ...♘c8 both seem playable. As long as he avoids giving White the opportunity for d4xc5, or wasting time with moves such as ...h7-h6, he should achieve a playable middlegame. White's attempts to clamp down on the queenside with a2-a3 and b2-b4 do not seem to be successful, but Lutz's plan of a very quick ♘bd2, ♖c1 and ♗b5 is well worth a look.

1 e4 c6 2 d4 d5 3 e5 ♗f5 4 ♘f3 e6 5 ♗e2 c5 6 0-0 ♘c6 7 c3

7...cxd4
       7...♘ge7 – *Game 8*
       7...♗g4 – *Game 9*
       7...h6 – *Game 10*
8 cxd4 ♘ge7 *(D)* 9 a3
       9 ♗e3 ♘c8
             10 ♘bd2 *(D)*
                 10...♗e7 – *Game 4*
                 10...♘b6 – *Game 5*
             10 ♘c3 ♘b6 11 ♖c1 ♗e7 12 ♘a4 ♘xa4 13 ♕xa4 0-0
                 14 a3 – *Game 6*
                 14 ♗b5 – *Game 7*
9...♘c8
       9...♗e4 10 ♘bd2 ♘f5 11 b4 *(D)*
             11...a5 – *Game 2*
             11...♕b6 – *Game 3*
10 ♘bd2 – *Game 1*

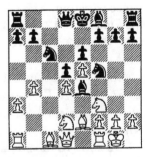

8...♘ge7   *10 ♘bd2*   *11 b4*

CHAPTER TWO

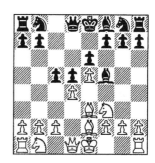

4 ♘f3 e6 5 ♗e2 c5 6 ♗e3

1 e4 c6 2 d4 d5 3 e5 ♗f5 4 ♘f3 e6
5 ♗e2 c5 6 ♗e3

6 ♗e3 has a very different philosophy from 6 0-0. White is suggesting that Black's play is a little slow and that the way to exploit this is with quick central action. 6 ♗e3 disdains the solid approach seen in Chapter 1 of 0-0 and c2-c3 and instead spoils for an immediate fight, usually with c2-c4 but sometimes with d4xc5.

Black must be careful after White opens the position with c2-c4 as his development lags slightly and the d6 square can prove vulnerable to a manoeuvre such as ♘a3-c4 or ♘f3-d4-b5. However, if he can negotiate the exchange of central pawns without suffering an early accident, he can look forward to a promising middlegame. He will have a useful square on d5 and the white pawn on e5 can become a liability. White, for his part, must look for ways to use his initiative as productively as possible. Even simple developing moves such as 0-0 are postponed in the interests of getting at

Black's position as quickly as possible. The strategy of these positions bears a similarity to that of certain lines of the Meran variation of the Semi-Slav.

When White chooses to capture with d4xc5, a different kind of struggle results. He may be planning to continue with the strategy of opening the position and follow up with c2-c4, but often has the plan in mind of trying to hold on to the c5-pawn, usually at the expense of the e5-pawn. Black has to waste time recapturing this pawn and White can use this to complete his development and gain a firm control over the central dark squares. However, if Black can keep the situation fluid, his central preponderence promises good long-term chances.

> *Game 11*
> **Kamsky-Karpov**
> *Dos Hermanas 1995*

1 e4 c6 2 d4 d5 3 e5 ♗f5 4 ♘f3 e6
5 ♗e2 c5 6 ♗e3 ♘d7 7 c4

Nigel Short's latest invention 7

♘bd2!? is discussed in Game 16.

7...dxc4 8 0-0 a6

This move is a little slow, given Black's already lagging development. However, as White has spent a tempo castling, he can probably afford this slight time loss. If White had played 8 ♘c3 instead, then 8...a6 in reply would be more dangerous, e.g. 9 ♗xc4 ♘e7 10 d5!? as in Spraggett-Magem (see Game 15). 8...♘e7 is considered (by transposition) in Game 13.

9 ♗xc4

Tempted by Black's lack of development, White opted for immediate violence with 9 d5 in Short-Adianto, Moscow Olympiad 1994, the result being an interesting draw after 9...♘e7 10 ♘c3 b5 11 ♖e1 exd5 12 ♘xd5 ♘xd5 13 ♕xd5 ♗e7 14 ♘g5 0-0 15 ♘xf7 ♖xf7 16 e6 ♖f6 17 exd7+ ♗e6 18 ♕e4 ♗f5 19 ♕d5+ ♗e6 20 ♕e4 ♗f5 ½-½.

9...♘e7 10 ♘c3 b5

10...♘c6 is considered in the next game.

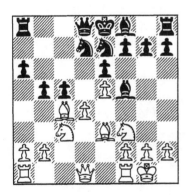

11 ♗d3

11 ♗e2 is possible, but after 11...b4! 12 ♘a4 ♘d5 13 ♗g5 ♕a5 14 ♖c1 (14 ♘d2 looks more dangerous) 14...h6 15

♗d2 ♗e7 16 b3 0-0 Black had nothing to complain about in Sulskis-Galkin, St Petersburg 1995.

11...c4 12 ♗c2

12 ♗xf5 ♘xf5 only speeds up Black's development, e.g. 13 d5 ♗b4 14 dxe6 fxe6 15 ♘d4 ♘xd4 16 ♕xd4 ♗xc3 17 bxc3 0-0 18 ♖fd1 ♖f7 19 a4 ♕c8 and Black was fine in Magem-Arlandi, Linares Zonal 1995.

12...♖c8 13 ♖e1 b4

Karpov suggests 13...♗xc2 14 ♕xc2 b4 15 ♘e4 ♘d5 as being unclear.

14 ♘e4 ♘d5 15 ♗g5 ♕a5

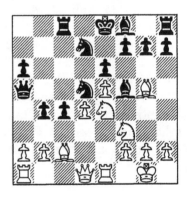

The position now resembles those that arise from the Meran variation of the Semi-Slav (1 d4 d5 2 c4 e6 3 ♘c3 ♘f6 4 ♘f3 c6 5 e3 ♘bd7 6 ♗d3 dxc4 7 ♗xc4 b5 8 ♗d3 a6 9 e4 c5 10 e5), except that the black bishop is outside the pawn chain. Black is winning the game on the queenside but White is placing his trust on his forthcoming kingside advance.

16 ♘h4 ♗xe4 17 ♗xe4 g6

This may be a mistake as it provides White with a target for his kingside attack and improves the activity of his dark-squared bishop. An alternative is 17...♘7b6, consolidating in the centre and on the queenside.

18 ♕g4 ♗g7 19 f4 ♕b6

This manoeuvre looks convoluted, but if 19...♘7b6 Karpov was probably concerned that he would come under a huge attack after 20 f5 gxf5 21 ♗xf5 h5 (21...exf5 22 ♘xf5 is too strong – Black must first deflect the white queen) 22 ♕f3 exf5 23 ♘xf5 ♗f8 and now both 24 e6 and 24 ♘d6+ come into consideration.

20 ♔h1

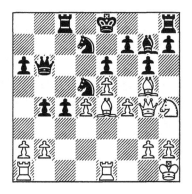

20...♕c6

Black makes way for his d7-knight to come to b6 and allows creates the possibility of ...0-0 which is, currently, unplayable (20...0-0? 21 ♗xd5 wins a piece).

21 f5 ♘7b6

Black must sit tight in the face of White's advance, e.g. 21...gxf5 22 ♗xf5 h5 23 ♕f3 exf5 24 ♘xf5 ♗f8 25 ♘d6+ and White has a huge attack.

22 ♗f6

Another line of play was to suffocate Black on the kingside via 22 f6 ♗f8 with an unclear position.

22...♗xf6 23 exf6 ♔d8

Karpov swiftly evacuates his king from the danger zone.

24 fxg6 hxg6 25 ♗xg6!?

25...♖c7?!

25...fxg6 26 ♘xg6 ♖h7 27 ♖xe6 gives White a strong attack but Karpov misses the best continuation: 25...♖g8! 26 ♕f3 and now 26...fxg6 is no good on account of 27 f7 ♖f8 28 ♘xg6 winning, but 26...♖xg6! 27 ♘xg6 fxg6 28 f7 ♔e7 keeps the position balanced. Now White gets on top.

26 ♗e4 ♔c8 27 ♘f3 ♘xf6 28 ♕g7 ♘xe4

Alternatively, Black could engineer a curious exchange of his b-pawn for White's h-pawn with 28...♖xh2+ 29 ♔xh2 ♘xe4 30 ♕f8+ ♔b7 31 ♕xb4 but White, with his extra exchange, would remain well on top although the position is complicated.

29 ♕xh8+ ♔b7 30 ♕h4 ♘d6 31 ♖ac1 a5 32 ♕g5 ♘d5 33 h4

This plan of advancing the h-pawn is very natural, but in fact it becomes something of a liability. Kamsky had an alternative, and possibly stronger, plan of 33 ♘e5 and general consolidation in the centre.

33...♖c8 34 h5 ♖h8 35 ♔g1 ♖h7 36 h6 ♕c7 37 ♘d2 ♕b6 38 ♕g4 1-0

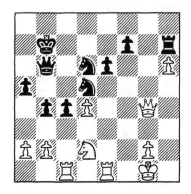

Here Karpov lost on time but the position was not yet completely clear, e.g. 38...f5 39 ♕h4 f4 40 ♕f2! c3 41 ♘b3 when White is on top but Black is still fighting.

Game 12
Wells-Engqvist
Isle of Man 1995

1 e4 c6 2 d4 d5 3 e5 ♗f5 4 ♘f3 e6
5 ♗e2 c5 6 ♗e3 ♘d7 7 0-0 a6 8 c4
dxc4 9 ♗xc4 ♘e7 10 ♘c3 ♘c6

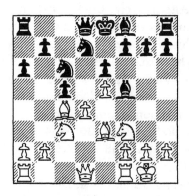

11 d5!?

White decides to stir up immediate complications with an adventurous move that more or less commits him to a piece sacrifice. A more restrained

alternative was 11 a4, but advancing with d4-d5 is always worth considering when it seems as if Black has wasted a little time.

11...♘cxe5 12 ♘xe5 ♘xe5 13 ♕a4+ b5

After this White gets a tremendous attack. A more circumspect, and probably better, defence would have been 13...♘d7 14 dxe6 fxe6 15 ♖ad1 (White throws more fuel onto the fire, but 15 ♕b3 is met by 15...♕b6 and it is hard to see how White can generate play for his pawn) 15...b5 16 ♘xb5 axb5 17 ♕xb5 ♖a7 18 ♖d2 (now Black consolidates, so Razuvaev suggests instead 18 b4! ♕b8 19 bxc5 ♖b7! which he assesses as unclear) 18...♕b6 19 ♖fd1 ♕xb5 20 ♗xb5 e5 21 b4 ♖b7 22 ♗c6 ♖c7 23 b5 c4 and Black went on to win in Bologan-Razuvaev, Biel 1995.

14 ♘xb5 axb5 15 ♗xb5+ ♔e7

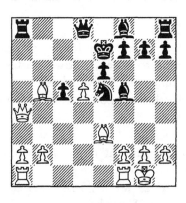

16 d6+!

This neat trick guarantees White an enduring initiative.

16...♔xd6

16...♔f6 17 ♕h4+ ♔g6 18 ♕g3+ ♘g4 19 ♗xc5 looks very bad for Black.

17 ♖fd1+ ♔c7 18 ♕f4!?

White decides to play for the middlegame attack, despite having a piece less. There was a perfectly reasonable alternative with 18 ♖xd8 ♖xa4 19 ♖xf8, when White's bishops should give him a small edge in the endgame.

18...♕f6 19 ♖ac1 ♗g4

19...♗g6 could be quite a testing move for White, e.g. 20 ♕g3 ♔b6! and it is not clear how White continues his attack, although he obviously retains good practical chances.

20 ♕e4

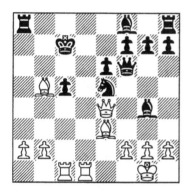

20...♗f3

Black must now bale out into an endgame otherwise he will be wiped out, e.g. 20...♖d8 21 ♖xd8 ♔xd8 22 ♕a8+ and mate soon follows.

21 gxf3 ♕g6+ 22 ♕xg6 ♘xf3+ 23 ♔g2 ♘h4+ 24 ♔f1 hxg6 25 a4

White will now regain the pawn on c5 when his bishops and queenside pawn majority guarantee him good winning chances.

25...♘f5 26 ♗xc5 ♗xc5 27 ♖xc5+ ♔b6 28 ♖c6+ ♔a5 29 ♖dc1 ♔b4 30 ♖1c3 ♖h4 31 ♗e2 ♖b8 32 ♗d1 ♘d4 33 ♖3c4+ ♔a5 34 b4+ ♖xb4 35 ♖6c5+ ♘b5 36 ♖xh4 ♖xh4 37

♖xb5+ ♔a6 38 ♔g2 ♖d4 39 ♖b1 ♔a5 40 h3 1-0

Game 13
Ehlvest-Vyzmanavin
Novosibirsk 1995

1 e4 c6 2 d4 d5 3 e5 ♗f5 4 ♘f3 e6 5 ♗e2 c5 6 ♗e3 ♘d7 7 0-0 ♘e7

A very sensible alternative to 7...a6.

8 c4 dxc4 9 ♘a3

This is a good alternative to 9 ♗xc4. White develops another piece and has ideas of ♘xc4-d6(+).

9...♘d5

9...c3!? can be met by the remarkable 10 ♗g5!? (10 bxc3 ♘d5 11 ♕b3 is a more straightforward response) 10...f6 (10...♕c8 11 bxc3 h6 12 ♗e3 ♘d5 13 ♖c1 ♗e7 is possible, while after 10...cxb2 White's idea is revealed, e.g. 11 ♘b5 and now in *Informator*, Nisipeanu gives 11...♘d5 12 ♗xd8 bxa1♕ 13 ♕xa1 ♖xd8 14 ♘d6+ with the advantage, but he does not mention 11...♘xe5!?, which seems very unclear, e.g. 12 dxe5 bxa1♕ 13 ♕xa1 ♕b8 14 ♘d6+ when White has a strong attack but is the exchange and two pawns down) 11 exf6 gxf6 12 ♗c1

♘d5 13 ♘h4 ♗g6 14 ♗f3 cxb2 15
♗xb2 ♘7b6 16 ♖c1 ♖c8 17 ♖e1 ♔f7
18 ♗g4 f5 19 dxc5 ♕xh4 20 cxb6? (20
♗xh8 was unclear) 20...♗xa3 21 ♖xc8
♖xc8 22 ♗f3 ♗xb2 23 ♗xd5 ♔g7 24
♗xb7 ♖d8 25 ♕c2 ♗d4 26 ♕c7+ ♗f7
27 g3 ♕f6 0-1 Del Rio-Nisipeanu, Sio-
fok 1996.

10 ♘xc4

Also playable is 10 ♗g5 ♗e7 (or
10...♕b8 11 ♗xc4 h6 12 ♗h4 ♘7b6 13
♖c1 a6 14 ♖e1 ♗e7 15 ♗xe7 ♔xe7 16
♗d3 with an edge, thanks to Black's
displaced king in Smirin-Vyzmanavin,
Elenite 1994) 11 ♗xe7 ♕xe7 12 ♘xc4
0-0 13 ♘d6 ♘f4 14 ♘xf5 exf5 15 ♗b5
(White is a little better) 15...♘b6 16
♖c1 ♖ac8 17 ♕d2 ♘bd5 18 ♗c4 cxd4
19 g3 ♘b6 20 ♗xf7+ ♕xf7 21 ♕xf4
♕xa2 22 ♖xc8 ♘xc8 23 ♕xd4 f4 24
♕e4 fxg3 25 hxg3 and White went on
to win in Tkachiev-Nikolaidis,
Cannes 1995.

10...h6

A familiar move, preparing an escape square for the bishop. Alternatives are:

a) 10...♗e7 11 ♘d6+ ♗xd6 12 exd6
0-0 13 dxc5 ♘xe3 14 fxe3 ♘xc5 15
♕d4 ♕b6 16 ♖ac1 ♘e4 17 d7 ♖fd8 18
♕xb6 axb6 19 ♘e5 with a promising
endgame for White, as in the encoun-
ter Smirin-Vyzmanavin, Novosibirsk
1995.

b) 10...b5 11 ♗g5 ♕b8 12 ♘e3 h6
13 ♗h4 ♘xe3 14 fxe3 a6 15 a4! (this
exposes serious weaknesses in Black's
position) 15...cxd4 16 axb5 g5 17 ♗g3
dxe3 18 ♘d4 ♗g6 19 bxa6 ♗c5 20
♘b5 ♔e7 21 ♔h1 and White soon
won in Kveinys-Velicka, Cappelle la
Grande 1996.

11 a4

This is perhaps a little slow and
Ehlvest recommends instead 11 dxc5!
♘xc5 12 ♘d4, when the threats to
capture on f5 or enter on b5 and d6
give White a good game. It is very
dangerous for Black to play 12...♗g6
13 ♘b5 ♘xe3 14 fxe3, when the open
d- and f-files and active white knights
create serious difficulties for Black.

**11...a6 12 ♖c1 ♖c8 13 ♕b3 cxd4
14 ♘xd4 ♘c5 15 ♕d1**

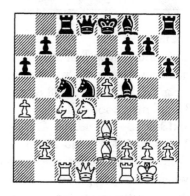

If Black could develop his king's
bishop and get castled he would have a
good game as White's e-pawn and his
queenside would then be a little weak.
However, Ehlvest now plays very dy-
namically to prevent Black from

coordinating his forces.

15...♗h7

15...♗g6 16 ♗h5! creates promising pressure on the central light squares.

16 ♗h5! ♕d7

16...♗e7? runs into 17 ♘d6+ (17 ♘xe6 is more speculative, e.g. 17...♘xe6 18 ♘d6+ ♗xd6 19 ♕xd5 g6) 17...♗xd6 18 exd6 ♕xd6 19 ♘xe6 ♕xe6 20 ♗xc5, with a continuing attack.

17 ♕f3

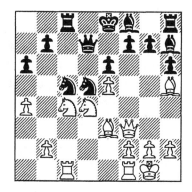

17...♖d8

A good idea of White's possibilities in this position is provided by the variations after 17...♗d3, e.g. 18 ♘xe6! ♘xe6 (18...♕xe6 19 ♗g4) 19 ♗xf7+ ♔d8 (19...♔e7 20 ♘d6) 20 ♘b6 ♘xb6 21 ♗xb6+ ♔e7 22 ♖xc8 ♕xc8 23 ♗h5 with a winning attack.

18 ♕g3

Again preventing Black from developing his king's bishop.

18...♘e4 19 ♕h3 ♘xe3

19...♗e7 is again impossible, this time because of 20 ♘xe6.

20 fxe3 ♘g5 21 ♕g3 g6

see following diagram

22 ♘b6!

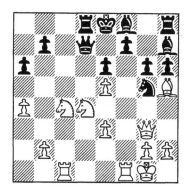

This unexpected move (the knight was usefully eyeing the d6 square) exposed a hidden weakness in the black position – the c8 square.

22...♕e7 23 ♗e2 ♘e4

23...♗g7 24 ♘c8 wins.

24 ♕g4 g5 25 ♘xe6!

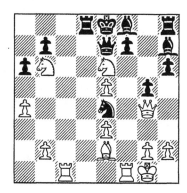

25...h5

This move strongly reminds me of the Polugayevsky variation of the Sicilian Najdorf where Black, faced with a devastating attack along open central files, calmly advances his pawns on the kingside to harry the white queen. However, here there is a more specific reason for this advance as 25...♕xe6 26 ♕xe6+ fxe6 27 ♗h5+ ♔e7 28 ♖f7+ ♔e8 29 ♖xh7 is checkmate.

26 ♕xe4!

Ehlvest plays this attack very accurately. 26 ♕xh5 ♕xe6 27 ♗c4 looks overwhelming but 27...♗g6! hangs on for Black.

26...♗xe4 27 ♘c7+ ♕xc7 28 ♖xc7

Although Black has succeeded in exchanging queens, White retains a huge initiative.

28...♖d2 29 ♗f3 ♗xf3 30 gxf3 ♗e7 31 ♖xb7 ♖xb2

This loses a piece, but Black's position was beyond hope anyway.

32 ♖b8+ ♗d8 33 ♖d1 0-0 34 ♖dxd8 1-0

Game 14
Vasiukov-Vyzmanavin
Elista 1995

---

1 e4 c6 2 d4 d5 3 e5 ♗f5 4 ♘f3 e6 5 ♗e2 c5 6 ♗e3 ♘d7 7 c4

With this move White tries to save time by delaying castling. He hopes that by blasting open the centre immediately, he can create problems for Black before he has time to develop.

7...cxd4

7...dxc4 is seen in the next game.

8 ♘xd4 ♗xb1 9 ♖xb1 ♗b4+

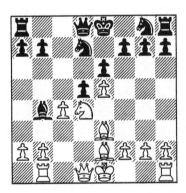

10 ♔f1!?

White hopes the loss of the opportunity to castle will be compensated for by the disorganised nature of Black's forces. 10 ♗d2 ♗xd2+ 11 ♕xd2 ♘e7?! 12 cxd5 ♘xd5 13 f4 0-0 14 0-0 ♕b6 15 ♗f3 ♘b4 16 a3 ♘c6 17 ♖bd1 ♖fd8 18 ♗xc6 bxc6 19 ♕f2 gave White a small edge in Anand-Gulko, Riga 1995. However, 11...♘xe5 would have left the onus on White to justify his play.

10...♘e7 11 ♕a4 ♕a5 12 ♕xa5 ♗xa5 13 f4

Black has an easier time of it after 13 b4, e.g. 13...♗c7 14 f4 dxc4 15 ♗xc4 0-0 16 ♗b3 ♗b6 17 ♔e2 ♖fd8 18 ♖hd1 with a balanced position in Ehlvest-Gulko, Riga 1995.

13...♗b6 14 ♔f2

14...♘c5?

Black is seduced by the idea of getting his knight to e4, but simpler was 14...0-0 15 ♖bc1 ♖ac8 16 ♔f3 ♘c6 17 ♖hd1 ♘xd4+ 18 ♗xd4 ♗xd4 19 ♖xd4 f6 with an equal game.

15 ♔f3! dxc4 16 ♗xc4 0-0 17 ♖hd1 ♖fd8 18 ♘b5

Black's knight on c5 has now become something of a target.

18...♘f5 19 ♗f2 h5 20 h3 ♘a4 21 b3 ♗xf2 22 ♔xf2 ♘c5 23 g4 hxg4 24 hxg4 ♘e7 25 b4 ♘a4 26 ♗b3 ♘b6 27 f5

White's active pieces give a very good endgame.

27...♘bd5 28 ♘d6 ♖d7 29 ♖bc1 ♘c6 30 ♘xb7 ♘xe5 31 ♘c5 ♖e7 32 fxe6 ♘xb4 33 exf7+ ♘xf7 34 ♘e6 ♔h7 35 a3 ♖ae8 36 ♖h1+ ♔g6 37 axb4 ♖xe6 38 ♗xe6 ♖xe6 39 ♖he1 ♖b6 40 ♖e4 ♖a6 41 ♖c7 ♘h6 42 ♔g3 ♘g8 43 ♖e8 ♔h7 44 g5 1-0

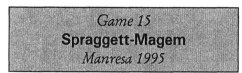

Game 15
Spraggett-Magem
Manresa 1995

1 e4 c6 2 d4 d5 3 e5 ♗f5 4 ♘f3 e6 5 ♗e2 c5 6 ♗e3 ♘d7 7 c4 dxc4 8 ♘c3

8 0-0 allows Black to transpose to Games 11-13 with 8...a6 9 ♗xc4 ♘e7. As usual, 8...♘e7 is a perfectly reasonable alternative, planning to meet 9 ♗xc4 with 9...♘c6.

8...a6 9 ♗xc4 ♘e7

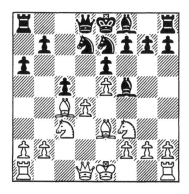

10 d5!?

10 0-0 would again transpose back to familiar positions, but Spraggett has

an imaginative idea in mind to put the tempo saved by not castling to good use.

10...♘b6

10...exd5 11 ♘xd5 ♘b6 12 ♘xb6 ♕xb6 13 0-0 gives White a small plus thanks to his lead in development. After the text move White's idea is revealed.

11 d6 ♘xc4 12 ♕a4+ b5 13 ♘xb5 axb5 14 ♕xb5+ ♕d7 15 ♕xc4

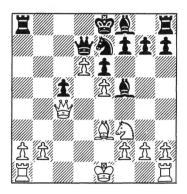

With two pawns, including a big passed one on d6, and an active position White has good compensation for the piece.

15...♘c6

An interesting psychological choice in this position would have been 15...♕a4!? 16 ♕xa4+ ♖xa4 17 dxe7 ♗xe7, when White would have to change his perspective from attack to defence – not always an easy thing to do in the heat of battle.

16 0-0 f6 17 ♖fd1 ♘xe5 18 ♘xe5 fxe5 19 ♗xc5 g5!? 20 a4

White's queenside pawns are well supported by his pieces and will prove difficult for Black to stop.

20...♗g7 21 a5 0-0 22 b4 ♖fb8

This is rather passive. A better try is

22...e4!? 23 ♖a3 ♗e5, planning ...♕f7-h5 with kingside counterplay.

23 a6 ♗g6 24 ♖a5 ♗f6

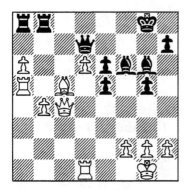

25 h3!

White's weak back rank makes further advances on the queenside tactically suspect as the following variation shows: 25 b5?! ♗d8 26 b6 ♗xb6 27 ♗xb6 ♖xb6 28 ♕c7 ♕c6! 29 ♕xc6 ♖xc6 30 d7 ♗d3!

25...♗e8 26 ♗e3 ♖c8 27 ♕e4 ♖cb8 28 b5! ♗g6 29 ♕c6 ♗e8 30 ♕f3! ♗d8 31 b6 ♕c6 32 ♕g4 ♖xb6!? 33 ♗xb6 ♕xb6 34 ♖xe5 ♗g6 35 ♕xe6+ ♔g7 36 ♕d7+

36 d7! would have been easier.

36...♔h6 37 ♕b5 ♖xa6 38 ♕xb6 ♗xb6

38...♖xb6 39 d7 ♔g7 40 ♖e8 ♖b8 gave Black chances to hold.

39 d7 ♖a8 40 ♖e6! ♗c5?

Black is losing anyway, e.g. 40...♗a5 41 ♖a1 or 40...♗d8 41 ♖c6!

41 d8♕ 1-0

> ### Game 16
> ### Short-Adianto
> *Jakarta 1996*

1 e4 c6 2 d4 d5 3 e5 ♗f5 4 ♘f3 e6

5 ♗e2 c5 6 ♗e3 ♘d7

Note that after 6...♘c6?! a similar plan to the one Short adopts in this game is very promising as Black has got his knights into a slight tangle, e.g. 7 dxc5 ♘ge7 8 ♘bd2 ♘g6 9 ♘d4 and Black is struggling to regain his pawn with a satisfactory position.

7 ♘bd2!? ♘e7

7...cxd4 8 ♘xd4 ♘xe5 9 ♗b5+ ♘d7 10 ♘xf5 exf5 11 ♕f3 is not a great idea for Black but 8...♘e7 is possible.

8 dxc5 ♘c6

9 ♘b3

Short's idea is to give up the centre to gain time and force the black pieces onto awkward squares in order to regain the pawn.

9...♗g4?!

9...♘dxe5 10 ♘xe5 ♘xe5 11 ♘d4 gives White a useful initiative. Short suggests 9...♗e4!, giving the variation 10 ♘g5!? (10 0-0 ♗xf3 11 ♗xf3 ♘cxe5 is probably about equal) 10...♗xg2 11 ♖g1 ♗e4 as unclear.

10 ♘fd4 ♗xe2 11 ♕xe2 ♘dxe5

11...♘cxe5, in order to retain the d7-knight to put pressure on the e5-pawn, seems more logical, e.g. 12 0-0-0 ♘c4! 13 ♖he1 ♖c8 with a balanced position, Bologan-Galkin, Russia 1996. Now Short swiftly gains control of the position.

12 f4 ♘c4 13 ♘xc6 bxc6 14 ♗d4

The white bishop dominates the board making it difficult for Black to develop.

14...♕h4+ 15 g3 ♕e7 16 0-0 h5 17 ♖ae1 0-0-0 18 ♘c1!

Suddenly the black knight on c4 is seriously embarrassed.

18...♕b7 19 ♘d3 h4 20 g4 h3 21 a4 ♕c7 22 b3 ♗e7 23 g5 ♔b7 24 ♕f2 e5 25 fxe5 ♗xg5 26 bxc4 dxc4 27 ♘f4 ♗h4 28 ♖b1+ ♔a8 29 ♕e3 ♕d7 30 c3 ♗g5 31 e6 ♕c8 32 exf7 ♖h4 33 ♕e6 1-0

1 e4 c6 2 d4 d5 3 e5 ♗f5 4 ♘f3 e6 5 ♗e2 c5 6 ♗e3 cxd4

A common alternative to 6...♘d7.

7 ♘xd4 ♘e7 8 0-0

The more direct 8 c4 is seen in the next game and the unusual 8 ♗g5 in Game 19.

8...♘bc6 9 ♗b5

9 c4 has been tried many times but it seems to be equal for White at best, e.g. 9...♘xd4 10 ♗xd4 ♘c6 11 cxd5 ♕xd5 12 ♗c3 (12 ♗f3 ♗e4 13 ♗xe4 ♕xe4 14 ♗c3 ♖d8 15 ♘d2 ♕d5 and Black has a very comfortable game, Tseitlin-Finkel, Beersheba 1996) 12...♕xd1 13 ♖xd1 ♗c2 14 ♖e1 ♗e4 15 ♗f1 ♗d5 16 ♘d2 ♗e7 17 ♘c4 0-0-0 18 a3 ♔b8 and, if anything, Black has slightly the better of the endgame, as in Iordachescu-Leko, Erevan Olympiad 1996.

9...a6 10 ♗xc6+ bxc6 11 c4

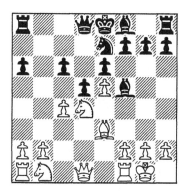

11...♕d7

The immediate 11...dxc4!? is also possible. Play can then continue 12 ♘xf5 ♕xd1 13 ♖xd1 ♘xf5 14 ♘d2 ♘xe3 15 fxe3, when White has an edge in the endgame as his pieces will quickly become active and his doubled e-pawns are not a problem.

12 ♘c3 dxc4 13 ♘a4

Although 13 ♘xf5 ♕xd1 would give White an extra tempo over the previous note, it is more of a hindrance than a help as his knight is misplaced on c3.

13...♘d5 14 ♘xf5 exf5 15 ♗d4 ♖d8

White has succeeded in holding up

Black's development as 15...♗e7?! is met by 16 e6 fxe6 17 ♗xg7 ♖g8 18 ♕h5+ ♔d8 19 ♕xh7 and White stands well.

16 ♕f3

Now 16...♗e7 still runs into 17 e6, but Karpov finds a clever way to exploit the unprotected nature of the white minor pieces.

16...c5! 17 ♘xc5 ♕b5!

This is a very accurate move from Karpov as 17...♕c6 18 ♖fc1! ♘b4 19 ♖xc4 ♖xd4 20 ♖xd4 ♕xf3 21 gxf3 ♗xc5 22 ♖c4 ♘d3, when in *ChessBase Magazine*, Ftacnik gives 23 ♖d1 ♗xf2+ 24 ♔f1 ♘xb2 25 ♖c8+ ♔e7 26 ♖c7+ ♔e6 27 ♖d2 with an edge, but 23 ♖c3 seems crushing.

18 a4 ♕b4

Not 18...♕c6 19 ♖fc1! as in the previous note. Now White seems to be in trouble as 19 ♘xa6 ♕a5 leaves his knight trapped. However, Gelfand finds a way to maintain the balance with a piece sacrifice.

19 e6! ♗xc5 20 ♗xg7 ♖g8 21 exf7+ ♔xf7 22 ♗c3 ♘xc3

22...♕b7 23 ♕xf5+ ♔e8 24 ♖ae1+ ♘e7 25 ♖e4 would be very risky for Black so Karpov settles for a draw.

23 ♕xf5+ ♔g7 24 ♕g5+ ♔f7 25 ♕f5+ ♔g7 26 ♕g5+ ½-½

1 e4 c6 2 d4 d5 3 e5 ♗f5 4 ♘f3 e6 5 ♗e2 c5 6 ♗e3 cxd4 7 ♘xd4 ♘e7 8 c4 ♘bc6 9 ♕a4 dxc4

Or 9...a6 10 ♘a3 ♕a5+ 11 ♕xa5 ♘xa5 12 cxd5 exd5 13 0-0 ♘ac6 14 ♖ad1 ♘xd4 15 ♗xd4 ♘c6 16 ♗b6 ♗e6 17 f4 ♗xa3 18 bxa3 g6 19 ♗f3 ♘e7 20 ♖c1 ♖c8 21 ♖xc8+ ♘xc8 22 ♗c5 and White's bishops were strong in Gallagher-Krueger, Bern 1995.

10 ♘a3 ♕a5+ 11 ♕xa5 ♘xa5 12 ♘ab5

Gelfand plays to complicate the position but the simple 12 ♘xc4 ♘xc4 13 ♗xc4 looks slightly better for White.

12...♘d5 13 ♘xf5 exf5 14 ♗d2 a6

Despite the exchange of queens the position remains tactically complex, e.g. 14...♗b4 15 ♘c7+ (15 ♗f3 0-0-0 16 ♗xb4 ♘xb4 17 ♘d6+ ♖xd6 18 exd6 ♘c2+ is good for Black) 15...♘xc7 16 ♗xb4 ♘c6 17 ♗d6 ♘b5 18 ♗xc4 ♘xd6 19 exd6 0-0-0 20 0-0-0 ♖d7 and White has an edge.

15 ♘d4

After 15 ♘d6+ ♗xd6 16 exd6 c3 17 bxc3 ♖c8 White has the bishop pair but the black knights are more active.

15...♗b4

More combative than 15...♘c6 16 ♘xc6 bxc6 17 ♗xc4, which leaves White with a simple advantage.

16 ♘xf5 0-0 17 ♗xb4

17 0-0-0 is tempting but Black can keep the balance with 17...c3!, e.g. 18

bxc3 ♘xc3 19 ♗xc3 ♗xc3 20 f4 ♖fd8.

17...♘xb4 18 0-0 b5 19 f4 ♖fd8 20 ♖ad1

White's kingside pawn majority is balanced by Black's three to two on the opposite wing. However, White has the better chances because his minor pieces are more active, his bishop will be better than a black knight and his outpost on d6 is more relevant than Black's on d3.

20...♔f8 21 ♘d6 ♖ab8

The white a-pawn is immune, e.g. 21...♘xa2 22 ♖a1 and the knights are skewered.

22 a3 ♘bc6 23 ♗f3 ♖d7 24 ♖fe1 ♖c7 25 f5 ♖d8 26 ♗g4 h5??

Gelfand has consolidated his position skilfully and now Karpov, unusually, cracks under the pressure. Much better was 26...♖e7!, when he remains only slightly worse after 27 e6 fxe6 28 fxe6 g6. Not good, though, is 26...♖cd7 27 f6 ♖c7 28 fxg7+ ♔xg7 29 ♘f5+ when White has a clear advantage. With the text move Karpov may have been hoping to use the pin that he obtains on the d-file but Gelfand can power his way to a winning endgame.

27 ♗xh5 ♖cd7 28 ♗xf7 ♖xd6

28...♘xe5 29 ♖xe5 ♖xd6 30 ♖xd6 ♖xd6 31 ♗g6 is hopeless for Black.

29 ♖xd6 ♖xd6 30 exd6 ♔xf7 31 d7 ♘b7 32 ♖e8 ♘bd8 33 ♔f2

Two knights are usually more than a match for a rook, but not when they are completely hamstrung.

33...a5 34 ♔e3 ♔f6 35 g4 ♔g5 36 h3 b4 37 axb4 axb4 38 ♔d2 ♔f6 39 h4 g6 40 fxg6 ♔xg6 41 h5+ ♔h6 42 ♔c1 ♔g5 43 ♖h8 ♔f6 44 ♖g8 ♔f7

45 ♖e8 1-0

1 e4 c6 2 d4 d5 3 e5 ♗f5 4 ♘f3 e6 5 ♗e2 c5 6 ♗e3 cxd4 7 ♘xd4 ♘e7 8 ♗g5!?

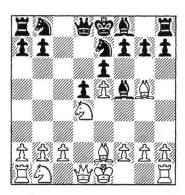

An interesting move, trying to disrupt Black's development by threatening to take on f5.

8...♕a5+ 9 ♘c3 ♗g6 10 0-0 ♘ec6?

After this White gains time by attacking the black queen. It would have been better to play either 10...a6 or 10...h6.

11 ♘b3! ♕b6 12 ♗e3 ♕d8 13 f4 ♘d7 14 g4 f5

As White has a big lead in development, Black is trying desperately to keep the position closed.

15 ♗d3 fxg4 16 ♕xg4

16 ♗xg6+ hxg6 17 ♕xg4 ♔f7 18 ♘xd5 ♖h4 19 ♕g2 exd5 20 ♕xd5+ is a promising sacrifice for White.

16...♗f7

see following diagram

17 ♘xd5

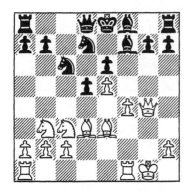

White has an excellent position but here he gets slightly carried away. It was better to mobilise his last piece with 17 ♖ae1, when the threats of ♘xd5 and f4-f5 would have been very difficult to meet.

17...exd5 18 e6 ♘f6 19 exf7+ ♚xf7 20 ♕h3 ♗d6 21 ♖ae1 ♕c7 22 ♗d2

Despite his small lapse on move 17, White still retains a very good position.

22...♖ae8 23 ♖xe8 ♖xe8 24 ♗xh7 ♘e7 25 ♗d3 ♕c8 26 ♕xc8 ♖xc8 27 ♗e3 b6 28 ♘d4?

This careless move allows Black to regain his lost pawn with a quick attack against the weak white pawns on the kingside.

28...♘g4 29 ♘b5 ♗b8 30 ♗d4 ♖h8 31 ♗e2 ♖h4! 32 h3 ♖xh3 33 ♚g2 ♖h2+ 34 ♚f3 ♖h4 35 ♗d3 ♘h2+ 36 ♚g3 g5 37 ♖f2 ♘g4 38 ♖f1 ♘h2 39 ♖f2 ♘g4 ½-½

Game 20
Adams-Brunner
Garmisch 1994

---

1 e4 c6 2 d4 d5 3 e5 ♗f5 4 ♘f3 e6 5 ♗e2 c5 6 ♗e3 ♘e7

This could simply transpose into the variation 6...cxd4 7 ♘xd4 ♘e7 but by delaying the exchange, Black gives his opponent an extra opportunity.

7 dxc5

Another way to try to exploit Black's move order is 7 c4 but this did not prove very effective in Shirov-Anand, Dortmund 1996, after 7...dxc4 8 ♘c3 ♘bc6 9 dxc5 ♘d5 10 ♘xd5 ♕xd5 11 0-0 ♗d3 12 ♖c1 ♖d8 13 ♗xd3 cxd3 and Black had no problems.

7...♘ec6

7...♘d7 8 ♘bd2 ♘c6 9 ♘b3 would transpose into Short-Adianto, Game 16. Now 8 ♘bd2 is prevented (8...d4), but Adams finds a different plan.

8 c4 dxc4 9 ♕xd8+ ♚xd8 10 ♘c3 ♘d7 11 0-0-0 ♚c8 12 ♗xc4 ♘dxe5

12...♗xc5 13 ♗xc5 ♘xc5 14 ♘b5 leaves Black with a rather prospectless position.

13 ♘xe5 ♘xe5 14 ♗e2 ♗e7

Black's only problem in this position is that it is not easy for him to develop his queen's rook. This looks likely to be only a temporary difficulty as it seems improbable that White will find a way to generate an attack quickly enough to exploit his better mobilisation. However, Adams finds an ingenious way to break open the kingside before Black can coordinate his rooks.

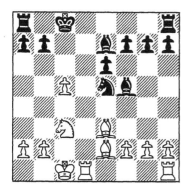

15 h3 g5

15...h5 16 f4 ♘d7 17 b4 keeps White on top. With 15...g5 Black is hoping to keep his knight on its strong central post but Adams quickly drives it back.

16 g4 ♗g6 17 h4! gxh4 18 f4 ♘d7 19 ♖hf1 f5

This unpleasant move is forced as White was threatening to win a piece with f4-f5. Now, however, Black's position is becoming dangerously exposed.

20 ♗c4 ♘f8 21 ♗d4 ♖g8 22 g5 ♗h5 23 ♖de1 ♖g6 24 ♖h1 ♗g4 25 ♖xh4 ♖xg5 26 ♗xe6+ ♔d8 27 ♗d5 ♖g6 28 ♖h2 ♖c8

Black finally activates his queen's rook but it immediately has to give itself up for White's bishop.

29 ♗xb7 ♖xc5 30 ♗xc5 ♗xc5 31 ♖d2+ ♔c7 32 ♗h1 ♘e6 33 b4 ♗f8 34 ♘d5+ ♔c8 35 ♔b1 ♗d6 36 ♘b6+ axb6 37 ♖xd6 ♘xf4 38 ♖c1+ 1-0

Summary

After 6 ♗e3 ♘d7 7 c4 dxc4 8 0-0 ♘e7, 9 ♘a3 seems quite promising. Black has not had an easy time of it after 9 ♘a3, but maybe the idea of 9...c3!? is the way to go. Black can side-step this possibility by means of an early ...a7-a6 (instead of ...♘e7), when 9 ♘a3 is not an option (9...b5) but this gives White the chance for a quick d4-d5 (see note to White's ninth move in Game 11). However, whether this brings any advantage is unclear.

If Black decides to clear up the central tension with 6 ♗e3 cxd4 7 ♘xd4 ♘e7 then the most promising line for White seems to be 8 c4 ♘bc6 9 ♕a4, while Kveinys' 8 ♗g5!? is also worth a look.

1 e4 c6 2 d4 d5 3 e5 ♗f5 4 ♘f3 e6 5 ♗e2 c5 6 ♗e3
6...♘d7
> 6...cxd4 7 ♘xd4 ♘e7 *(D)*
>> 8 0-0 – *Game 17*; 8 c4 – *Game 18*; 8 ♗g5 – *Game 19*
> 6...♘e7 – *Game 20*

7 c4 *(D)*
> 7 ♘bd2 – *Game 11*
> 7 0-0
>> 7...a6 8 c4 – see *Games 11 and 12* (by transposition)
>> 7...♘e7 8 c4 dxc4 – see *Game 13* (by transposition)

7...dxc4
> 7...cxd4 – *Game 14*

8 0-0
> 8 ♘c3 – *Game 15*

8...a6
> 8...♘e7 – *Game 13*

9 ♗xc4 ♘e7 10 ♘c3 *(D)* **b5**
> 10...♘c6 – *Game 12*

11 ♗d3 – *Game 11*

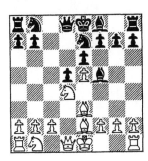

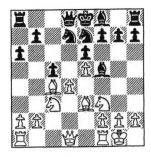

7...♘e7   *7 c4*   *10 ♘c3*

CHAPTER THREE

4 ♘f3 e6 5 ♗e2 ♘d7
6 0-0 ♘e7

1 e4 c6 2 d4 d5 3 e5 ♗f5 4 ♘f3 e6 5 ♗e2 ♘d7 6 0-0 ♘e7

With this scheme of development, Black renounces an immediate ...c6-c5, although this move often follows before too long. As with all things in life, this idea has its good and bad points. On the plus side, Black is less vulnerable to a swift opening of the position with c2-c4 or d4xc5. However, the flip side is that he places less immediate pressure on White's centre, who is thus able to maintain flexibility for longer than in lines with 5...c5.

The most critical try for White is 7 ♘h4(!), hunting down the exposed black bishop. After this bishop drops back to g6, White exchanges with ♘xg6 and Black recaptures with the h-pawn. The resulting structure is very interesting. Black has a solid position but is rather passive and must be careful not to drift into a position where he has no hope of active play. Castling kingside is, surprisingly, very dangerous. As we see in Game 21, White has a ready-made plan to attack with the advance of his h-pawn and it is hard for Black to get his counterplay on the queenside going. The important lesson here is that Black can use his kingside pawn front aggressively with ...f7-f6 and/or ...g6-g5 and must not commit his king too early.

If White does not take the opportunity for 7 ♘h4 Black should gain a decent game as he has time to preserve the bishop with either ...h7-h6 (Game 26) or, for example, 7 ♘bd2 c5 8 c3 ♘c6, holding up ♘h4 (Game 27).

Game 21
Hellers-Berg
Copenhagen Open 1991

1 e4 c6 2 d4 d5 3 e5 ♗f5 4 ♗e2 e6 5 ♘f3 c5 6 0-0 ♘d7 7 c3

Although this game soon transposes to our main line, note that the combination of ...♘d7 and ...c6-c5 is not a happy one for Black. The correct way for White to exploit this is 7 c4! – see Game 33. The lesson for Black is that if he wants to play a quick ...c6-c5, he nearly always needs either to have his queen's knight on c6, or at least have the option of moving it there.

7...♘e7 8 ♘h4 ♗g6 9 ♘d2 ♘c6

See Game 23 for 9...♖c8.

10 ♘xg6 hxg6 11 ♘f3 cxd4

The immediate 11...♗e7 is considered in the next game.

12 cxd4 ♗e7

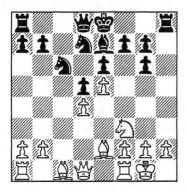

13 g3

White creates the possibility of gaining space on the kingside with h2-h4 and waits to see how Black will complete his development. Also possible is 13 ♗d2 0-0?! (This provides White with a clear plan of attack. As we shall see in other examples, Black must keep the option of castling queenside to maintain flexibility in his position.) 14 ♗d3 a6 15 g3 ♕b6 16 ♗c3 ♖ae8 (already Black has no play at all and can only watch as White builds up at leisure on the kingside) 17 ♕d2 ♕d8 18 ♔g2 ♘b6 19 b3 ♗a3 20 ♖ad1 ♕e7 21 ♕f4 ♘d7 22 ♕g4 ♖c8 23 ♗d2 ♖fe8 24 h4 and White won quickly in Gallagher-Polak, Bern 1995.

13...♕b6 14 ♖b1

This move, testing Black's resolve about placing his king on the queen-side, is more combative than 14 ♔g2, after which Black had no problems in Lau-Borik, German Bundesliga 1995/96: 14...0-0-0 (despite the open c-file, the black king is actually much safer on this wing) 15 a3 f6 16 exf6 gxf6 17 b4 ♔b8 18 ♗e3 g5 (Black now threatens to gain a big initiative on the kingside with ...♖dg8, ...f6-f5 and ...g5-g4. White manages to mount a holding operation, but Black has a very comfortable game) 19 ♖h1 ♖dg8 20 h4 gxh4 21 ♖xh4 ♖xh4 22 ♘xh4 f5 23 ♘f3 ♗d6 24 ♕d2 ♘f6 25 ♗f4 ♕c7 26 ♗xd6 ♕xd6 27 ♔f1 ♘e4 28 ♕e3 ♖h8 29 ♔g2 ♖g8 30 ♔f1 ♖h8 31 ♔g2 ½-½.

14...♖c8?

This move, eliminating the possibility of ...0-0-0, is a bad mistake as now Black is never able to co-ordinate his position. Much better were either 14...f6 or 14...g5, exploiting the slight weakness of the white d-pawn.

15 h4

White prevents ...g6-g5 and leaves Black with nothing much to do.

15...0-0

It would have been better to try 15...f6 16 exf6 gxf6 but, compared with Lau-Borik, Black will have long-term problems with his king.

16 ♔g2 ♖c7 17 ♖h1 ♖fc8 18 h5 g5 19 ♗e3 ♘f8 20 h6 g6 21 h7+ ♘xh7 22 ♖h6

White's successful kingside attack stems from the fact that his centre is rock solid and Black has no counterplay.

22...g4 23 ♕h1 gxf3+ 24 ♗xf3 ♔f8 25 ♖xh7 ♔e8 26 ♗xd5! ♘b4

26...exd5 27 ♖h8+ ♗f8 28 ♗h6 wins.

27 ♗b3 ♕c6+ 28 ♔h2 b5 29 ♕xc6+ ♖xc6 30 ♔g2 ♘c2 31 ♗h6 ♘xd4 32 ♖d1

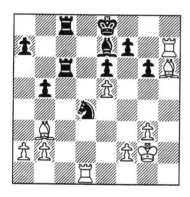

Black has managed to survive to an endgame but now his king is caught in the crossfire of the white pieces.

32...♗c5 33 ♗e3 ♘xb3 34 ♖h8+ ♗f8 35 axb3 ♖c2 36 ♗h6 ♔e7 37 ♗g5+ ♔e8 38 ♖dh1 ♔d7 39 ♖1h7 ♔e8 40 ♖xf8+ 1-0

Game 22
Khalifman-Lobron
Munich 1992

---

1 e4 c6 2 d4 d5 3 e5 ♗f5 4 ♘f3 e6 5 ♗e2 ♘e7 6 0-0 ♘d7 7 ♘h4 ♗g6

The most natural move for Black.

7...♗e4 is considered in Game 24 and 7...♕b6 in Game 25.

8 ♘d2 c5 9 c3 ♘c6 10 ♘xg6 hxg6 11 ♘f3 ♗e7 12 ♗e3 a6 13 g3

13...g5

This move does not signify the start of an optimistic kingside attack; it is a space gaining manoeuvre, played before White prevents the idea with h2-h4. Black plans to play ...f7-f6, and does not want to be left with a weak pawn on g6.

14 ♔g2 cxd4 15 cxd4 ♘f8 16 ♖c1

White's passive play in this game allows Black to co-ordinate his position successfully by castling queenside. At least he should make Black think twice about this by advancing on the queen's wing, e.g. 16 a3 f6 17 h3 ♕d7 18 b4 when ...0-0-0 is suddenly a much less attractive proposition. Smirin-Li Wenliang, Beijing Cup 1996, continued 18...♗d8 19 ♖c1 ♘g6 20 ♗d3 ♘ge7 21 ♖e1 ♗c7 22 ♗d2 ♗b6 23 ♗c3 ♖c8 24 a4 ♔f7 25 ♖c2 ♘d8 26 a5 ♗a7 27 ♕b1 ♖c7 28 ♖ec1 ♕c8 29 b5 (White has managed to keep Black's central and kingside ambitions in check while advancing himself on the queenside) 29...axb5 30 ♕xb5 ♕d7 31

♕b1 ♘f5 32 ♗b5 ♕c8 33 ♗b4 ♖xc2 34 ♖xc2 ♘c6 35 a6 ♕b8 36 axb7 ♘cxd4 37 ♘xd4 ♗xd4 38 ♗d6 ♘xd6 39 exd6 ♗b6 40 ♗e8+ ♖xe8 41 ♕xb6 1-0.

16...f6 17 h3 ♕d7 18 ♖c3 ♗d8 19 a3 ♘g6

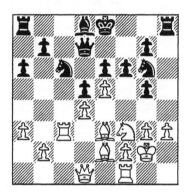

20 ♖h1

White decides to break Black's clamp on the kingside with h2-h4 at some point, but this is a very unambitious. A plan with b2-b4 followed by doubling rooks on the c-file must be better.

20...♗b6 21 ♗d3 ♘ge7 22 ♗c2 0-0-0 23 exf6 gxf6 24 h4 gxh4 25 ♖xh4 ♔b8

White has carried out his plan but it has not got him very far. He has a weak d-pawn, his king is rather vulnerable and he must watch out for a black advance with ...e6-e5.

26 ♕h1 ♕c8 27 b4 ♖xh4 28 ♕xh4 ♖f8 29 ♗f4+ ♔a8 30 ♗h6 ♖f7 31 ♗e3 ♕g8 32 ♗d3 e5 33 dxe5 ♗xe3 34 e6

This small tactic enables White to break up the black centre. However, this is of little relevance as the key features of the position are the activity of

the black forces and the broken white kingside.

34...♖g7 35 fxe3 ♕xe6 36 ♔f2 ♘e5 37 ♘xe5 fxe5 38 e4 ♖f7+ 39 ♔g2 d4 40 ♖c5 ♕b3 41 ♕h5 ♖f8 42 ♗c4 ♕e3 43 ♖xe5 ♘g6 0-1

A model game for Black in this line.

Game 23
Short-Yudasin
Erevan Olympiad 1996

1 e4 c6 2 d4 d5 3 e5 ♗f5 4 ♘f3 e6 5 ♗e2 ♘e7 6 0-0 ♗g6 7 c3 ♘d7 8 ♘h4 c5 9 ♘d2

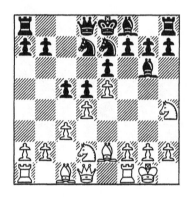

9...♖c8

A similar scheme of development to the one Black adopts in this game was seen in Lutz-Rogers, German Bundesliga 1995/96: 9...♘c6 10 ♘xg6 hxg6 11 ♘f3 ♕b6 12 ♖b1 ♗e7 13 ♗e3 ♖c8 14 g3 cxd4 15 cxd4 ♕a5 16 a3 a6 17 h4 b5 18 ♖a1 ♕b6 19 b3 ♗d8 20 ♕d3 ♘db8 21 ♖fc1 ♕b7 22 ♖c2 and again Black found himself in a position with very few prospects. The lesson that Black must keep options open for his king and look for counterplay with ...f7-f6 and ...g6-g5 should now be clear.

10 ♘xg6 hxg6 11 ♘f3 ♕b6 12 ♖b1

a6

Having taken away the possibility of ...0-0-0, Black again finds himself slightly stuck for a plan. 12...♘c6 is met simply by 13 b4! thanks to the pressure on the b-file.

13 b4 cxd4 14 cxd4 ♘f5?!

This leaves Black with a lifeless position as his best minor piece is now exchanged off. His only chance to generate some activity was 14...f6 15 b5 a5 16 ♗d3 g5, although this loosening of his position obviously entails certain risks.

15 g4 ♘h4 16 ♘xh4 ♖xh4

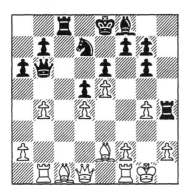

17 b5

This is an important component in White's plan. Black clearly does not want to allow the b-file to become opened as then his b-pawn would be terminally weak. He therefore has to allow the white pawn to remain on b5, where it takes away the key square c6 from Black's knight. If Black had been able to regroup this knight via b8 to c6 his prospects would have been much improved. Now, however, this piece is devoid of possibilities and remains a spectator until the end of the game.

17...a5 18 ♗e3 f5

Black later regrets this loosening on his position. However, sitting around and waiting for White to roll him up with f2-f4-f5 was not an attractive proposition either.

19 ♖c1 ♖b8

This is very passive, but with his other rook out of the game on h4 Black cannot afford to let White in on the c-file, e.g. 19...♖xc1 20 ♕xc1 ♗e7 21 ♕c8+ ♕d8 22 ♕xb7 and White is winning

20 ♗g5 ♖h7

Black plays his rook to this square, rather than h8, in the hope of creating trouble later by doubling rooks with ...♖bh8.

21 gxf5 exf5 22 ♗f3 ♗e7

Black's position is falling apart, e.g. 22...♕xb5 23 a4 ♕a6 24 ♗xd5 and the centre pawns will win the game for White.

23 ♕d2 ♗xg5 24 ♕xg5 ♖h6 25 ♕f4

White loses a little momentum after this. Stronger seems to be 25 ♗xd5 ♕xd4 26 ♖fd1 when Black will surely not survive long.

25...♖d8 26 ♗xd5 ♘f8 27 ♖c5 ♘d7 28 ♖c2 ♘f8 29 ♖c5 ♘d7 30 ♖c4 ♕xb5

After 30...♘f8 White would certainly not repeat but instead play 31 ♕f3 ♕xb5 32 ♖c5 with a continuing initiative.

31 ♗g8 ♖h8

see following diagram

32 ♕g5!

White's bishop was actually getting in the way of the advance of his central pawns. Short therefore sacrifices it to clear a path for their winning advance.

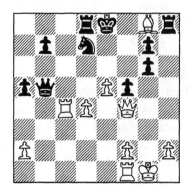

32...♖xg8 33 ♕xg6+ ♔e7 34 ♕d6+ ♔e8 35 ♕e6+ ♔f8 36 ♖fc1 ♕b6?!

In *ChessBase Magazine*, Psakhis points out the best defence which consists of the surprising 36...♘f6! This is best met by 37 ♖c7 (37 exf6 ♕d7! 38 ♕xd7 ♖xd7 39 ♖c8+ ♔f7 gives Black drawing chances in the rook endgame) 37...♕e8 38 ♕xf5 ♕h5 39 ♕xh5 ♘xh5 40 e6 ♔e8 41 ♖xb7 when White has three pawns for the knight and his rooks are very active.

37 ♕xf5+ ♔e7

37...♔e8 38 e6 ♘f6 39 ♕g6+ ♔e7 40 ♖c7+ ♔d6 41 ♕g3+ ♔xe6 42 ♕e5 is checkmate.

38 d5!

Now there is no defence to the advance of the white d- and e-pawns.

38...♕h6 39 d6+ ♔e8 40 e6 ♘f6 41 ♖c8 ♕h5 42 ♖xd8+

It makes no difference to the outcome of the game, but Short actually misses a forced mate with 42 ♕xh5+ ♘xh5 43 ♖1c7 and the doubled rooks swiftly combine to finish off the black king.

42...♔xd8 43 e7+ ♔e8 44 ♖c8+ 1-0

1 e4 c6 2 d4 d5 3 e5 ♗f5 4 ♘f3 e6 5 ♗e2 ♘d7 6 0-0 ♘e7 7 ♘h4 ♗e4!?

This is an interesting try from Adams. Black places his bishop on a slightly insecure post but it will prove difficult for White to exploit this directly.

8 ♘d2 ♘f5 9 ♘hf3 c5

9...♗e7 10 c3 0-0 11 ♘e1 c5 12 ♘xe4 dxe4 13 g4 led to complex play in Bologan-Polak, Vienna 1996. The game was eventually drawn after 13...♘h4 14 ♕c2 cxd4 15 cxd4 f5 16 ♗c4 ♘b6 17 ♗xe6+ ♔h8 18 d5 ♘xd5 19 gxf5 ♘c7 20 ♗b3 ♘xf5 21 ♕xe4 ♗c5 22 ♘f3 ♕e8 23 ♗c2 ♘e6 24 ♗e3 ♕g6+ 25 ♔h1 ♗xe3 26 fxe3 ♕h6 27 ♖g1 ♘xe3 28 ♖ac1 ♘c5 29 ♕xh7+ ♕xh7 30 ♗xh7 ♖xf3 31 ♖xc5 ♔xh7 32 ♖c7 ♘f5 33 ♖xb7 ♖c8 34 e6 ♖c2 35 ♖f7 ♖ff2 36 ♖g5 ♖f1+ ½-½.

10 c3 ♗e7

Shirov suggests that this is a little slow and prefers 10...cxd4 or 10...♕b6.

11 g4

As we saw in Game 2, Shirov likes to gain kingside space with this advance.

11...♗xf3 12 ♘xf3 ♘h4 13 ♘xh4 ♗xh4 14 f4 cxd4 15 cxd4 ♗e7 16 ♗e3 ♕b6 17 ♗d3 0-0 18 ♕e2

With his two bishops and obvious plan of a kingside attack, White has a good game. However, the exchange of two pairs of minor pieces has eased Black's cramp and White must be careful not to become too over-exposed.

18...f6

19 ♔g2?!

Shirov criticises this move and prefers 19 ♔h1! to free g1 for the white rook. The tactical justification of this plan can be seen in the following variation: 19...fxe5?! 20 fxe5 ♖xf1+ 21 ♖xf1 ♖f8 22 ♖c1 ♕d8 23 g5! ♗xg5? 24 ♕h5 ♗h6 25 ♖g1 ♔h8 26 ♗xh6 gxh6 27 ♗xh7 with a winning attack. Compare this to what actually happens in the game.

19...fxe5 20 fxe5 ♖xf1 21 ♖xf1 ♖f8 22 ♖c1 ♕d8 23 ♕c2

Now, with his king on g2, White has to continue in more circumspect fashion, as 23 g5!? ♗xg5 24 ♕h5

allows Black to defend, e.g. 24...♗h6! 25 ♗xh6 gxh6 26 ♕xh6 ♖f7! with an unclear position.

23...♗g5!

Adams is on the ball and finds a sharp pawn sacrifice. In comparison 23...h6 24 ♕c7 ♗g5 25 ♕xd8 ♗xd8, leaving White with a pleasant endgame edge, would be feeble.

24 ♗xh7+ ♔h8 25 ♖e1 ♗xe3 26 ♖xe3 ♖f4?

This enables Black to regain his pawn but unfortunately it allows his king to come under a very strong attack. Black's best plan, again indicated by Shirov, was to keep the initiative with 26...♕g5 which should be enough to hold the balance, e.g. 27 ♖g3 ♕f4 28 ♗d3 ♔g8 (but not the immediate 28...♕xd4? when 29 ♖h3+ ♔g8 30 ♗h7+ ♔f7 31 ♕g6+ ♔e7 32 ♕g5+ wins for White) 29 ♗h7+ (White is well advised to settle for a draw as after 29 ♕c3?! ♘b8! the d-pawn will prove indefensible) 29...♔h8 30 ♗d3 ♔g8 with a drawn position.

27 ♖g3

27...♖xd4?

Now the white attack breaks

through. A better defensive try was 27...♕h4 28 ♗d3 ♔g8 29 ♕c7 ♘f8 when White is on top but Black's active pieces mean that he should be able to set problems.

28 ♕f2! ♖b4 29 ♗g6 ♕h4

After 29...♕e7 30 ♖h3+ ♔g8 31 ♗f7+ ♕xf7 32 ♖h8+ the black queen goes.

30 ♕f7 ♖xb2+ 31 ♔f1 ♘f6 32 ♕f8+

Also winning was 32 exf6 ♕xf6+ 33 ♖f3.

32...♘g8 33 ♖c3 ♖b1+ 34 ♗xb1 ♕xg4 35 ♕f3 1-0

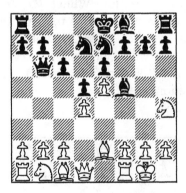

Game 25
Short-Adams
English Championship 1991

1 e4 c6 2 d4 d5 3 e5 ♗f5 4 ♘f3 e6 5 ♗e2 ♘d7 6 0-0 ♘e7 7 ♘h4 ♕b6

This typical queen thrust aims to put pressure on the slightly sensitive d4 and b2 squares. A further alternative is 7...c5 8 c3 (but not 8 ♘xf5? ♘xf5 9 c3 cxd4 10 cxd4 ♕b6) and now:

a) 8...♕b6 is natural but appears to be well met by 9 ♘a3, threatening ♘b5, e.g. 9...a6 10 dxc5 ♕xc5 11 ♗e3

♕c7 12 c4 (White has a lead in development and so, as usual, he blasts open the centre) 12...♗e4 13 f3 ♘f5 14 ♗f2 ♘xh4 15 fxe4 ♗c5 16 cxd5 0-0 17 ♖c1 ♗xf2+ 18 ♖xf2 ♕xe5 19 g3 ♕g5 (or 19...♘g6 20 dxe6 ♘f6 21 exf7+ ♔h8 22 ♗f3 with a solid plus for White, although Black has counterchances) 20 ♖c7 ♘e5 21 ♖xb7 ♖ac8 22 ♘c2 exd5 23 exd5 ♖c5 24 d6 and White had a big plus in Yudasin-Malisauskas, Chigorin Memorial 1996.

b) 8...♗xb1 9 ♖xb1 cxd4 10 cxd4 ♘c6 11 ♘f3 ♗e7 12 ♗d2 0-0 13 b4 a6 14 ♗d3 (White has a very pleasant game) 14...g6 15 a4 ♕b6 16 a5 ♕a7 17 ♗c3 ♖fc8 18 ♕d2 b5 19 ♕b2 ♖c7 20 ♖fe1 ♖ac8 21 ♗d2 ♗f8 22 g4 h6 23 h4 and White has all the chances, as in Rivero-Arencibia, Capablanca Memorial 1995.

8 ♘xf5

8 c3 is also possible and perhaps slightly more flexible. 8...c5 in reply gives White the opportunity for 9 ♘a3, as in Yudasin-Malisauskas given above, and 8...♗xb1 9 ♖xb1 also gives White a comfortable edge.

8...♘xf5 9 c3 c5 10 ♗d3 ♘e7

Or 10...g6 11 ♖e1 ♘b8 (As we have seen in earlier games, this is a very natural manoeuvre. Here, however, it leaves Black well behind in development and Nunn is very quick to exploit this.) 12 ♗xf5 gxf5 13 c4 dxc4 14 d5 ♘d7 15 ♘a3 0-0-0 16 ♗g5 ♖e8 17 ♘xc4 and White had an excellent position in Nunn-Adams, Brussels SWIFT 1992.

11 dxc5 ♕xc5 12 ♕e2 ♕c7 13 f4 g6 14 ♘d2 ♘f5 15 ♘f3 ♗c5+ 16 ♔h1 h5

17 g3

White chooses to prevent ...h5-h4 as after 17 ♗d2 h4 (with the unsubtle threat of 18...♘g3+) 18 ♗xf5 gxf5 19 h3 ♗e7 20 ♗e1 ♖c8 21 ♘d4 ♕c4 22 ♕f3 ♘c5 Black has an equal game, A.Rodriguez-Soppe, Villa Gesell 1996.

17...♘b8

17...h4 is now met simply by 18 g4.

18 ♗d2 ♘c6 19 b4 ♗b6 20 ♖ac1 ♔f8 21 c4

White opens the position, hoping to capitalise before Black can fully co-ordinate his forces.

21...dxc4 22 ♖xc4 ♕d7 23 ♗e4 ♔g7 24 a4 ♘cd4! 25 ♘xd4 ♗xd4 26 ♖f3

Black's 24th move has freed his position. It concealed the clever tactical point 26 ♖d1 h4! and if 27 g4? ♘g3+ 28 hxg3 hxg3+ 29 ♔g2 ♖h2+.

26...♖ac8 27 ♖xc8 ♕xc8

Black now has a comfortable game.

28 ♔g2 ♖d8 29 a5 ♗b2 30 ♖d3 ♕c4 31 ♕f3 ♘d4 32 ♕d1 b5 33 axb6 axb6 34 ♔h3 ♖c8 35 ♕b1 ♘c2 36 ♕h1 ♘xb4

Black has played well and won a pawn. Now, however, Short manages to cause sufficient confusion to

eventually force a draw.

37 ♖d7 ♕b5

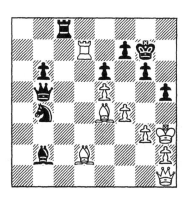

38 ♖xf7+!? ♔xf7 39 ♗xg6+! ♔e7

39...♔xg6 40 ♕e4+ and ♕b7+ follows.

40 ♕b7+ ♔d8 41 f5 ♕f1+ 42 ♔h4 ♕c4+ 43 ♔g5 ♘d5 44 fxe6

White is a whole rook down but his tremendous activity makes life difficult for Black.

44...♘c7?

44...♗a3, planning to regroup with ...♗e7+, was the right way and should win for Black.

45 ♕xb6 ♗a3 46 ♔f6! ♗c5

If 46...♗e7+ 47 ♔f7 White has the amazing threat of 48 ♕d6+! mating.

47 ♗g5!

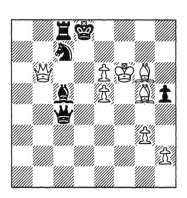

47...♖a8!

Adams finds an accurate move. One way to go wrong (apart from 47...♗xb6 48 ♔f7 mate) was 47...♕g4? 48 ♕xc5 and now the apparently crushing 48...♕xg5+ is neatly side-stepped by 49 ♔f7! and White wins.

48 ♔f7+ ♔c8 49 ♕c6 ♖a6 50 ♕d7+ ♔b8 51 ♗f5

Although he is still a rook down, White's three pawns and wonderful bishop pair provide good compensation. Adams is now content to force a draw.

51...♖a7 52 ♔g6 ♖a6 ½-½

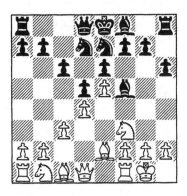

Game 26
Anand-Karpov
Candidates (5), Brussels 1991

1 e4 c6 2 d4 d5 3 e5 ♗f5 4 ♘f3 e6 5 ♗e2 ♘d7 6 0-0 ♘e7 7 c3 h6

This is a good reply to White's overly passive seventh move. Black ensures that he will either preserve his queen's bishop or that White will have to expend time exchanging it. Now it will be difficult for White to prove an advantage.

8 ♘a3 a6

This is a useful precaution as after 8...c5 9 ♘b5 ♘c6 10 c4 White takes the initiative in the centre.

9 ♘c2 ♗h7

A more risky strategy was seen in Bojkovic-A.Maric, Belgrade 1992, when after 9...♕c7 10 ♗e3 ♗h7 11 ♖c1 ♘f5 12 ♗f4 g5 13 ♗d2 ♗e7 14 ♘e3 0-0-0 15 c4 ♘xe3 16 fxe3 dxc4 17 ♗xc4 ♗e4 the position was unclear.

10 ♘ce1 c5 11 ♗d3 ♗xd3 12 ♘xd3 ♘g6 13 g3 ♗e7 14 h4 h5 15 ♖e1 ♖c8 16 ♗e3

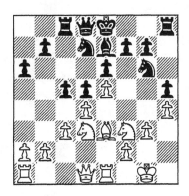

16...c4

16...cxd4 17 cxd4 leaves White with a small edge as his minor pieces are functioning slight better than Black's.

17 ♘c1

The black knight on g6 is poorly placed and so exchanging it off with 17 ♘f4 would not be a good idea.

17...♖c6 18 ♕c2 ♘b6 19 ♘e2 ♕d7 20 ♘g5 ♗d8 21 ♘h3 ♘c8 22 ♘ef4 ♘xf4 23 ♘xf4 ♘e7 24 ♕d1

White forces ...g7-g6, so that after an exchange of bishops Black will have a permanent weakness on the dark squares.

24...g6 25 ♘h3 ♘f5 26 ♗g5 ♗xg5 27 ♘xg5 ♕e7 28 ♔g2 b5 29 ♕d2

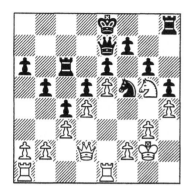

29...♖b6?

After this White is able to gain a small advantage by fixing the pawn structure on the queenside. Better would have been 29...a5 which would have kept the position about level.

30 b4 cxb3

If 30...0-0 31 a4 and White has the initiative.

31 axb3 ♖c6 32 b4 0-0 33 ♖eb1 ♖a8 34 ♖b3 ♔g7 35 ♘f3 ♕d8 36 ♖a5 ♘e7 37 ♕f4 ♖c7 38 ♕f6+ ♔g8 39 ♖a1 ♖ca7 40 ♖ba3 ♘c6 41 ♕f4 ♕f8 42 ♘g5 ♘e7 43 f3 ♘f5 44 g4 ♘g7 45 ♘h3 ♖c7

46 ♖xa6?

Here Anand misses a good chance with 46 ♖b3! ♖c6 (if 46...♕c8 47 ♖aa3

and ♕h6 follows) 47 ♘f2 ♖ac8 48 ♖aa3 and White can bring his knight round to c5.

46...♖xa6 47 ♖xa6 ♕c8 48 ♖a1 ♖xc3 49 ♘g5

White now has only a small edge. After further adventures, during which Anand again missed chances, Karpov eventually hung on for a draw.

49...♖c7 50 ♔g3 ♕b7 51 ♖a2 ♕c6 52 ♖a3 ♘e8 53 ♕d2 ♔g7 54 ♖a2 ♕c3 55 ♕xc3 ♖xc3 56 ♖a8 ♔f8 57 gxh5 gxh5 58 ♖b8 ♔e7 59 ♖xb5 f6 60 ♖b7+ ♔c7 61 exf6+ ♔xf6 62 ♖b8 ♘d6 63 ♔f4 ♖c1 64 ♖b6 ♔e7 65 ♖a6 ♖e1 66 ♖a7+ ♔e8 67 ♖h7 ♘b5 68 ♘f7! ♘xd4 69 ♘e5 ♖b1 70 ♔g5 ♖xb4 71 ♔f6 ♔d8 72 ♖xh5 ♖b3 73 ♖g5 ♖e3 74 ♖g4?

74 h5 ♘xf3 75 ♘f7+ ♔c7 76 ♖g7 ♘d4 77 ♘g5+ ♔d6 78 h6 was winning for White.

74...♘xf3 75 ♘f7+ ♔d7 76 h5 ♖e4 77 ♖xe4 dxe4 78 h6 e3 79 h7 e2 80 h8♕ e1♕ 81 ♕d8+ ♔c6 82 ♕a8+ ♔c7 83 ♕xf3 ♕h4+ 84 ♔g6 ♕d4 85 ♕g3+ ♔b7 86 ♘e5 ♕d5 87 ♔f7 ♔b6 88 ♕c3 ♔b5 89 ♕b2+ ♔a6 90 ♕e2+ ♔b6 91 ♔e7 ♔c5 92 ♘d7+ ♔b4 93 ♕b2+ ♕b3 94 ♕xb3+ ½-½

1 e4 c6 2 d4 d5 3 e5 ♗f5 4 ♘f3 e6 5 ♗e2 ♘d7 6 0-0 ♘e7 7 ♘bd2

A further recent try for White here is 7 ♗e3, as in Shirov-Anand, Wijk aan Zee 1996, which continued 7...♗g6 (a continuation which suggests itself is 7...h6, as in previous examples) 8 ♘h4 ♘f5 9 ♘xf5 ♗xf5 10 g4 ♗g6 11 f4 f5 12 g5 h6 13 h4 hxg5 14 hxg5 ♔f7 15 ♘d2 ♗e7 16 ♔g2 ♕c7 17 ♖h1 ♖ag8 18 ♗f3 ♖xh1 19 ♕xh1 ♕d8 20 ♕d1 ♖h8 and the blood-letting on the h-file has left the position equal.

7...c5

Others:

a) 7...♗g6 8 c3 ♘f5 9 g4?! (This move can, as we have seen, be the prelude to a powerful kingside advance. Here, however, it only creates weaknesses in the white kingside) 9...♘e7 10 ♔g2 h5 11 h3 c5 12 a3 cxd4 13 cxd4 ♖c8 14 b4 ♗c2 15 ♕e1 hxg4 16 hxg4 ♘g6 17 ♖h1 ♘f4+ 18 ♔g1 ♘xe2+ 19 ♕xe2 ♖xh1+ 20 ♔xh1 ♘b6 and Black is better, Szalanczy-Groszpeter, Bucharest 1993

b) 7...h6 8 ♖e1 ♗h7 9 ♘f1 ♕b6 10 a4 ♕c7 11 a5?! c5 12 a6?! c4 13 axb7 ♕xb7 14 ♘g3 ♘c6 15 ♗f1 a5 16 c3 ♘b6 17 ♗e3 a4 18 ♘d2 ♘a5 19 f4 ♘b3 20 ♘xb3 axb3 and Black has a good game, Gelfand-Brunner, Biel 1995.

8 c3 ♘c6 9 b3 cxd4 10 cxd4 ♗e7 11 ♗b2 ♕b6

Black has developed his pieces very smoothly and has no real problems.

12 a3 0-0 13 b4 ♖fc8

---

see following diagram

---

14 ♖c1

In Chapter 1 we saw how White can often try to take the initiative in such positions by getting a knight to c5. Here, however, the immediate execution of this plan would fail tactically, e.g. 14 ♘b3? ♘xb4 15 axb4 ♗c2 16 ♕d2 ♗xb3.

14...♕d8 15 h3 a5 16 b5 ♘a7 17 ♕b3

In this game White eventually winds up with an unpleasant weakness in the form of the pawn on a3. He may therefore have done better to take the opportunity to eliminate this potential problem with 17 a4, although after 17...♖xc1 18 ♕xc1 ♗b4 Black has plenty of room to manoeuvre on the queenside and has a completely equal game.

17...♖xc1 18 ♖xc1 ♖c8 19 ♖c3 ♘b6 20 ♘e1 a4 21 ♖xc8 ♕xc8 22 ♕e3 h6 23 ♗f1

Rogers' play in this game is unusually passive. A better chance to generate play was the immediate 23 g4 ♗h7 24 f4, although after 24...♕c7 Black's queenside play is more relevant than White's on the opposite wing.

23...♕c7 24 g3 ♘d7!

Now Black's queen invades and the white queenside becomes indefensible.

25 ♔h2 ♕a5 26 g4 ♗g6 27 f4 ♘xb5 28 ♘ef3 ♘c7 29 ♔g3 ♕b6 30 ♕c3 ♘b8 31 ♕c1 ♘c6 32 ♗a1 ♘a5 33 ♗c3 ♘b3 34 ♕b2 ♘b5 35 ♗b4 ♗xb4 36 ♘xb3 ♘xa3 37 ♘c1 ♗e1+ 0-1

Summary

The main lesson to be learnt from this chapter is that White should play 7 ♘h4, as more restrained continuations do not pose serious problems for Black. After 7...♗g6 and the inevitable exchange ♘xg6 h7xg6, Black must be very wary of committing his king too early, or playing a move such as ...♖c8, which amounts to the same thing. However, if he makes the most of his options with ...f7-f6 and ...g6-g5 he has good chances to obtain counterplay.

Adams' idea 7 ♘h4 ♗e4!? (Game 24) is interesting but should be slightly better for White.

1 e4 c6 2 d4 d5 3 e5 ♗f5 4 ♘f3 e6 5 ♗e2 ♘d7 6 0-0 ♘e7

7 ♘h4 *(D)*
> 7 c3 – *Game 26*
> 7 ♘bd2 – *Game 27*

7...♗g6
> 7...♗e4 – *Game 24*
> 7...♕b6 – *Game 25*

8 ♘d2 c5 9 c3 *(D)* **♘c6**
> 9...♖c8 – *Game 23*

10 ♘xg6 hxg6 11 ♘f3 *(D)* **cxd4**
> 11...♗e7 – *Game 22*

12 cxd4 – *Game 21*

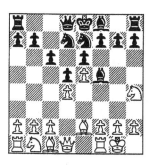

7 ♘h4

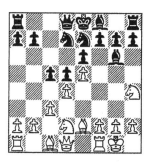

9 c3

11 ♘f3

CHAPTER FOUR

4 ♘f3 e6 5 ♗e2: Alternative Fifth and Sixth Moves

1 e4 c6 2 d4 d5 3 e5 ♗f5 4 ♘f3 e6 5 ♗e2

In this chapter we look at Black's alternatives to 5...c5 and 5...♘d7 6 0-0 ♘e7.

If Black does not want to relinquish his queen's bishop after 5...♘d7 6 0-0 ♘e7 7 ♘h4 then his main try is 6...h6, preparing a retreat for this piece on h7 and this sequence is the subject of Games 28-31. Black's play is a little slow (...c7-c6 and ...h7-h6) but, as he has not yet committed himself to ...c6-c5, White is not in a position to exploit this by blowing open the centre and a manoeuvring game is in prospect.

White has generally tried to use his extra time to claim space with 7 b3 and 8 c4 and hope that Black struggles to find counterplay. This plan has been quite successful and is seen in Games 28-30, while White's other plan, 7 c3, is considered in Game 31.

Another attempt to preserve the light-squared bishop, temporarily at least, is with 6...♗g6 (Game 32). Black

has in mind the idea of developing the king's knight on h6 (not fearing ♗xh6 which would leave Black with a strong pair of bishops) and thus cutting across White's idea of ♘h4.

Karpov is an enthusiastic defender of the Caro-Kann Defence and so his ideas should always be looked at closely. His latest is the combination of 5...♘e7 and 6...c5 (Games 34-36), delaying the development of the queen's knight, which he has used with success against Kamsky and Shirov. However, note that 5...♘d7 and 6...c5 is a bad combination of moves, as shown in Game 33.

The final game in this chapter (Game 37) features Nigel Short's latest invention, 5 a3.

Game 28
Topalov-Timman
Amsterdam 1996

1 e4 c6 2 d4 d5 3 e5 ♗f5 4 ♘f3 e6 5 ♗e2 ♘d7 6 0-0 h6 7 b3 ♘e7 8 c4 ♘g6

For 8...g5 see Game 30.

9 ♘a3

White plans the knight's tour ♘a3-c2-e3 to annoy Black's bishop on f5. Others:

a) The more straightforward 9 ♘c3 is well met by 9...♗b4, e.g. 10 ♗d2 ♗xc3 11 ♗xc3 ♘f4 and Black is comfortably equal.

b) 9 ♗e3 ♗b4 (why not 9...♗e7 at once?) 10 a3 ♗e7 11 ♘c3 ♘h4 12 ♘xh4 ♗xh4 13 g4 ♗h7 14 f4 f6 15 f5 exf5 16 e6 ♘b6 17 gxf5 and White's pawn on e6 is a monster, Savon-Guliev, Orel 1992.

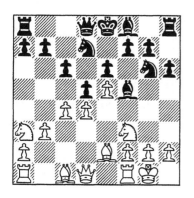

9...♘f4 10 ♗xf4 ♗xa3 11 ♗d3 ♗g4

11...♗xd3 12 ♕xd3 ♕e7 (12...♗e7 is more circumspect) 13 c5 ♗b4 14 a3 ♗a5 15 b4 ♗d8 16 b5 ♘b8 17 ♖ab1 0-0 18 ♖b3 ♗a5 19 a4 ♖c8 20 ♕e3 and White has developed an impressive initiative on the queenside, Xie Jun-Hort, Prague 1995.

12 ♖b1 ♗e7

Before the bishop becomes inconvenienced by c4-c5. 12...a5 is considered in the next game.

13 h3 ♗h5 14 ♕e2 0-0 15 ♕e3 a5?

Slightly surprisingly, this loses by force. The correct way for Black to

play is 15...♗g6 and now 16 ♗xg6 (or 16 ♖fd1 a6 17 ♖bc1 ♗xd3 18 ♖xd3 ♔h7 19 g4 ♖c8 20 ♔g2 and White's intended kingside advance gave him a slight initiative in Fiorito-Bacrot, Erevan Olympiad 1996) 16...fxg6 17 ♕d2 g5 18 ♗e3 ♕e8 19 ♘h2 ♕g6 20 ♕a5 ♖fc8 21 ♖bc1 ♘f8 22 ♕d2 ♕h7 23 ♕e2 a5 (with two minor pieces having been exchanged, White now experiences some difficulties defending all his territory) 24 ♗d2 ♗a3 25 ♖ce1 ♕c2 26 ♗c1 ♕xe2 27 ♖xe2 ♗e7 28 ♗e3 a4 29 c5 axb3 30 axb3 b6 31 b4 ♖cb8 32 ♖c2 and the endgame is about equal, Lutz-Adams, German Bundesliga 1995/96.

16 cxd5 cxd5

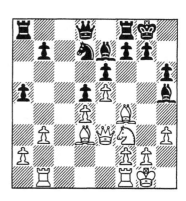

17 ♗xh6! ♗xf3

If 17...gxh6 18 ♕xh6 ♗g6 19 ♗xg6 fxg6 20 ♕xg6+ ♔h8 21 ♕h6+ ♔g8 22 ♕xe6+ and White will have five(!) pawns and an attack for the piece.

18 gxf3 ♗h4

18...gxh6 19 ♕xh6 f5 20 ♔h1 and with the white rook coming to the g-file, Black will not last long.

19 ♔h1 f5 20 ♖g1 ♖f7 21 ♗xg7!

21 ♖g6 is also very strong but this sacrifice is more in Topalov's combat-

21...♖xg7 22 ♕h6 ♗g5 23 ♕xe6+ ♔h8 24 ♕xf5 ♕e7 25 ♕g4 ♘xe5 26 dxe5 ♕xe5 27 ♖be1 ♕f4 28 ♕h5+ ♔g8 29 ♖xg5! ♖xg5 30 ♕h7+ ♔f8 31 ♕h6+ ♔f7 32 ♗g6+ 1-0

Black is either mated in two moves or loses his queen.

Game 29
Kindermann-Dautov
Vienna 1996

---

1 e4 c6 2 d4 d5 3 e5 ♗f5 4 ♘f3 e6 5 ♗e2 ♘d7 6 0-0 h6 7 b3 ♘e7 8 c4 ♘g6 9 ♘a3 ♘f4 10 ♗xf4 ♗xa3 11 ♗d3 ♗g4 12 ♖b1 a5

Black keeps his options open.

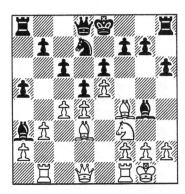

13 ♕e2 ♗h5 14 ♕e3 ♗e7

Not 14...0-0? 15 ♗xh6 as in Topalov-Timman. However 14...♕e7 is playable, but White has a good game after 15 ♗g3 0-0 16 ♘h4 with the idea of f4-f5.

15 ♘d2 ♗g6 16 ♗xg6 fxg6 17 ♕d3 ♔f7 18 ♗e3

As we saw from the extract Lutz-Adams in the previous game, this pawn structure can be quite playable for Black. Here, however, he has seri-

ous problems with his king.

18...♖e8 19 g4 ♘f8

White's last move was based on the tactical point 19...dxc4 20 bxc4 ♘xe5 21 ♕e4 ♘d7 22 ♖xb7 and White regains the pawn with an excellent position.

20 f4 ♕d7 21 f5?!

White blows open the position too soon. He would have been better advised to continue his build up. One possibility is 21 h4 ♔g8 (21...♗xh4? 22 g5 leaves the bishop stuck offside) 22 h5 gxh5 23 f5 exf5 24 gxf5 with a promising attack.

21...gxf5 22 gxf5 exf5 23 ♖xf5+ ♔g8 24 ♔h1 ♘e6

This position demonstrates why the knight is the best piece to use as a blockader.

25 ♘f3 ♖f8 26 ♖g1 ♔h8

An unfortunate blunder which loses at once. Black could have held the balance with 26...♖xf5 27 ♕xf5 ♖f8 28 ♕h3 ♔h7 29 ♕g4 ♔h8 30 ♕h3 ♔h7 with a draw.

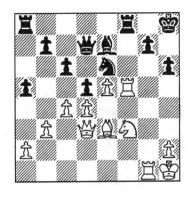

27 ♗xh6! ♖xf5

27...gxh6 28 ♖h5 ♗g5 29 ♘xg5 ♘xg5 30 ♖gxg5 wins.

28 ♕xf5 gxh6 29 ♖g6 ♘f8 30

♖xh6+ ♔g8 31 e6 1-0

> ### Game 30
> ### Shirov-Brunner
> *Biel 1995*

1 e4 c6 2 d4 d5 3 e5 ♗f5 4 ♗e2 e6
5 ♘f3 ♘d7 6 0-0 h6 7 b3 ♘e7 8 c4
g5!?

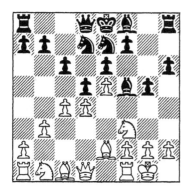

We have seen Black get away with such a move in previous games. It looks rather amateurish but the centre is blocked and White's play has been a little slow, so such a wing advance is not unreasonable. Nevertheless, it takes some courage to play like this against Shirov.

9 ♘c3 ♗h7

9...♘g6 10 cxd5 cxd5 11 ♗d3 ♗b4 12 ♘xd5?! ♗xd3 13 ♕xd3 exd5 14 e6 ♘b8 15 h4 (this looks rather hopeful but 15 ♕b5+ ♘c6 16 ♕xb7 ♘ge7 is solid enough for Black) 15...♕e7 16 exf7+ ♕xf7 17 h5 ♘e7 18 ♘e5 ♕f5 19 ♕b5+ ♘bc6 20 ♘xc6 ♘xc6 21 ♕xb7 ♖c8 22 ♗e3 ♕d7 and Black soon consolidated his extra material in A.Rodriguez-Garcia Palermo, Villa Gesell 1996.

10 ♘e1 ♘g6 11 ♘d3?!

This allows Black to undermine the white centre. Shirov gives 11 cxd5 cxd5 12 ♘d3 ♖c8 13 ♗b2 f5 as better, but assesses it as no better than unclear.

11...dxc4 12 bxc4 c5!

Now the white centre is swept away.

13 dxc5

13 d5 ♘dxe5 14 ♘xe5 ♘xe5 15 dxe6 ♕xd1 16 exf7+ ♘xf7 17 ♗xd1 ♗g7 is also fine for Black.

13...♗g7 14 ♗a3

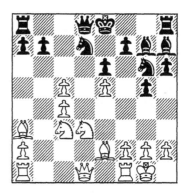

14...♘gxe5?!

This impetuous move allows White to gain time and coordinate his position. The cold-blooded 14...0-0! 15 c6 bxc6 16 ♗xf8 ♕xf8 gives Black excellent play for the exchange.

15 ♘xe5 ♘xe5 16 ♕a4+ ♘c6 17 ♖ad1 ♕c8 18 ♘b5 0-0 19 ♘d6 ♕c7 20 ♗f3 ♖ab8?

Now White gets on top. Shirov gives 20...♘d4 21 ♖xd4 ♗xd4 22 ♘b5 ♕f4 23 ♘xd4 ♕xd4 24 c6 bxc6 25 ♖d1 as unclear.

21 ♘xb7 ♘e5 22 ♘d6 ♘xf3+ 23 gxf3 ♗e5 24 ♖fe1 ♗f4 25 ♔g2 ♖fd8 26 h3

White has such a firm grip on the

queenside that his own kingside weaknesses are irrelevant.

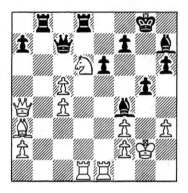

26...♗g6 27 ♘e4 ♗e5 28 ♖xd8+ ♖xd8 29 ♘d6 ♗f4 30 ♕b4 ♖b8 31 ♕c3 e5 32 ♖xe5! ♗xe5 33 ♕xe5 ♔h7 34 ♗b2 ♖g8 35 ♗d4 ♗c2 36 ♕d5 ♗a4

Black's loss of time with his last move is fatal as after 36...♗g6 37 c6 ♘b5 follows and White's front c-pawn will win the game.

37 ♘xf7 ♕c6 38 ♘e5 ♕xd5 39 cxd5 ♔g7 40 c6 ♔f6 41 ♘c4+ ♔e7 42 ♗xa7 ♗b5 43 ♗c5+ ♔f6 44 ♘b6 ♔e5 45 c7 1-0

> ### Game 31
> ### Kir.Georgiev-Vogt
> *Altensteig 1995*

1 e4 c6 2 d4 d5 3 e5 ♗f5 4 ♘f3 e6 5 ♗e2 ♘d7 6 0-0 h6 7 c3

This quiet looking move has been played several times with, generally, unimpressive results. White can only create problems for Black by adopting the plan used by Georgiev in this game. 7 c4 is often seen in the Advance variation with ♘f3 (e.g. Game 33) but here, where Black has not yet

committed himself to ...c6-c5, it loses much of its point, e.g. 7...dxc4 8 ♗xc4 ♘b6 9 ♗b3 ♘e7 10 ♘c3 ♘ed5 11 ♕e2 ♗e7 12 ♘e4 0-0 with a comfortable position for Black in Lau-Schaack, Bad Worishofen 1992.

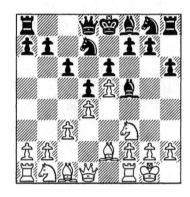

7...♘e7

7...♕c7, envisaging a quick ...0-0-0, is a perfectly reasonable alternative, e.g. 8 a4 (8 ♗e3 0-0-0 9 ♘bd2 ♘e7 10 c4 dxc4 11 ♘xc4 ♘d5 12 ♗d2 ♘7b6 13 ♘a5 g5 14 ♖c1 ♔b8 and Black's excellent central control gives him good counterplay, Kindermann-W.Watson, Prague 1992) 8...g5 9 ♘a3 f6 10 ♗d3 ♗xd3 11 ♕xd3 0-0-0 12 exf6 ♘gxf6 13 ♖e1 ♖e8 14 c4 ♘e4 15 ♘d2 ♗b4 16 ♖xe4 dxe4 17 ♘xe4 ♖d8 18 ♘c2 ♗e7 with unclear play, as in Anand-Timman, Paris 1991. Of course White could consider 8 ♘h4 and follow Georgiev's plan.

8 ♘h4 ♗h7 9 ♗d3 ♗xd3 10 ♕xd3 g5

Again we see this kingside advance. Here it has a specific point as White was threatening to gain a strong attacking position with f2-f4.

11 ♘f3 ♘g6 12 ♗e3 ♗e7 13 ♘bd2 ♕c7

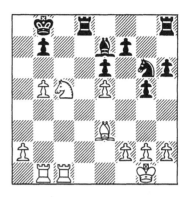

14 c4

White opens up lines on the queenside, the probable eventual destination of the black king.

14...dxc4 15 ♘xc4 0-0-0 16 ♕e4 ♖dg8

This is very decentralising and leads to serious problems for Black. It would have been better to play 16...♔b8, maintaining an influence on the d-file.

17 ♖fc1 ♔b8 18 b4 ♕d8 19 ♖ab1

White's attack is very imposing while Black's counterplay is stillborn. Black now finds a plan to bale out into a bad ending.

19...♘b6 20 ♘xb6 axb6 21 b5 ♕d5 22 ♘d2 ♕xe4 23 ♘xe4 c5 24 dxc5 bxc5 25 ♘xc5

Georgiev seems to lose track of the position around here. 25 ♗xc5 seems much simpler.

25...♖d8

see following diagram

26 ♖d1

This is really feeble. 26 ♘a6+! would surely win, e.g. 26...♔a8 (26...bxa6 27 bxa6+ ♔a8 28 ♖c7) 27 ♖c7 ♖he8 28 ♘c5.

26...♘xe5 27 f3 ♖xd1+ 28 ♖xd1 ♖d8 29 ♖xd8+ ♗xd8 30 ♔f1 ♘c4 31 ♔e2 ♘a3 32 ♘d7+ ♔c8 33 ♘e5 f6 34 ♘f7 ♘xb5 35 ♘xh6 ♘c3+ 36 ♔d3 ♘d5 37 g3 ♔d7 38 ♗d2 b5 39 ♘g4 ♗c7 40 ♘e3 ♘e7 41 ♗c3 e5 42 ♗b4 ♘c6 43 ♗c5 ♔e6 44 ♔e4 ♘a5 45 ♘f5 ♘c4 46 ♗b4 ♗a5 47 ♗xa5 ♘xa5 48 f4 gxf4 49 gxf4 b4 50 fxe5 fxe5 51 ♘g7+ ♔f6 52 ♘e8+ ♔g5 53 ♔xe5 ½-½

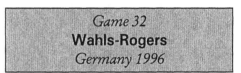

> ### Game 32
> ### Wahls-Rogers
> *Germany 1996*

1 e4 c6 2 d4 d5 3 e5 ♗f5 4 ♘f3 e6 5 ♗e2 ♘d7 6 0-0 ♗g6!?

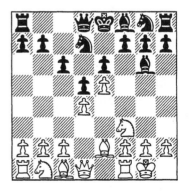

This semi-waiting move is an inter-esting try from the imaginative Aus-tralian grandmaster. The main idea is to avoid the 6...♘e7 7 ♘h4(!) variation by bringing the knight to f5 via the h6 square.

7 b3

White continues with the usual space gaining plan. Others:

a) 7 ♘bd2 ♘h6 does not seriously test Black's idea.

b) 7 c3, perhaps planning to capture on h6, is possible.

c) 7 c4 dxc4 8 ♗xc4 ♘b6 9 ♗e2 ♘e7 10 ♘c3 ♘ed5 11 ♗d3 ♗e7 12 ♗xg6 fxg6 (this is an ambitious recap-ture; the normal 12...hxg6 should be about equal) 13 ♘e4 0-0 14 ♘e1 ♘f4 15 ♗e3 ♘bd5 16 ♘d3 ♘xd3 17 ♕xd3 g5 18 ♕e2 ♘f4 19 ♗xf4 ♖xf4 20 ♖ad1 ♕d5 21 ♘c3 ♕d7 22 ♕c4 with a bal-anced position, as in Magomedov-Rogers, Erevan Olympiad 1996.

7...♘h6 8 c4 ♘f5 9 ♘c3 ♗b4

9...♗e7 10 ♗b2 0-0 11 ♕d2 a6 12 c5 (12 cxd5 cxd5 13 g4, as in the main game, is an alternative continuation) 12...b6 (Black doesn't get anywhere on the queenside so it would have better to look for counterplay with the ...f7-f6 break) 13 b4 a5 14 a3 ♕b8 15 h3 h5 16 ♗d3 ♘h4 17 ♘xh4 ♗xd3 18 ♕xd3 ♗xh4 19 ♖ab1 axb4 20 axb4 b5 21 f4 and White is in complete control, Kal-lai-Metz, Budapest 1995.

10 ♗b2 0-0 11 a3 ♗e7 12 cxd5 cxd5 13 g4! ♘h6

Or 13...♘h4 14 ♘xh4 ♗xh4 15 f4 and White has a useful space advan-tage.

14 ♘e1 f6 15 exf6 gxf6 16 h4 f5!?

After 16...♔h8 17 f4 White is gain-ing a bind on the position. Rogers is a player who likes to have the initiative and his solution to Black's problems is typically ingenious.

17 g5

17...♗xg5! 18 hxg5 ♕xg5+ 19 ♘g2 f4 20 ♕d2 ♖f7 21 a4?

White wants to prevent Black dou-bling on the f-file (♗a3), but this loses time and the queen's rook has a fine future on the g-file. The best way to counter Black's gambit was 21 ♗b5! ♖af8 22 ♖ae1 ♖g7 23 f3, as pointed out by Rogers.

21...♔h8 22 f3 ♖g8 23 ♖f2 ♗h5 24 ♗d3 ♕h4! 25 ♖e1

It is not easy for White to untangle the traffic jam in his position, e.g. 25 ♘e2 ♖xg2+! 26 ♖xg2 ♗xf3 and Black wins.

25...♕h3! 26 ♕e2

This loses, but White's position was already beyond repair. Other varia-tions given by Rogers are: 26 ♖ef1 ♖fg7 27 ♕e2 ♗xf3; 26 ♗e2 ♖fg7 27 ♗f1 ♗xf3; 26 ♘e2 ♖xg2+ 27 ♖xg2 ♗xf3 and Black wins immediately in all cases.

26...♖xg2+! 27 ♖xg2 ♗xf3 28 ♕xf3 ♕xf3 29 ♗b5 ♘f8 30 ♘d1 ♖g7 0-1

Game 33
Nunn-Adams
Oviedo (rapid) 1992

1 e4 c6 2 d4 d5 3 e5 ♗f5 4 ♘f3 e6 5 ♗e2 ♘d7 6 0-0 c5?!

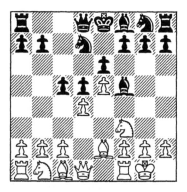

7 c4!

White breaks open the centre at a moment when Black is not well placed to meet this. The lesson, as mentioned previously, is that if Black wants to play a quick ...c6-c5 he needs his queen's knight to be able to go to c6. On d7, it severely restricts Black's pressure on the centre.

7...dxc4

The notes in this game demonstrate some terrifying experiences for Black. The first of these is 7...♘e7 8 ♘c3 dxc4 9 ♗xc4 ♘c6 10 d5 ♘cxe5 (this is really asking for it: 10...exd5 11 ♘xd5 must be better, but White still has an alarming lead in development) 11 ♘xe5 ♘xe5 12 ♗b5+ ♘d7 13 g4 ♗g6 14 ♖e1 ♗e7 15 dxe6 fxe6 16 ♖xe6 ♗f7 17 ♖e1 a6 18 ♗xd7+ ♕xd7 19 ♗g5 ♗e6 20 ♕xd7+ ♔xd7 21 ♖ad1+ 1-0 L.Hansen-V.Johansson, Stockholm Open 1993.

8 ♘c3

8 d5 is less ambitious for White but is still enough to guarantee a good game, e.g. 8...exd5 9 ♕xd5 ♕c7 10 ♗xc4 ♗e6 11 ♕e4 ♗xc4 12 ♕xc4 ♘b6 13 ♕e4 ♘e7 14 e6 f6 15 ♖d1, as in Tkachiev-Hatanbaatar, Moscow Olympiad 1994.

8...cxd4 9 ♘xd4 ♗g6 10 ♗xc4 ♖c8 11 ♗b3

Also possible is 11 ♕e2 with the plan of quickly bringing the king's rook to the d-file.

11...♗c5 12 ♖e1 a6

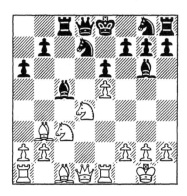

12...♘e7 13 ♘db5 0-0 14 ♘d6 gives White a strong initiative.

13 ♗xe6!?

White decides to strike quickly before Black can get his king to safety.

13...♗xd4

If instead 13...fxe6 14 ♘xe6 ♕e7 15 ♕g4 and White has an 'octopus' knight on e6.

14 ♗xf7+ ♔xf7 15 ♕xd4

With two pawns and a strong attack, White has excellent compensation for the piece.

15...♗e6

This very natural move is probably a mistake. Black needs to blockade with a knight on e6 while dealing with the threat of ♘c3-e4-d6(+) and the way to do this is 15...♖c4!, hitting the white queen at an awkward moment, e.g. 16 ♕d3 (16 ♕d6 ♘c5) 16...♘c5 17 ♕g3 ♘e6 18 b3 (not 18 ♘e4 ♖xe4) and, with the white bishop entering the fray, White maintains good attacking chances.

16 ♘e4 ♘e7 17 ♘d6+ ♔f8 18 ♗g5

18 ♘xc8 is also strong for White.

18...♖c6

18...♖c7, guarding the second rank, was a better defence but White keeps all the chances after 19 ♖ad1 or 19 ♕e4.

19 ♕f4+ ♔g8 20 ♕h4 ♘g6

Unfortunately for Black, 20...♔f8 21 ♖e4 ♘xe5 22 ♘xb7 ♕c7 23 ♗xe7+ wins easily for White

21 ♗xd8 ♘xh4 22 ♗xh4 g6 23 ♘xb7 ♔g7 24 ♖ad1 ♖b8 25 ♘d8 ♖xd8 26 ♗xd8 ♖c2 27 ♖b1 ♗xa2 28 ♖bc1 ♖xc1 29 ♖xc1 ♘xe5 30 ♖c7+ ♔g8 31 ♗f6 ♘d3 32 ♖g7+ ♔f8 33 ♖xh7 ♗c4 34 ♖c7 ♗b5 35 h4 ♘f4 36 ♖a7 ♘d5 37 ♗e5 ♔e8 38 f3 ♘b4 39 ♖g7 ♗d3 40 g4 ♘c6 41 ♗c3 ♘e7 42 h5 gxh5 43 gxh5 ♘f5 44 ♖c7 ♔f8 45 h6 ♘xh6 46 ♗g7+ ♔e8 1-0

Game 34
Kamsky-Karpov
Groningen 1995

---

1 e4 c6 2 d4 d5 3 e5 ♗f5 4 ♘f3 e6 5 ♗e2 ♘e7

This may will often transpose straight back to lines with 5...♘d7 but by developing the king's knight first, Black creates the possiblity of follow-

ing an independent path.

6 0-0 ♗g6

The sharper 6...c5 is considered in the next two games.

7 ♘bd2

Other possibilities are:

a) 7 ♘h4 is well met by 7...c5 (less convincing is 7...♘f5 8 ♘xf5 ♗xf5 9 g4 ♗g6 10 f4 ♕d7 11 ♗e3 ♗e7 12 ♘d2 ♘a6 13 c3 and White keeps the advantage, as in Novikov-Kaunas, Vilnius 1996) 8 c3 ♘bc6 9 ♗e3 ♕b6 10 b3 ♘f5 11 ♘xf5 ♗xf5 12 ♗d3 ♗xd3 13 ♕xd3 ♗e7 with a totally equal position, Sutovskij-Yudasin, Haifa 1996.

b) 7 c3!? is perhaps the best move as if 7...♘d7 8 ♘h4 transposing to the previous chapter, and if 7...c5?! 8 dxc5 and it will not be easy for Black to complete his development and regain the pawn.

7...c5 8 c4 cxd4 9 ♘xd4

Note the small trick 9 cxd5? d3.

9...♘ec6 10 ♘2f3 dxc4 11 ♗xc4

Black's smooth development makes it difficult for White to generate activity here; e.g. 11 ♗g5 ♕b6 12 ♗xc4 ♗c5 13 ♘b3 ♗e7 14 ♕e2 0-0 15 ♖fd1 ♗h5 16 ♗xe7 ♘xe7 17 ♕e4 ♘bc6 18

♘g5 ♗g6 19 ♕f4 ♖ad8 20 ♖d6 h6 21
♘f3 ♘f5 and Black has fully equalised,
Fedorov-Nielsen, Minsk 1996.

**11...♗e7 12 ♗e3 0-0 13 ♖c1 a6 14
a3 ♕e8 15 ♗a2 ♔h8 16 ♖e1 ♘xd4
17 ♕xd4 ♘c6 18 ♕g4 ♖c8 19 h4 h6
20 ♗b6 ♘b8**

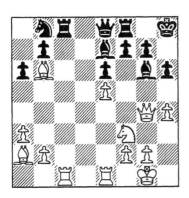

21 ♗c7

Kamsky's highly accurate play has
kept some initiative but Karpov's position is very solid.

**21...♕d7 22 ♗a5 ♖xc1 23 ♖xc1 ♖c8
24 ♗c3 ♘c6 25 ♗b3 ♗c5 26 ♖d1
♕e7 27 h5 ♗h7 28 ♕f4 ♕c7 29 ♖d2
♔g8 30 ♔h2 ♖d8 31 ♗c2 ♗xc2 32
♖xc2 ♕b6 33 ♕h4 ♖d5! 34 b4?!
♗e7 35 ♕e4 ♗d8 36 a4 ♕c7 37 g3
♕d7 38 ♔g2 ♗c7 39 ♖e2 ♘e7 40
♕c4 ♗b6 41 a5 ♗c7 42 g4?!**

Kamsky gets over-ambitious. He
could easily have held the balance
with 42 ♖d2 ♖xd2 43 ♗xd2 ♗xe5 44
♗xh6! ♗xg3 45 ♗xg7.

**42...♘c6 43 ♖e4 ♗d8 44 ♘e1 ♗e7
45 ♘c2**

see following diagram

45...♘xa5! 46 bxa5 ♖c5

The white pieces have got into a
tangle on the c-file.

47 ♕d4

Or 47 ♕b4 ♕c6 48 f3 ♖xc3 49
♕xe7 ♖xc2+ 50 ♔h3 ♕b5.

47...♕xd4 48 ♖xd4 ♖xc3 49 ♘e3

With his extra pawn Black should
win the game. Kamsky, however, is a
tremendous fighter and he hangs on
for a draw.

**49...♔f8 50 ♔f3 ♔e8 51 ♔e4 ♖b3
52 ♘c4 ♗c5 53 ♖d2 ♖b4 54 ♔d3
♖b3+ 55 ♔e4 ♖b4 56 ♔d3 ♔d7 57
♔c3+ ♔e7 58 f3 ♖b1 59 ♔c2 ♖b4
60 ♔c3 ♖b5 61 ♖a2 f6 62 exf6+
gxf6 63 f4 ♗b4+ 64 ♔d3 ♖d5+ 65
♔e4 ♗c3 66 ♔e3 ♗d4+ 67 ♔f3 ♖b5
68 ♔e4 ♗a7 69 ♖a3 f5+ 70 gxf5
exf5+ 71 ♔f3 ♔e6 72 ♖d3 ♗c5?**

In his notes Karpov suggests
72...♗b8! as the correct way to maintain Black's winning chances.

**73 ♖d8 ♖b3+ 74 ♔g2 ♖b4 75 ♘e5
♖xf4 76 ♘d3 ♖g4+ 77 ♔f3 ♗e7 78
♖b8 ♖d4 79 ♔e2 ♖e4+**

One point of White's play is
79...♖d7? 80 ♖h8 ♗g5? 81 ♘c5+.

**80 ♔f3 ♖h4 81 ♖xb7 ♖h3+ 82 ♔e2
♗g5 83 ♘c5+ ♔e5 84 ♘xa6 ♖xh5
85 ♖b5+ ♔f4 86 ♖b4+ ♔g3 87 ♖b3+
♔g4 88 ♘c5 ♖h2+ 89 ♔f1 ♖a2 90
♖b4+ ♔f3 91 ♖a4 ♖c2 92 ♘d3 ♗d2**

93 ♘e1+ ♗xe1 94 ♔xe1 ♖c1+ 95 ♔d2 ♖c7 96 a6 ♖a7 97 ♔e1 f4 98 ♔f1 ♔g3 99 ♖a3+ f3 100 ♖a5 ♖c7 101 ♖a1 ½-½

Game 35
Shirov-Karpov
Vienna 1996

1 e4 c6 2 d4 d5 3 e5 ♗f5 4 ♘f3 e6 5 ♗e2 ♘e7 6 0-0 c5

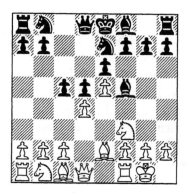

Karpov, a frequent champion of the Caro-Kann Defence, has faced the advance with ♘f3 many times. This plan, combining ...♘e7 and ...c6-c5 is his latest thought to counter the system.

7 c4

This is the standard aggressive try, but Black is well prepared to meet it. Several other moves have also been tried:

a) 7 ♘c3!?, blocking the c-pawn, is a strange looking idea. Smirin-Karpov, European Rapid Championship 1996, continued 7...♘ec6 8 ♗g5 ♕a5 (8...f6!?) 9 a3 ♘xd4 10 ♘xd4 cxd4 11 ♘b5 h6 12 ♗d2 ♕b6 13 ♗b4 ♗xb4 14 axb4 ♘c6 15 ♘d6+ ♔e7 16 ♘xf5+ exf5 17 b5 ♘xe5 18 ♖a4 ♘c4 19 ♗xc4

dxc4 20 ♖xc4 ♖hd8 21 ♕h5 ♕xb5 22 ♕h4+ ♔f8 23 ♖xd4 ♖xd4 24 ♕xd4 ♔g8 and Black was a pawn up, although the game was later drawn.

b) 7 c3 ♘ec6! (7...cxd4 8 cxd4 ♘bc6 transposes back into Chapter 1) 8 ♗e3 ♘d7 9 a3 c4 10 ♘bd2 b5 11 ♘e1 h5 12 g3 ♗h3 13 ♘g2 g6 14 ♖e1 ♗xg2 15 ♔xg2 with a balanced position, Short-Ljubojevic, Amsterdam 1991.

c) 7 dxc5 is the subject of the next game.

7...♘bc6

This seems to be more precise than 7...dxc4 8 ♘a3 ♘ec6 9 dxc5 ♕xd1 10 ♖xd1 ♗xc5 11 ♘xc4 ♘d7 12 ♗f4 ♘b6 13 ♖ac1 ♘xc4 14 ♗xc4 ♗b6 15 ♗b5 ♖c8 16 ♘d2 with a useful initiative, as in Bologan-Adianto, Manila Olympiad 1992.

8 ♘c3

Karpov equalises against this, so a better try for White might be 8 dxc5:

a) 8...dxc4 and now Bologan suggests 9 ♕a4 ♘g6 (9...♘d5 10 ♘d4) 10 ♕xc4 ♗e7 (10...♘gxe5 11 ♘xe5 ♘xe5 12 ♕a4+ with an edge) 11 ♕c3 0-0 12 ♘a3 ♕b8 13 ♘c4 ♗xc5 14 ♗e3 and White will expose the d6 square, gaining a useful outpost for his knight.

b) 8...d4 9 ♗d3 (not 9 ♕a4 ♘g6 10 b4 a5 11 b5 ♘b4 12 b6+ ♘c6 13 ♗a3 ♗e7 14 ♖d1 0-0 15 ♘c3 and Black has a clear advantage, Bologan-Haba, German Bundesliga 1992/93) 9...♗xd3 10 ♕xd3 ♘g6 11 ♕e4 ♗xc5 12 ♘bd2 0-0 13 ♘b3 ♗b6 14 ♗g5 with an edge for White, Bologan-Razuvaev, Reggio Emilia 1996.

8...dxc4

8...a6 is also possible, e.g. 9 cxd5 ♘xd5 10 ♘xd5 (10 ♗g5 ♘xc3 11 bxc3

♗e7 12 ♗e3 0-0 was fine for Black in Yermolinsky-Gulko, USA Championship 1994) 10...♕xd5 11 ♗e3 cxd4 12 ♘xd4 ♘xd4 13 ♕xd4 ♕xd4 14 ♗xd4 ♗e4 15 ♖ac1 and White retains a small pull.

9 dxc5 ♘d5 10 ♘d4 ♘xc3 11 bxc3 ♗xc5 12 ♘xf5 exf5

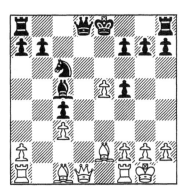

13 ♗xc4

Exchanging queens would only be equal so Shirov plays an ambitious sacrifice.

13...♗xf2+! 14 ♔h1

Forced as 14 ♔xf2 ♕h4+ 15 ♔g1 ♕xc4 is poor for White and 14 ♖xf2 ♕xd1+ is worse.

14...♕xd1 15 ♖xd1 ♘xe5 16 ♗b5+ ♘c6 17 ♗a3 f6 18 ♖ab1

White has a good initiative for his two pawns but all he can really do with it is regain his material. In the meantime Black fully coordinates his position and gains good chances.

18...♔f7 19 ♖d7+ ♔g6 20 ♖f1 ♗e3 21 ♗d3 ♘e5 22 ♗xf5+ ♔h6 23 ♖xb7 ♖ab8 24 ♖c7 g6 25 ♗c2 f5 26 ♗d6 ♖be8 27 ♖e1 f4 28 c4 g5!

Despite the fact that the black king has been kicked around in this game it is now the white king, stuck away on

h1, which is in greater danger.

29 h3 ♘g6 30 c5 ♗f2 31 ♖f1 ♖e2 32 ♗xg6 ♔xg6 33 ♖xa7 ♖he8 34 ♖e7 ♖8xe7 35 ♗xe7 ♖xa2 36 c6 ♖c2

Despite the reduced material White is curiously helpless against the advance of the black kingside pawns.

37 ♖d1?

This loses at once. The best defence was 37 c7 ♗e3 38 ♗d6 (38 ♗d8 h5 39 ♖d1 g4 40 ♖f1 g3 and ...f4-f3 follows) 38...♔f5 (38...h5 39 h4) 39 g4+ ♔e6 with a clear advantage.

37...h6 38 ♗a3 ♗e3 39 ♖d7 h5 40 ♖d1 g4 0-1

> **Game 36**
> **Shirov-Teske**
> *Vienna 1996*

1 e4 c6 2 d4 d5 3 e5 ♗f5 4 ♘f3 e6 5 ♗e2 ♘e7 6 0-0 c5 7 dxc5!? ♘ec6 8 ♗e3 ♘d7 9 c4 dxc4 10 ♘a3 ♗xc5

10...c3 led to a bizarre conclusion in Jovanovic-Shovunov, Budapest 1996: 11 b4 ♘xb4 12 ♕a4 ♘d5 13 ♘d4 ♘xe3 14 c6 ♘b6?? (14...bxc6 15 fxe3 ♗c5 was unclear) 15 cxb7+ ♘xa4 16 ♗b5+ 1-0. Despite being a queen up,

Black will soon be a queen down!

11 &xc5!

Shirov analyses 11 ♘xc4 &xe3 12 ♘d6+ ♔e7 13 ♘xf5+ exf5 14 ♛d6+ ♔e8 15 e6 fxe6 16 ♛xe6+ ♛e7 17 ♛xe7+ ♔xe7 18 fxe3 as leading to an equal ending.

11...♘xc5 12 ♘xc4 0-0

Exchanging queens is dangerous: 12...♛xd1 13 ♖fxd1 ♔e7 14 ♖ac1 and Black must be very careful

13 ♛c1!

The only move to try for the advantage.

13...♛e7 14 ♛e3 ♖ad8 15 ♘d6 b6?

This is a mistake as Black weakens the c6 square. After 15...♘d7! 16 ♘xb7 ♖b8 Black would keep the balance, e.g. 17 ♘d6 ♘dxe5 18 ♖ad1 ♛f6 19 ♖d2.

16 &b5!

Shirov immediately latches on to the weakness.

16...♘b4

Surprisingly, Black is already in some trouble, e.g. 16...♛c7 17 &xc6 ♛xc6 18 ♘d4.

17 ♘d4 &d3 18 &xd3 ♘cxd3 19 f4!

Now Black's knights are stuck and he must lose material.

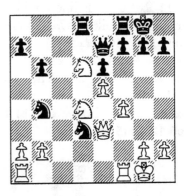

19...f6 20 a3 fxe5 21 fxe5 ♘xe5

21...♖xf1+ 22 ♖xf1 ♘xe5 23 ♛xe5 ♛xd6 24 ♛xd6 ♖xd6 25 ♘b5 ♖d5 26 ♘c7 ♖d7 27 ♘xe6 with a mate threat on f8 is a neat variation.

22 ♛xe5 ♛xd6 23 ♖xf8+ ♔xf8 24 ♘xe6+ ♔e7 25 ♛xg7+ 1-0

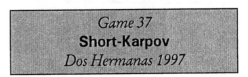

Game 37
Short-Karpov
Dos Hermanas 1997

1 e4 c6 2 d4 d5 3 e5 &f5 4 ♘f3 e6 5 a3

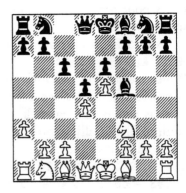

This finesse is Short's latest idea in his patent line. 5 a3 is a useful waiting move and can sometimes threaten (after ...c6-c5) d4xc5 quickly supported

by b2-b4. The drawback is, of course, that it is rather slow.

5...♘e7

Short has also faced:

a) 5...♘d7 6 ♗e2 ♘e7 7 0-0 c5 8 dxc5! ♘xc5 9 b4 ♘d7 10 ♘bd2! (not 10 ♗b2? when 10...♖c8 11 ♗d3 ♗xd3 is fine for Black, as in Short-Adianto, Jakarta 1996) 10...♕c7 11 c4 ♘xe5 12 cxd5 with an obscure position.

b) 5...c5 6 c4 ♗xb1 (this looks very odd) 7 ♖xb1 ♘c6 8 ♕b3 ♕b6 9 ♕xb6 axb6 10 cxd5 exd5 11 ♗b5 ♘ge7 12 0-0 ♘f5 13 ♖d1 0-0-0 14 dxc5 bxc5 15 ♗xc6 bxc6 16 g4 ♘h6 17 h3 with a good position for White, Short-Leko, European Rapid Championship 1996.

6 ♘bd2 ♘d7

White gains the advantage after this move. 6...h6, preserving the bishop, should be considered.

7 ♘h4 c5 8 c3 a6 9 ♘xf5 ♘xf5 10 ♘f3 ♖c8 11 ♗d3 cxd4

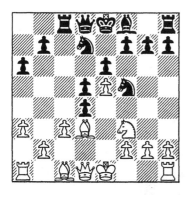

12 ♗xf5

This capture is very tempting but, with hindsight, the simple 12 cxd4 might have been better. White would then maintain many options, including an advance with g4 or a later capture on f5. After 12 cxd4 ♕b6 White

could consider maitaining the tension with 13 ♕a4!?

12...exf5 13 ♘xd4 g6

White's problem is the e5-pawn. Black can easily attack it and if at any stage he decides to bolster it with f2-f4, he will donate Black a huge outpost on e4 for his knight. Of course, Black has his own weakness on d5, but this pawn proves more difficult to get at.

14 0-0 ♘c5 15 ♗e3 ♗g7 16 ♘f3 0-0 17 ♖e1 ♖e8 18 ♖e2 ♘e4 19 ♕b3 b5 20 ♖d1 ♖c4 21 ♗d4 ♕b8

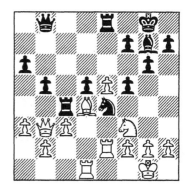

It is remarkable how swiftly Karpov has taken control of the position.

22 ♖d3 f4 23 ♕d1 ♖c6 24 ♘e1 ♖ce6 25 ♘c2 ♕b7 26 f3

White finally evicts the knight from e4, but it soon finds another tempting outpost on e3.

26...♘d6 27 b3 ♘f5 28 ♕d2 h5 29 ♖e1 a5 30 ♔f1 ♕c7 31 ♔g1 ♔h7 32 b4

This move, relinquishing the c4 square, is easy to criticise but it is less easy to suggest a good alternative.

32...a4 33 ♔f1 ♕c4 34 ♔g1 ♗xe5 35 ♗xe5 ♖xe5 36 ♖xe5 ♖xe5 37 ♘d4 ♖e3 38 ♖xe3 fxe3 39 ♕d1 ♕xc3 0-1

Summary

The lines with 6...h6 are quite pleasant for White, who can develop his forces unmolested and obtain a useful space advantage with the simple plan of b2-b3 and c2-c4. Additionally, Georgiev's simple looking plan of ♘h4 and ♗d3 (Game 31) is surprisingly difficult to meet.

Rogers' 6...♗g6 (planning ...♘h6) is solid but suffers from the same drawback as 6...h6 – White obtains a pleasant position with simple developing moves.

So it seems that Karpov's idea of 5...♘e7 and 6...c5 is the most promising way for Black to avoid the main lines. It is far from clear how White can obtain the advantage against this set-up. Finally, Short's 5 a3 is an interesting attempt to take the game off the beaten track that will appeal to non-theoretical players.

1 e4 c6 2 d4 d5 3 e5 ♗f5 4 ♘f3 e6

5 ♗e2
> 5 a3 – *Game 37*

5...♘d7
> 5...♘e7 6 0-0 *(D)*
>> 6...♗g6 – *Game 34*
>> 6...c5
>>> 7 c4 – *Game 35*; 7 dxc5 – *Game 36*

6 0-0 h6
> 6...♗g6 – *Game 32*; 6...c5 – *Game 33*

7 b3
> 7 c3 – *Game 31*

7...♘e7 8 c4 *(D)* ♘g6
> 8...g5 – *Game 30*

9 ♘a3 ♘f4 10 ♗xf4 ♗xa3 11 ♗d3 ♗g4 12 ♖b1 *(D)* ♗e7
> 12...a5 – *Game 29*

13 h3 – *Game 28*

6 0-0   *8 c4*   *12 ♖b1*

CHAPTER FIVE

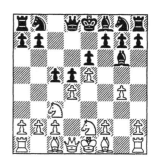

4 ♘c3 e6 5 g4 ♗g6 6 ♘ge2 c5

1 e4 c6 2 d4 d5 3 e5 ♗f5 4 ♘c3 e6 5 g4 ♗g6 6 ♘ge2 c5

4 ♘c3 e6 5 g4 ♗g6 6 ♘ge2 is the most aggressive way to exploit the exposed position of the bishop on f5. 4 ♘c3 eliminates ...♗f5-e4, which Black might play after 4 g4, and waits for 4...e6, blocking the retreat back down the c8-h3 diagonal. After 5 g4 ♗g6 6 ♘ge2 is necessary to disarm the positional threat ...h7-h5, and 6...h5 would now be met by 7 ♘f4 and 8 ♘xg6 crippling Black's structure (7...♗h7 drops the h5-pawn). White will then continue rolling down the kingside pawns starting with h2-h4-h5, forcing Black either to weaken his position or accept a kingside cramp. If Black does not react vigorously White will push him off the board.

The advanced white pawns give Black three prospective areas for counterplay: ...c6-c5, ...f7-f6, and ...h7-h5. White needs to consider how to answer each of these at any juncture. The major drawback of 4 ♘c3 is that White is unable to reinforce the centre by c2-c3 if (when!) Black attacks it with ...c6-c5. Instead White has to support it with pieces (♘ge2, ♗e3, ♕d2, 0-0-0) and risk, should Black play ...c5xd4, giving up the e5-pawn after ♘xd4. If White is forced to answer ...h7-h5 (or ...h6-h5) by g4-g5 then, with the kingside immobilised, Black can attack the centre at leisure. Years of theoretical investigation have uncovered some extraordinary plans for Black, but they all involve one of these three breaks in the end. In this chapter we consider 6...c5. Black's other sixth move possibilities are considered in the next chapter.

6...c5 is the most thematic move according to Nimzowitschian tenets; ...c6-c5 strikes at the base of the pawn chain while White is unable to support it by c2-c3. But there are dangers for Black too as he has still only developed one piece. If White succeeds in removing the e6-pawn by f4-f5 and f5xe6 or ...e6xf5 then the d5-pawn will be vulnerable.

White's two logical moves are 7

♗e3 and 7 h4. Given that after 7 h4 h6 White generally plays 8 ♗e3 in any case, the pertinent question is: why play 7 h4 at all? – especially as 7 h4 allows Black options which would not be viable after 7 ♗e3 (because ♗e3 is clearly a more useful developing move than h2-h4); e.g. 7...h5 or 7...cxd4 8 ♘xd4 h5. And with the inclusion of ...h7-h6 Black no longer has to capture the pawn when it arrives at f5 and can instead retreat the bishop to h7.

For White the advantages of 7 h4 are as follows: Without h2-h4 the possibility of ...♕h4(+) at some point can be quite irksome, and if White plays ♘f4 (e.g. after 7 h4 h6 8 ♗e3 ♘c6 9 dxc5 ♘xe5 10 ♘f4) this now threatens to destroy the black pawn structure with ♘xg6 f7xg6. Also, while it is not usually advantageous to play h4-h5 too readily since the bishop is more exposed on g6, if White can find a good time to push then there will be no need ever again to worry about Black playing ...h7-h5. In general the advantages of 7 h4 do outweigh those of 7 ♗e3, and that is why modern theory is heavily focused on 7 h4.

For both players it is important always to bear in mind the strike at the kingside pawn formation with ...h7-h5 (or ...h6-h5). The idea of 6 ♘ge2 was to meet this by ♘f4 and ♘xg6, but at some point the knight may not be able to go to f4. It may, for example, be needed to defend d4. It would be strategically disastrous for White to meet ...h7-h5 with g4-g5 as this would leave the pawns fixed and weak, and Black could attack d4 at leisure. So if ♘f4 is not possible, White has to rely

on the counter-strike f2-f4-f5. Then ...e6xf5 closes the bishop's diagonal and leaves the d5-pawn without infantry support, while White has the f4 square for a piece and the possibility of e5-e6. White can sometimes answer ...e6xf5 with g4-g5, resolving the kingside before proceeding further.

Also, as in any position in which there is conflict in the centre, players must at every move consider what happens if the tension is suddenly resolved; e.g. if White plays d4xc5 or Black plays ...c5xd4. Will the evacuation of d4 leave White's position full of holes, or will it merely allow the white pieces to come flooding forwards? And if the black queen is on b6, can she capture on b2? The answer to all these questions will lie in the relative activity of the white pieces. If they are very active then Black can often finish on the receiving end of a miniature. If they are not active White can spend the rest of the game surveying his wreck of a position and regretting all those pawn advances.

After 7 h4, 7...h6 is the most solid reply. Black's seventh move alternatives are seen in Games 38-42. If Black chooses the main line of 7...h6, White continues 8 ♗e3 and now Black has three moves, 8...cxd4, 8...♘c6 and 8...♕b6 which are seen in Games 43-45 respectively. Finally, the unimpressive 7 ♗e3 is the subject of Game 46.

Game 38
Kotronias-Djuric
Corfu 1993

1 e4 c6 2 d4 d5 3 e5 ♗f5 4 ♘c3 e6

5 g4 ♝g6 6 ♞ge2 c5 7 h4 ♞c6

Black ignores the threat of h4-h5 and develops a piece. Now 8 ♝e3?! runs into 8...h5! (for which see 7 ♝e3 ♞c6 8 h4?! h5!). So White has to continue as planned.

8 h5

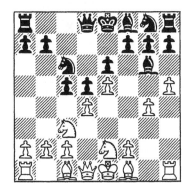

8...♝xc2

8...♝e4 is met by 9 ♖h3!

9 ♛xc2 cxd4 10 ♞b1?!

10 ♞d1! seems better and if 10...♖c8 11 f4! ♞xe5 12 ♛a4+ ♛d7 13 ♛xd7+ ♞xd7 14 ♞xd4 with a clear advantage. So it seems that 7...♞c6 is unsound.

10...♖c8 11 ♛a4 ♛b6

In a later game against Sax at Saint Affrique 1993, Djuric tried 11...♛d7!? 12 ♞a3 ♞xe5 13 ♛xd7+ ♞xd7 14 ♞xd4 and now he should have taken the g-pawn straightaway (14...♞xg4); instead he inserted 14...♝c5? 15 ♞ac2 ♞xg4 16 ♖g1 with a clear advantage since the g7-pawn is undefended behind the knight, and after 16...♞8f6 17 ♝e2 ♞xf2 18 ♔xf2 e5 19 ♖xg7 exd4 Black had merely devalued his pawns.

12 ♞f4 ♛b4+ 13 ♛xb4 ♝xb4+ 14 ♔d1 ♞xe5

Black now has three pawns for the piece, but they aren't going anywhere; whereas White has two useful bishops, no weaknesses, and can attack the d4-pawn.

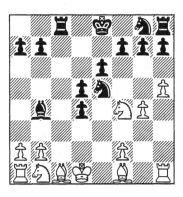

15 ♞d3 ♞xd3

Not 15...♞xg4? 16 f3 winning a piece.

16 ♝xd3 ♞f6 17 f3 h6?!

This wastes time and allows White to attack the e5 square. Kotronias prefers 17...0-0.

18 ♝f4 ♞d7

Black cannot allow ♝f4-e5.

19 ♞d2 ♔e7 20 ♞b3 e5 21 a3 ♝d6 22 ♖e1 ♔d8 23 ♝g3 ♖c6 24 ♞a5 ♖c7 25 ♔d2 ♖e8 26 ♖ac1 ♞f6 27 ♝f5

Intending ♞b3 and ♞xd4 winning a pawn. Instead Black makes it easier.

27...♖ee7?? 28 ♞xb7+ 1-0

Game 39
Vodicka-Stluka
Czech Team Championship 1995

1 e4 c6 2 d4 d5 3 e5 ♝f5 4 ♞c3 e6 5 g4 ♝g6 6 ♞ge2 c5 7 h4 f6!?

Cocozza sprung this tricky move on Nunn at the 1984 Thessaloniki Olympiad and very quickly obtained a good position (which he later managed to lose). It is worth noting that this position could also arise via 6...f6 7 h4 c5!?

8 h5

The point is that 8 ♘f4 ♗f7 9 exf6 is met by 9...cxd4! (Cocozza) 10 ♕xd4 gxf6 11 ♕a4+ ♘c6 and the black centre is strong, and 10 ♕e2 is answered by 10...♔d7! (Nunn). If 9 ♘cxd5?!, intending 9...exd5 10 e6 ♗g6 11 h5 ♗e4 12 f3, then 9...♘c6! (Beliavsky) and the white centre disappears.

8 exf6!? hopes for 8...gxf6?! 9 ♘f4! ♗f7 10 ♕e2 etc, or 8...♘xf6 9 ♘f4 ♗f7?! 10 g5! In Sax-Adorjan, Budapest Zonal 1993, Black was wise to this and responded 8...♘xf6 9 ♘f4 cxd4! 10 ♕xd4 ♘c6 11 ♕e3 e5 12 ♘xg6 hxg6 and the players agreed a draw.

Kotronias suggests 8 ♗g2!? ♘c6 9 f4 ♘ge7 10 f5!? exf5 11 exf6 gxf6 12 g5! with excellent compensation on the dark squares, or if 9...fxe5 10 dxe5 ♘ge7 11 ♘b5!? with the initiative.

8...♗f7 9 f4

Cocozza had reached this position in an earlier game and played 9...♗e7!? 10 ♗e3? fxe5 11 fxe5 ♗h4+ 12 ♔d2 ♘c6 13 ♗g2 ♗g5! 14 ♘b5 ♗xe3+ 15 ♔xe3 ♕g5+ 16 ♘f4 cxd4+ 17 ♔f3

♘xe5+ 18 ♔g3 ♘h6 0-1 Ciuffoletti-Cocozza, Latina 1981. 10 exf6 was necessary, and Nunn has even suggested 9 exf6!?, not bothering to try and defend the centre.

9...♘c6 10 ♗e3 fxe5 11 fxe5

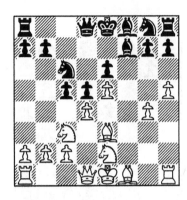

11...cxd4?!

11...♗e7 is more accurate and if 12 ♕d2!? (or 12 ♗f2 ♘h6!) 12...♗h4+ 13 ♔d1 ♗e7!, keeping ...c5xd4 as a threat. Speelman's 11...♘h6!? has the same idea.

12 ♘xd4 ♗e7

12...♘xe5!? is at least consistent. In my booklet *A Line for White* (T.U.I. 1988) I gave 13 ♗b5+ ♘d7 14 ♕f3 with excellent compensation. Tait-J.G. Wilson, York 1991, continued 14...♕f6?! (14...a6 15 ♖f1 ♘gf6 is better) 15 ♗xd7+ ♔xd7 16 ♕e2 a6 17 0-0-0 ♗d6 18 g5 ♕e7 19 ♕g4 ♔c7 20 ♖he1 ♕d7?! 21 ♖f1 ♖e8 22 g6! hxg6 23 hxg6 ♘f6 24 ♖xf6 gxf6 25 gxf7 ♕xf7 26 ♘db5+! (the point of 22 g6) 26...axb5 27 ♘xb5+ ♔c6 28 ♘xd6 ♔xd6 29 ♕b4+ ♔c7 30 ♗b6+ ♔c8 31 ♕c5+ ♔b8 32 ♕d6+ ♔c8 33 ♖d3 ♖h1+ 34 ♔d2 ♖h4 35 ♖a3 ♖h2+ 36 ♕xh2 e5 37 ♕h3+ ♕e6 38 ♖c3+ 1-0.

13 ♗b5 ♗h4+ 14 ♔d2 ♖c8 15 ♕f3

♘h6 16 g5

16 ♕f4!?, intending 17 g5, was also possible.

16...♗xg5 17 ♖ag1 ♗xe3+ 18 ♕xe3 ♖g8 19 ♔c1

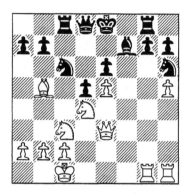

19...♔e7?

This exposes the king on the dark squares and in fact loses immediately to 20 ♘xc6+! bxc6 21 ♕c5+. It would have been better to leave the king on e8 and play 19...a6 20 ♗d3 ♘xd4 21 ♕xd4 ♘f5 when White does not have ♕b4+.

20 ♗d3?! ♘xd4 21 ♕xd4 ♘f5 22 ♕b4+ ♔e8 23 ♗b5+ ♖c6 24 ♘e2 ♕b6 25 ♗xc6+ bxc6 26 ♕f4 ♔e7

That move again! But if 26...♕a6?! 27 ♘g3! ♕xa2 28 ♘xf5 exf5 29 ♕xf5 ♕a1+ 30 ♔d2 ♕xb2 31 ♕c8+ and White is winning.

27 ♘g3 ♕e3+ 28 ♕xe3 ♘xe3

Black has only one pawn for the exchange.

29 b3 ♘g4 30 ♖e1 ♖b8 31 a3 c5 32 ♖h4 ♘h6 33 ♖f1 ♗e8 34 ♖hf4 ♗d7 35 ♔d2 a5 36 a4 ♗e8 37 ♖1f2 ♗d7 38 ♘f1 ♘f5 39 ♘e3 g6 40 hxg6 hxg6 41 ♖h2 ♖f8 42 ♘g4 g5 43 ♖ff2 ♘h4 44 ♖xf8 ♔xf8 45 ♖h3 d4 46 ♘f6 ♗c6 47 ♘h7+ 1-0

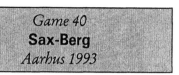
1 e4 c6 2 d4 d5 3 e5 ♗f5 4 ♘c3 e6 5 g4 ♗g6 6 ♘ge2 c5 7 h4 h5

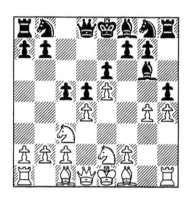

Compared with 6...h5 (see the next chapter), Black reckons the inclusion of 6...c5 7 h4 is in his favour, which is, of course, correct. Nevertheless 8 ♘f4 forces Black to sacrifice either a pawn (with 8...♗h7) or his kingside structure, and it is unclear as to whether or not the demolition of White's centre provides sufficient compensation.

8 ♘f4 ♗h7

Seirawan's 8...♘c6 is considered in the next game.

9 ♘xh5 cxd4

9...♘c6 is met by 10 ♗b5.

10 ♘b5!

Black has been causing problems in the older line 10 ♕xd4 ♘c6 11 ♗b5; e.g. 11...♘e7 12 ♗h6 ♖g8! 13 0-0-0 a6 14 ♗xc6+ ♘xc6 15 ♕f4 ♕a5 transposes to analysis by Kotronias, who gives 16 ♖h3!? d4 17 ♖xd4! or 16...♘b4 17 ♖d4! ♘xc2 18 ♖a4 and 16...♖c8! 17 ♖f3 ♗g6 as unclear.

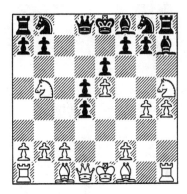
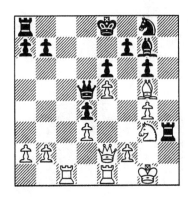

10...♘c6 11 ♘xd4 ♕c7?!

If Black wants to revive this line he will have to try 11...♘xe5!? and hope to survive after 12 ♗b5+ ♘d7 13 ♗g5. It is too soon for 11...♘xd4?! 12 ♕xd4 as White is then threatening 13 ♗b5+, and against other moves White will consolidate his extra pawn.

12 ♘xc6!

Berg had reached this position before, against Westerinen at Malmo 1988. Westerinen played 12 f4 and Black regained his pawn after 12...♘xd4 13 ♕xd4 ♗c5 14 ♕c3 ♖c8 15 ♗e3 ♗xe3 16 ♕xe3 ♕xc2. Although he later lost, Berg must have been happy with his game, and had obviously prepared an improvement. Unfortunately for him, Sax improved first.

12...♕xc6 13 ♗d3! ♗xd3 14 cxd3 d4 15 0-0 g6 16 ♘g3 ♗g7 17 ♖e1 ♕d5 18 ♕e2 ♖xh4

Denied the more valuable e-pawn, Black finally decides to make do with the h-pawn.

19 ♗g5 ♖h3 20 ♖ac1

see following diagram

20...♗h6

If 20...♕xa2?! White comes in with 21 ♖c7 and if 22...♕a5 22 ♖ec1 ♕xe5 23 ♕f3! wins. While 20...♘e7 21 ♗xe7 ♔xe7 22 ♖c7+ ♔f8 23 23 ♕e4! is similar to the game.

21 ♗xh6 ♘xh6 22 ♕e4! ♕d8 23 ♔g2 ♖h4 24 ♖h1! ♖xh1 25 ♖xh1 ♘g8 26 ♕xb7 ♖b8 27 ♕xa7 ♕d5+ 28 ♘e4 ♕xe5 29 ♖h7 ♘e7 30 ♘d6+! 1-0

If 30...♕xd6 31 ♖h8+ wins everything.

Game 41
Timman-Karpov
Jakarta (m/17) 1993

1 e4 c6 2 d4 d5 3 e5 ♗f5 4 ♘c3 e6 5 g4 ♗g6 6 ♘ge2 c5 7 h4 h5 8 ♘f4 ♘c6

An idea of Yasser Seirawan's. Black abandons the kingside and concentrates on demolishing the white centre. 8...cxd4 is similar: 9 ♘xg6 fxg6 10 ♘b5 ♗c5 11 ♗d3 ♘e7 12 ♗f4! ♕a5+? 13 ♗d2 ♕b6? 14 b4! winning a piece in Borge-Shahzad, Manila Olympiad 1992. Instead 10...♘c6 11 ♘xd4 would transpose to 8...♘c6 9 ♘xg6 fxg6 10

♘e2 cxd4 11 ♘xd4 below, or if 10 ♕xd4 ♘c6 11 ♕f4 ♕b8!?

9 ♘xg6 fxg6 10 ♘e2!

This is Seirawan's suggestion against his own line. As the knight will have to move in any case after ...c5xd4, White prophylactically moves it at once, intending to recapture on d4 (after 10...cxd4) or otherwise to place it on f4 to attack the kingside.

10...♘ge7

In Nunn-Seirawan, Monaco (rapid) 1994, Black forgot his own analysis and was wiped out after 10...hxg4? 11 ♘f4! ♘h6 12 ♘xg6 ♘xd4 13 ♘xh8 ♘f3+ 14 ♕xf3! gxf3 15 ♗b5+ ♕d7 16 ♗xd7+ ♔xd7 17 ♗xh6 gxh6 18 ♘g6 h5 19 ♖h3 ♗h6 20 ♖xf3 ♖g8 21 ♖f7+ 1-0. Against Seirawan's 10...cxd4 11 ♘xd4 ♘xd4 12 ♕xd4 ♘e7 Kotronias gives 13 ♗d3! ♘c6 14 ♕a4! hxg4 15 ♗d2 ♖xh4 16 0-0-0 ♖xh1 17 ♖xh1 ♕b6 18 ♕xg4 ♔d7 19 f4 with a clear advantage. Beliavsky suggests 10...♕b6 11 ♘f4 cxd4 12 ♘xg6 ♗b4+ 13 ♗d2 ♗xd2+ 14 ♕xd2 ♖h6, which is good for Black, so White should try 13 ♔e2!? ♖h7 14 ♕d3.

11 ♘f4 cxd4

12 ♗h3 ♘xe5 13 ♕e2 ♘7c6! 14

♘xe6 ♕a5+ 15 ♔f1 hxg4

Since White was now ready to play g4xh5.

16 ♗xg4 ♗d6

By covering the c7 square, Black prepares to exchange queens with 17...♕a6. On 17 f4 ♘xg4 18 ♕xg4 ♘e7 19 ♘xg7+ ♔f7 20 ♘e6 Karpov intended 20...♕b5+ 21 ♔g1 ♕d7.

17 ♔g2! ♕a6 18 ♕d1

18...♘xg4?

18...d3 was better and if 19 ♗f4 ♕a4! 20 cxd3 ♕xd1 21 ♗xd1 ♔e7 (Karpov), or 19 cxd3 ♘xg4 20 ♕xg4 ♘e5 and 21...♕xd3 (Adianto) with a slight advantage.

19 ♕xg4 ♘e5 20 ♕xd4 ♕c4 21 ♕xc4 dxc4?!

Now White could have gained a very strong position with 22 ♗f4 ♔d7 23 ♘g5! ♖ae8 24 ♖ad1 ♔c6 25 ♖he1, intending ♖e4 and ♖de1. So, objectively, it would have been better to accept the inferior endgame with 21...♘xc4 22 b3.

22 ♗e3?! ♔d7 23 ♘g5 ♗e7

Karpov was worried about 23...♔c6 24 ♗d4!, so he transfers the bishop to the long diagonal.

24 ♖ad1+ ♔c6 25 ♘e6?

25 ♖d4 ♗f6 26 ♖e1 (intending ♖e4 and ♗f4) was much stronger as the knight cannot be maintained on e5. And if 26...b5 27 ♖e4 ♘d7 28 a4! a6 29 ♖e6+ ♔c7 30 ♗f4+ ♔b7 31 axb5 axb5 32 ♘f7, or 29...♔b7 30 ♖d6, intending 31 axb5 axb5 32 ♖b6+ after the knight moves from d7.

25...♗f6 26 ♘d4+ ♔b6 27 ♘f3+ ♔c6 28 ♘d4+ ♔b6 29 ♖he1 ♖ae8 30 ♘e6+ ♔c6 31 ♘d4+ ♔b6 32 ♗g5 ♘f7 33 ♗e3 ♔a6 ½-½

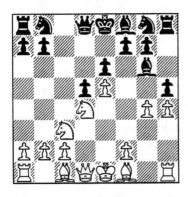

Game 42
Carleton-Pyrich
Correspondence 1994-95

1 e4 c6 2 d4 d5 3 e5 ♗f5 4 ♘c3 e6 5 g4 ♗g6 6 ♘ge2 c5 7 h4 cxd4 8 ♘xd4 h5

Having deflected the knight, Black no longer has to fear ♘f4xg6. The drawback is that the white pieces are now very active. White will seek to increase his initiative by once again jettisoning pawns to open lines for his pieces.

9 ♗b5+

9 f4 hxg4 10 ♗b5+ ♘d7 is slightly inaccurate in that it allows Black other

serious ninth move defences; e.g. 9...♗e7!? (Varnusz) or 9...♕d7 10 ♗b5 ♘c6. After 9 ♗b5+ ♘d7 10 f4 White intends f4-f5 against everything, and the only way to defuse this threat is by capturing the g-pawn.

9...♘d7 10 f4 hxg4 11 f5

White has to break through before his position falls apart. 11 ♕xg4?! is not in the spirit of the position. Then the natural 11...♘h6 does not gain time as after 12 ♕g2 (or 12 ♕g1) Black must answer the threat of 13 ♘xe6. Instead 11...♘e7! is solid, supporting the bishop and the central light squares. Black can then get on with developing the queenside.

11...♖xh4!

Alternatives are bad:

a) 11...exf5? 12 e6 fxe6 13 ♘xe6 ♕e7 14 0-0! is now very strong; e.g. 14...♕xe6 15 ♖e1 or 14...♕xh4 15 ♗xd7+ or 14...♕d6 15 ♗f4 or 14...♘f6 15 ♖e1 ♘e4 16 ♘xd5.

b) 11...♗xf5? 12 ♘xf5 exf5 13 ♕xd5 ♕c7 14 e6! fxe6 15 ♕xe6+ ♗e7 16 ♗e3 ♕g3+ 17 ♗f2 ♕d6 18 ♕xf5 ♘h6 19 ♕e4 0-0-0 20 ♘d5 ♘f6 21 ♘xe7+ ♔b8 22 ♕e3 ♕b4+ 23 c3 ♕xb5 24 ♕xa7+ ♔c7 25 ♗g3+ ♔d7 26 ♕e3! ♔e8 27 ♘f5+ 1-0 Krempel-Elfving, Correspondence 1990-92.

12 ♖f1

12 ♖g1 is clearly inferior since the rook is doing nothing on this square. And White's other moves are worse still: 12 ♗xd7+ ♔xd7 13 ♖f1 exf5 and White has nothing; e.g. 14 ♘xf5 ♔c8! Or 12 0-0 exf5! 13 e6 fxe6 14 ♘xe6 ♕b6+ 15 ♔g2 ♗d6 16 ♗f4 ♗xf4 17 ♗xd7+ (17 ♘xf4 0-0-0 18 ♕xd5 ♘c5) 17...♔xd7 18 ♘xf4 and now 18...d4 or

18...♗f7 with a clear advantage to Black.

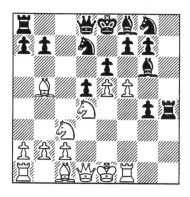

12...exf5!

The only move. Others:

a) After 12...♖h2? 13 ♗xd7+ ♔xd7 14 ♕xg4 exf5 15 ♘xf5 the black king is too exposed; e.g. 15...♗xf5 16 ♕xf5+ ♔c6 17 ♗g5 ♗e7 18 ♗xe7 ♕xe7 19 0-0-0 ♘h6 20 ♕d3 ♕c5 21 ♘xd5 a5 22 ♕e4 ♔b5 23 ♖f3 1-0 Krpelan-Durnik, Vienna 1991, or 15...♔e8!? 16 ♗g5 ♕d7 17 0-0-0 ♗h5 (if 17...♗xf5 18 ♖xf5! g6 19 e6) 18 ♕f4 ♗xd1 19 ♖xd1 ♖h7 20 ♘xd5 g6 21 ♕c4 1-0 Ruiz Sala-Romero Macias, Correspondence 1992.

b) 12...♗xf5? 13 ♘xf5 exf5 14 ♕xd5 is similar to 11...♗xf5, while 13...♖h5!? is refuted by 14 ♘xg7+! ♗xg7 15 ♕xg4 ♖xe5+ 16 ♔d1 ♔f8 17 ♖g1 with a clear advantage (Nunn); e.g. 17...♕f6 18 ♗xd7 ♖d8 19 ♗b5 ♘h6 20 ♗xh6 ♗xh6 21 ♕b4+ ♕e7 22 ♖g8+ 1-0 Kistner-Palma, Ladenburg 1992. Or if 15...♖h7 16 ♗g5 ♕c7 17 0-0-0 with a winning attack; e.g. 17...a6 18 ♘xd5! exd5 19 ♕f5 or 17...♖c8 18 ♖xd5! exd5 19 e6 or 17...♘h6 18 ♕a4 a6 19 ♘xd5! exd5 20 ♖xd5 etc.

c) Seirawan has suggested 12...♖h5!? obtaining three (or even four) pawns for the piece, but the piece seems to be more valuable; e.g. 13 fxg6 ♖xe5+ (13...♕h4+ 14 ♔e2 ♖xe5+ 15 ♗e3 – Kotronias) 14 ♘ce2 ♕h4+ 15 ♔d2 (intending c2-c3 and ♔c2 – Kotronias) and now 15...♕h6+ 16 ♘f4 ♖e4 17 exf7+ ♔xf7 18 ♘xe6 is good for White. Tait-Derouineau, Correspondence 1995-96, concluded instead 15...f5?! 16 c3 a6 17 ♗xd7+ ♔xd7 18 ♕a4+ ♔c8 19 ♔c2 ♘f6 20 ♗f4 ♖xe2+ (20...♖e4 21 ♖h1 ♕f2 22 ♖h2) 21 ♘xe2 ♘d7 22 ♖ae1 ♕d8 23 ♘d4 ♘c5 24 ♘xe6 ♘xa4 25 ♘xd8 ♔xd8 26 ♗g5+ ♔c7 27 ♖xf5 ♔c6 28 ♗e7 1-0.

13 ♗f4?

This completes White's development (almost) but gives Black a crucial tempo, and the bishop does not belong on f4 in any case.

13 e6! fxe6 is the main line. By giving away four consecutive pawns White has brought the base of the black pawn chain up to e6, and now the cover for the black king is paper thin. Nevertheless, it seems that Black can defend: 14 ♘xe6 ♕e7 15 ♕e2 ♔f7! and now 16 ♘g5+ ♔e8 17 ♘e6 ♔f7 is a draw by repetition. White's only winning attempt is 16 ♗xd7 ♕xd7 17 ♘g5+ ♔f6 18 ♗e3!? (18 ♘ce4+ dxe4 19 ♘xe4+ ♔f7 20 ♘g5+ is another draw) and then Eveleens-Kuhlmann, Correspondence 1995-96, continued 18...♖e8 19 0-0-0 ♗f7 20 ♕f2 (20 ♘xf7 ♔xf7 21 ♖xd5 ♕e6 22 ♖dxf5+ ♘f6) 20...♖h5 21 ♘ge4+ ♔g6 22 ♘g3 ♖h3 23 ♘xf5 ♗e6 24 ♘d4 g3 25 ♕g2 ♗d6 26 ♘xe6 ♕xe6 27 ♗xa7 ♖h2 28 ♕f3 ♔h7 29 ♗g1 g2 30 ♖f2 ♖h3 31 ♕xd5

♕xd5 32 ♘xd5 ♖g3 33 c4 ♖e4 34 ♘c3 ♗f4+ 35 ♔c2 ♖xc4 36 ♔b3 b5 37 ♗h2 ♖gxc3+ 38 bxc3 ♗xh2 39 ♖xg2 ♗e5 40 ♖h1+ ♘h6 41 ♖h5 ♖xc3+ 42 ♔b4 ♖e3 43 ♔xb5 ♗f4 44 a4 g6 ½-½. White needs to find an improvement on this game.

If 14 ♕e2!? then 14...♕e7! (theory has shown that all other moves lose by force) and 15 ♘xe6 transposes. 15 ♗g5?! ♕xg5 16 ♘xe6 is worse after 16...♕f6! 17 ♗xd7+ ♔xd7 18 ♕b5+ (Spitz) 18...♔xe6! 19 ♕xd5+ ♔e7 20 0-0-0 ♕xc3!! 21 bxc3 ♔f6 (Revell) or 20 ♕xb7+ ♔e8! 21 ♕xa8+ ♔f7 and White is struggling to draw in both cases.

White has also tried 13 ♕e2!?, intending 14 e6 fxe6? transposing to winning lines of 13 e6, since by this move order the ...♕e7 defence is ruled out; i.e. 13...♕e7? 14 ♘xd5. Therefore 13...♗c5 is forced as it is the only move that allows Black to answer 14 e6 with something other than 14...fxe6. Fortunately for Black 13...♗c5 seems to be good enough; e.g. 14 e6 ♗xd4! or 14 ♗g5 ♕xg5 15 e6 ♔f8! or 14 ♘b3 ♗e7! 15 ♘xd5 g3! intending ...♗h5, ...♖h2 or ...♖e4.

13...a6! 14 e6 axb5 15 ♕e2

see following diagram

15...♗e7 16 ♘xd5 ♘c5 17 ♘c7+ ♔f8 18 0-0-0

Instead, if 18 ♖d1 ♖h3! (intending ...♗h4+), or 18 ♘xa8 ♕xa8 19 exf7 ♔xf7 20 ♕xb5 ♘f6 and Black has two knights and a pawn for a rook (Pyrich).

18...♖xa2!

Kamsky gave the single line 18...♕c8 19 exf7 ♗xf7 20 ♘xa8 ♕xa8 21 ♘xf5 ♘e6 22 ♗g3 ♖h3 23 ♘xe7 ♔xe7 24 ♗d6+ ♔e8 25 ♕b5 which has been quoted uncritically by recent books. Working backwards, 22 ♗g3 in fact loses to 22...♗g5+ 23 ♔b1 ♘d4!; instead 22 ♘xe7 ♘xe7 23 ♗b8! (threatening 24 ♕xe6) wins; but 21...♕xa2 is still a big mess; e.g. 22 ♘xh4 ♕a1+ 23 ♔d2 ♘b3+! But this is all irrelevant since 18...♖xa2! is much stronger than 18...♕c8.

19 ♔b1 ♖a4 20 ♘xf5

On 20 ♘c6 ♕xd1 21 ♖xd1 bxc6 22 ♗g5!? Pyrich had worked out another win: 22...♘f6! 23 ♗xh4 ♘b3!! 24 cxb3 f4+ 25 ♖d3 ♖d4 or 25 ♔c1 ♖a1+ 26 ♔d2 ♗b4 mate.

20...♕xd1+! 21 ♖xd1 ♘b3+ 22 cxb3 ♗xf5+ 23 ♔c1 ♖xf4 24 ♕xb5 ♖c4+! 0-1

And 25...♗g5+ leads to mate.

Game 43
Sax-Nisipeanu
Balatonbereny 1996

1 e4 c6 2 d4 d5 3 e5 ♗f5 4 ♘c3 e6 5 g4 ♗g6 6 ♘ge2 c5 7 h4 h6

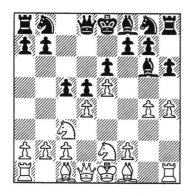

Black quietly answers the threat of h4-h5 by giving the bishop a refuge at h7, leaving it up to White to prove that the inclusion of h2-h4 and ...h7-h6 is a significant improvement on 7 ♗e3.

8 ♗e3

It is wrong to play 8 h5?! since White wants the bishop on g6 to be hit either by ♘e2-f4 or f4-f5.

8...cxd4

Black resolves the position in the centre in order to be able to develop smoothly. The drawback is that it solves White's problems as well, and brings the knight to a powerful central square.

Black's alternatives, 8...♘c6 and 8...♕b6, keeping the tension, are considered in the next two games.

9 ♘xd4 ♗b4

9...♘c6?! is worse; e.g. 10 f4 ♘xd4 11 ♕xd4 ♘e7 12 0-0-0 ♘c6 13 ♕a4 ♗e7 14 f5 ♗h7 15 fxe6 fxe6 16 g5 (threatening ♗h3) 16...♗f5 17 gxh6 gxh6 18 ♗e2 h5 19 ♖hf1 (threatening ♖xf5) 19...♗g6 20 ♖g1 ♗f5 21 ♖g7 ♕a5 22 ♕xa5 ♘xa5 23 ♖dg1 a6 24 ♘a4 ♖c8 25 ♖g8+ ♖xg8 26 ♖xg8+ ♗f8 27 ♗xh5+ ♔e7 28 ♗g5+ 1-0 Borge-

Ostergaard, Copenhagen 1993.

10 h5 ♗e4 11 f3 ♗h7 12 ♕d2!?

Kotronias' suggested improvement on Timman-Seirawan, Tilburg 1990, which continued instead 12 ♗d3 ♗xd3 13 ♕xd3 ♘d7 14 0-0-0!? (14 ♗d2! is better) 14...♗xc3 15 ♕xc3 ♖c8 16 ♕e1 ♘xe5 17 ♗f4 ♘c6 18 ♘f5 ♔f8 19 ♗d6+ ♘ge7 20 ♘xe7 ♘xe7 21 ♕e5 ♔g8 22 ♗xe7 ♕xe7 23 ♖xd5 ♕c7 24 ♕xc7 ♖xc7 and the game ended in a draw.

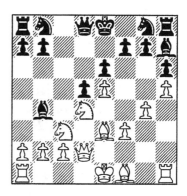

12...♘e7

Kotronias analysed 12...♘d7 13 a3! ♗xc3 14 ♕xc3 ♘xe5 15 ♗b5+ ♘d7 16 ♘f5! exf5 17 0-0-0! with a big attack, the point being that with the pawn on f3 Black cannot defend with ...♘f6-e4; e.g. 17...♘gf6 18 ♗c5 ♕c7 19 ♖he1+ ♔d8 20 ♗e7+ ♔c8 21 ♗xd7+ ♘xd7 22 ♕xg7 ♕f4+ 23 ♔b1 ♔c7 24 ♖xd5, intending ♗d6+ or ♖ed1 winning material.

13 a3 ♗xc3 14 ♕xc3 ♘bc6 15 ♗b5 0-0!?

Provocative since White now has a ready-made attack with the advance g4-g5.

16 ♗xc6 ♖c8! 17 g5 ♘xc6 18 g6!

18 gxh6 ♘xe5 19 ♕b3 ♘c4 20 ♖g1

is worse as Black can keep the g-file closed with 20...g6!, but not 20...e5?! 21 ♘e6! fxe6? 22 ♕xb7 wins.

18...fxg6 19 ♘xe6 d4 20 ♕c5 ♕e8!

21 ♕xf8+

Not 21 ♘xf8? ♘xe5 22 ♕d5+ ♔xf8 and Black's attack is worth at least a draw; e.g. 23 hxg6 ♗xg6 24 ♖xh6!? ♘f7 25 ♖xg6 ♕xe3+ 26 ♔f1 ♖xc2 27 ♖g2 ♕d3+.

21...♕xf8 22 ♘xf8 ♖xf8 23 ♗g1 g5 24 0-0-0 d3 25 cxd3 ♘xe5 26 ♗xa7 ♘xd3+ 27 ♔d2 ♖d8 28 ♔c3 ♖c8+ 29 ♔b3 b5 30 ♗e3 ♗f5 31 ♔a2 b4 32 a4 ♗e6+ 33 ♔a1 ♘e5 34 ♗b6 ♗b3 35 a5 ♗xd1 36 ♖xd1 ♔f7 37 b3 ♖c6 38 ♖d4 ♖c3 39 ♖xb4 ♘d3 40 ♖d4?

Here Hecht gave 40 ♖b5! intending simply to queen the a-pawn; e.g. 40...♖c1+ 41 ♔a2 ♖c2+ 42 ♔a3 ♖c1 (or 42...♘c1 43 ♗d4) 43 b4 ♖c3+ 44 ♔a2 ♖c2+ 45 ♔b3 and wins.

40...♖xb3 41 ♖d7+ ♔e6 42 ♖xg7 ♘b4 43 ♗c5 ♔d5 44 ♗f8 ♘c2+ 45 ♔a2 ♖xf3 46 ♖g8 ♔c4 47 a6 ♖f6 48 a7 ♖a6+ 49 ♔b2 ♖xa7 50 ♔xc2 ♖a8 51 ♔d2 ♖e8 52 ♖h8 ♔d5 53 ♔d3 g4 54 ♗g7 ♖xh8 55 ♗xh8 g3 56 ♗g7 g2 57 ♗d4 g1♕ 58 ♗xg1 ♔e5 ½-½

1 e4 c6 2 d4 d5 3 e5 ♗f5 4 ♘c3 e6 5 g4 ♗g6 6 ♘ge2 c5 7 h4 h6 8 ♗e3 ♘c6!?

This is probably not as bad as its reputation, even though it allows White to rush his pieces into action following his next move.

9 dxc5! ♘xe5

In Bliumberg-Wells, Budapest 1994, Black unsuccessfully tried 9...h5!? 10 ♘d4 hxg4 11 ♗b5 ♖c8 12 ♕xg4 ♗h5 (else White plays h4-h5) 13 ♕g3 a6 14 ♗a4 ♘h6 15 f3 g6 16 0-0-0 ♗xc5 17 ♗xh6 ♖xh6 18 ♕f4 ♖h8 19 ♘e4 ♗e7 20 ♗xc6+ bxc6 21 ♘d6+ ♗xd6 22 exd6 1-0.

10 ♘f4

White exploits the fact that 7...h6 has weakened the g6 square. If 10 ♘d4 then Black can play 10...♘d7 as after 7 ♗e3 ♘c6 etc. Both players have gained something from the inclusion of 7 h4 h6. White does not have to worry about ...♕h4+ and Black has a home for his bishop after f4-f5.

10...♗h7

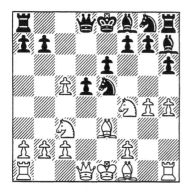

11 ♗b5+?!

This check achieves nothing. 11 ♕e2! intending 0-0-0 is better. Kotronias-Theoharis, Athens (simultaneous) 1992, continued 11...♘e7 12 0-0-0 ♕a5 13 ♖d4!? ♘c4 14 ♖xc4 dxc4 15 ♕xc4 0-0-0 16 ♗g2 ♘c6 and afterwards Kourkounakis pointed out 17 ♘xe6! fxe6 18 ♕xe6+ ♔b8 19 ♗f4+ ♔a8 20 ♕xc6! bxc6 21 ♗xc6 mate. Tait-Young, Correspondence 1994-95, saw instead 11...♕d7!? 12 0-0-0 0-0-0 13 ♘fxd5!? exd5 14 ♖xd5 ♕e6 15 ♖xd8+ ♔xd8 16 ♗g2 ♔c8 17 ♕b5 ♘c6 18 ♗d5 ♕d7 19 ♖d1 ♗e7 20 ♗xf7 ♕xg4 21 ♕b3 ♔b8 22 ♗e6 ♕g6? 23 h5 ♕xh5 24 ♖d7 ♘a5? 25 ♖xb7+ ♘xb7 26 ♗d5 ♕xd5 27 ♘xd5 ♔c8 28 c6 ♘a5 29 ♘xe7+ ♘xe7 30 ♕e6+ ♔b8 31 ♕xe7 1-0. Black should have played 22...♕b4! forcing 23 ♘d5 ♕xb3 24 ♗f4+ ♔a8 25 ♘c7+ with perpetual check.

11...♘c6 12 ♕e2 ♘e7 13 0-0-0 ♕a5

13...♕c7! looks better as the knight is then vulnerable on f4. White cannot storm forward with f2-f4-f5, while Black intends 14...0-0-0 and ...d5-d4.

14 ♖d4!? 0-0-0 15 ♖a4 ♕c7 16

♗xc6 ♘xc6 17 ♘b5 ♕b8 18 ♘d3 a6?!

After this Black faces some difficulties at the c6 square.

19 ♘d4 ♗xd3 20 ♕xd3 ♘e5 21 ♕c3 ♕c7 22 c6!

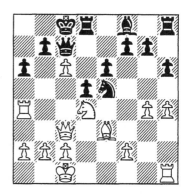

22...♘xc6?

It is difficult to resist the urge to remove the pawn from his throat. 22...♘c4? 23 ♘b5! ♕e7 24 ♘a7+ ♔b8 25 ♖xc4! dxc4 26 ♗b6 wins material, but perhaps 22...♔b8!? is playable.

23 ♘xc6 ♕xc6 24 ♕xc6+ bxc6 25 ♖xa6 c5?!

Black should have tried 25...♔d7! 26 ♖a7+ ♔e8, although White is clearly better with his passed a-pawn and active rook.

26 ♗xc5 ♔b7?! 27 ♖a7+ ♔b8 28 ♖a5 ♖c8 29 ♗xf8 ♖hxf8 30 ♖h3 ♖c4 31 ♖ha3 ♖fc8 32 ♖a8+ ♔b7 33 ♖3a7+ ♔b6 34 ♖xc8 1-0

Game 45
Magnusson-Anhalt
Correspondence 1991

1 e4 c6 2 d4 d5 3 e5 ♗f5 4 ♘c3 e6 5 g4 ♗g6 6 ♘ge2 c5 7 h4 h6 8 ♗e3 ♕b6 9 f4!

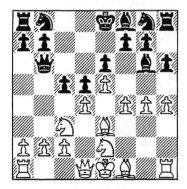

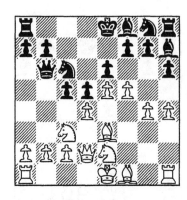

This was Nunn's recommendation after he learnt the hard way that inserting h4-h5 and ...♗h7 was inferior.

9...♘c6

It is foolhardy to take the b-pawn now that White can block the attack on c2; i.e. 9...♕xb2? 10 f5! exf5 11 ♘xd5 ♘a6 12 ♖b1 ♕a3 13 ♘ec3 and Black has no defence; e.g. 13...0-0-0 14 ♖b3 ♕a5 15 ♖b5 ♕a3 16 ♗c1 wins the queen, 13...cxd4 14 ♗xa6 bxa6 15 ♘c7+ ♚e7 16 ♕xd4 ♖d8 17 ♕c4, intending ♗c5+, wins the king, and 13...♖c8 14 ♗b5+ ♚d8 15 dxc5 wins everything.

If Black tries defending d5 first with 9...♘e7?! then after 10 dxc5! ♕xb2 White should forget about c2 and play 11 ♖b1! ♕xc2 12 ♕xc2 ♗xc2 13 ♖xb7 with a clear advantage since White has far more active pieces and is not even behind on material.

10 f5! ♗h7

The justification for this apparent internment of the bishop is that it is very difficult for White to make later progress without playing f5xe6, when the bishop will have its diagonal open again.

11 ♕d2

11...c4 12 0-0-0 0-0-0 13 ♘f4 ♕a6 14 fxe6 ♘b4!?

Black can also attack with the b-pawn: 14...b5!? 15 exf7 ♘ge7 16 ♘e6 b4 17 ♘xd8 ♚xd8 18 a3 bxc3 19 ♕xc3 ♘c8 20 g5 was the crazy game Timman-Seirawan, Hilversum (m/2) 1990, which White in fact won. Seirawan later analysed 18...bxa3! to be a win for Black in all lines; e.g. 19 ♚b1 ♘b4 20 ♖c1 ♘ec6 21 b3 ♘xc2 or 21...♘a5, or 19 ♕g2!? ♕a5!, or if 19 ♘a2 axb2+ 20 ♚xb2 (or 20 ♚b1 ♘c8 intending ...♘b4) 20...♘c8 21 c3 ♕b5+ 22 ♚a1 ♘a5 23 ♚c1 ♕b1 mate. This is by no means conclusive but it does seem as if the white king cannot survive alone on the queenside.

15 exf7 ♘e7

Not 15...♘xa2+? 16 ♘xa2 ♕xa2 17 ♕c3 ♘e7 18 ♕a3 when Black is a pawn down for nothing. Or if 17...♗e4 18 fxg8♕ ♖xg8 19 ♖h3! a5 20 ♗g1 and then if 20...b5 or 20...♗b4 21 ♕a3! and White emerges with two minor pieces for a rook.

16 a3

Attention has focused on 16 g5!? ♘xa2+ 17 ♘xa2 ♕xa2 18 ♕c3 ♘c6!? 19 ♘xd5 and now:

a) 19...♖xd5 20 ♗xc4 ♕a4 21 ♕b3
♕a1+ 22 ♔d2 ♕a5+ 23 ♔e2 ♖d8 24
gxh6 gxh6 25 ♖hg1 ♗e7 26 h5 ♘xe5?
27 dxe5 ♕xe5 28 ♗d5 ♕xh5+ 29 ♗f3
♕h2+ 30 ♖g2 ♕c7 31 ♗f4 ♕b6 32
♗g4+ 1-0 Neubauer-Hakulinen,
Paranana 1993. Black should have
played 26...♗g5 and the game would
still have been very unclear.

b) In his book *Beating the Caro-
Kann* Kotronias concentrated on
19...b5!?, and showed that White had
good play.

**16...♘xc2 17 ♕f2 ♘a1 18 ♖e1
♘c2!?**

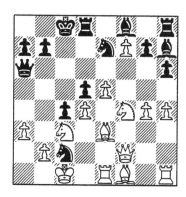

19 ♕xc2!??

Remarkable. In this particular in-
stance it may be unsound to sacrifice
the queen, but it is typical of the variation that White should consider doing
so, relying on the strength of the advance passed pawns.

19...♗xc2 20 ♔xc2 g6?

Black should have played 20...g5
himself, and then 21 hxg5 hxg5! 22
♖xh8 gxf4 23 ♗xf4 ♘g6 when nothing seems to work for White.

21 g5 ♔b8 22 ♗h3 h5

22...hxg5? 23 ♘e6 ♖c8 24 ♗xg5 ♘f5
25 ♗xf5 gxf5 26 ♘xf8 and e5-e6,

♖hf1xf5, e6-e7 wins.

**23 ♖hf1 ♕a5 24 ♘e6 ♖c8 25 ♖f6
♖c6 26 ♘xf8 ♖xf8 27 ♗d7**

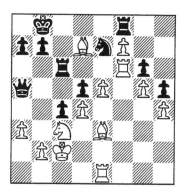

27...♖a6?

Black could still have made a draw
by 27...♖b6 28 e6 ♔a8 29 ♗c1 ♖b3 30
♖xg6 ♖xc3+! 31 bxc3 ♕b6 and
32...♕b3+ 33 ♔d2 ♕a2+ etc., or if 32
♗b2?! ♘xg6 33 e7 ♘xe7 34 ♖xe7
♕g6+ 35 ♔c1 ♖b8 36 ♗e8 ♕f5.

28 e6 ♔a8 29 ♗f4 ♖b6

Too late.

30 ♖xg6 ♖b3

Now if 30...♘xg6 31 e7 ♘xe7 32
♖xe7 and 33 ♖e8+ wins.

31 ♖g8 1-0

Game 46
Mortensen-Berg
Danish Championship 1994

**1 e4 c6 2 d4 d5 3 e5 ♗f5 4 ♘c3 e6
5 g4 ♗g6 6 ♘ge2 c5 7 ♗e3 ♘c6**

7...♕b6 is also critical. If then 8
♕d2 ♘c6 9 0-0-0 h5! is good, or if 9 f4
♕xb2 10 ♖b1 ♕xc2 11 ♕xc2 ♗xc2 12
♖xb7 c4, and 9...0-0-0 or 9...h5!? are
also possible. Finally, if 8 f4 ♘c6 9 f5?!
exf5 10 ♘xd5 ♕a5+ 11 ♗d2 ♕d8 and
Black will come in with ...♕h4+.

8 dxc5

It is too late now for 8 h4?! because of 8...h5! 9 ♘f4 cxd4 10 ♗xd4 ♘h6 11 ♘xg6 hxg6 12 gxh5 ♘f5 or 12 ♗d3 ♘xg4 13 ♗xg6+ ♔d7 and White's aggressive position has gone.

8...♘xe5

The lack of h2-h4 allows Black an alternative in 8...♕h4!? 9 ♘b5, when 9...♘xe5 10 ♘g3 ♖c8 11 ♘xa7 ♖xc5!? 12 c3 and 9...♗e4 10 ♖g1!? ♘xe5 11 ♘ed4 (intending ♗f4) 11...♕xh2 12 ♖g3!? are not entirely clear either.

9 ♘d4

9 ♘f4 is less effective without the inclusion of ...h7-h6, since after ♘xg6 Black can recapture with the h-pawn.

9...♘d7!

Theory regards this as the critical move, anticipating both f2-f4 and ♗b5. 9...♘c6 is less good since Black has to waste time protecting the knight after 10 ♗b5, while 9...a6 is not the most constructive move either. On d7 the knight also protects the bishop after ...♗xc5 so that ♘xe6 tricks are ineffective.

10 f4 ♗xc5

10...♘gf6 is also possible, preparing 11 f5 exf5 12 gxf5 ♗h5.

11 ♗b5 ♘e7

If now 11...a6 White can try 12 ♗xd7+ ♕xd7 13 f5!, although Black still seems fine after 13...e5!

12 ♕e2 0-0 13 0-0-0 a6 14 ♗xd7 ♕xd7 15 h4 ♖ac8

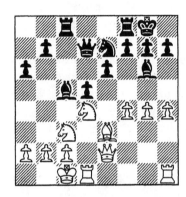

16 h5?

16 f5! exf5 17 h5 f4! 18 ♗xf4 ♗e4 19 ♘xe4 dxe4 20 ♕xe4 ♕d5 would have been roughly equal, and perhaps White might try 18 fxg6!? fxe3 19 gxh7+ ♔h8 20 ♕f3.

16...♗e4 17 ♘xe4 dxe4 18 h6 g6 19 ♘f5!?

White is a pawn down for not very much, so he tries to initiate some play on the dark squares by exchanging the bishops.

19...♘d5?!

This allows White access to the central dark squares. 19...♗xe3+ 20 ♘xe3 ♕a4 21 ♔b1 ♖fd8 was better.

20 ♗xc5 ♖xc5 21 ♕xe4 ♕c7 22 ♘e3 ♘xe3 23 ♕xe3 ♖xc2+ 24 ♔b1 ♖c4 25 ♖d4 ♖c8 26 a3 ♔f8 27 ♖hd1 ♖xd4 28 ♕xd4 ♔e8 29 g5 b5 30 ♔a1 ♖d8 31 ♕h8+ ♔e7 32 ♕f6+ ♔e8 33 ♖e1 ♕c2 34 ♖xe6+ fxe6 35 ♕xe6+ ♔f8 36 ♕f6+ ♔e8 37 ♕e6+ ½-½

Summary

6...c5 7 ♗e3 offers few prospects for an advantage, so White must concentrate on 7 h4, when 7...♘c6?! 8 h5 is good for White. After 7...h6 8 ♗e3 cxd4 seems too obliging, while 8...♘c6 9 dxc5 ♘xe5 has a dubious reputation (perhaps unwarranted), and 8...♕b6 9 f4 has scored well for White – although the main line is too sharp to be written off for Black just yet. 7...h5 8 ♘f4 ♘c6! and 7...f6 also lead to very complicated and unusual positions, and here too White has still to prove a definite advantage. 7...cxd4 8 ♘xd4 h5 9 ♗b5+ ♘d7 10 f4 hxg4 11 f5 ♖xh4 12 ♖f1 exf5 appears at the moment to be a forced draw. Theoretically that would be okay for Black, but if a draw is the object there are surely easier ways of going about it.

1 e4 c6 2 d4 d5 3 e5 ♗f5 4 ♘c3 e6 5 g4 ♗g6 6 ♘ge2 c5

7 h4
> 7 ♗e3 – *Game 46*

7...h6 (D)
> 7...♘c6 – *Game 38*
> 7...f6 – *Game 39*
> 7...h5 8 ♘f4 (D)
>> 8...♗h7 – *Game 40*
>> 8...♘c6 – *Game 41*
> 7...cxd4 8 ♘xd4 h5 – *Game 42*

8 ♗e3 (D) ♕b6
> 8...cxd4 – *Game 43*
> 8...♘c6 – *Game 44*

9 f4 – Game 45

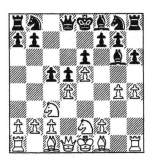

7...h6

8 ♘f4

8 ♗e3

CHAPTER SIX

4 ♘c3 e6 5 g4 ♗g6 6 ♘ge2: Sixth Move Alternatives

1 e4 c6 2 d4 d5 3 e5 ♗f5 4 ♘c3 e6 5 g4 ♗g6 6 ♘ge2

The lines with 6...c5 are certainly playable for Black but a great deal of theory must be known and there are many pitfalls along the way. It is therefore understandable that Black players may want to side-step this minefield with a solid sixth move alternative. If you are such a player, then you are in luck, because almost every legal move has been tried and most are playable.

The most theoretically significant of these is 6...f6 (Games 47-49), undermining the centre from the kingside rather than the queenside. This often results in an unbalanced position where White has a four to three pawn majority on the kingside and Black the same on the opposite wing.

The alternative sixth moves are seen in Games 50-56. An important point to bear in mind if choosing any of these continuations is that it means that counter-attacking against the centre with ...c6-c5 or ...f7-f6 has been

temporarily postponed. However, these thrusts must not be postponed too long. White has a clear plan in mind of advancing on the kingside and if Black does not react in the centre quickly, he can be overrun.

1 e4 c6 2 d4 d5 3 e5 ♗f5 4 ♘c3 e6 5 g4 ♗g6 6 ♘ge2 f6

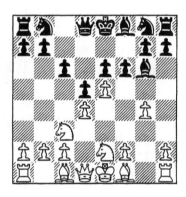

According to Nimzowitschian principles the strike at the pawn frontage is less accurate than the strike at the base. In its favour 6...f6 fulfils another useful purpose in this position: the bishop is simultaneously given a retreat square at f7. White can then either force the bishop from the b1-h7 diagonal by playing h2-h4-h5, or attack the weaknesses at e6 and g6 created by ...f7-f6 with 7 ②f4.

7 ②f4

The aggressive 7 h4 is considered in the next two games.

7...fxe5!

Black ignores the threats. 7...♝f7 is worse as White can then build on the e-file; e.g. 8 exf6 gxf6 9 ♕e2 ♕e7 10 ②d3 ②d7 11 f4 ♝g7 12 ♝e3 e5 13 fxe5 fxe5 14 dxe5 ②xe5 15 ②xe5 ♝xe5 16 0-0-0 ②f6 and now in *Informator 55* Sveshnikov recommends 17 ♝g5! ♝xc3 18 ♕xe7+ ♔xe7 19 bxc3 or 17...♖g8 18 h4 'with a clear advantage' due to the bishop pair and kingside pawn majority. But in fact this had been played before – by the author! Jacobs-Steinbacher, Lugano 1988, continued 17 ♝g5! ♖g8 18 h4 ♖xg5!? 19 hxg5 ♝f4+ 20 ♔b1 ♕xe2 21 ♝xe2 ♝xg5 22 ♝d3 h6 23 ♝f5 ♔f8 24 ♖de1 ♖d8 25 ②e2 c5 26 ♖hf1 d4 27 ②f4 c4 28 ♝e6 ♖d6 29 ♝xf7 ♔xf7 30 ②h5 with a small plus.

Timman's 8 ♕e2!?, aiming to recapture on e5 with a piece, may be even better. By White's refusal to vacate the e5 square Black is prevented from creating early counterplay in the centre. Timman-Anand, Amsterdam 1992, continued 8...fxe5 9 ♕xe5! ②d7 10 ♕e2 ♕e7 (10...♕f6 11 g5 ♕xd4 12 ②xe6 is very pleasant for White) 11 ②d3 ♝g6 12 h4 ♝xd3 13 ♕xd3 e5 14

♝g5 ♕f7 15 0-0-0 ♝d6 and now with 16 ♕g3! White could have claimed a big advantage. Instead he played 16 dxe5?! ②xe5 17 ♕e2 ♕f3 18 ♕xf3? ②xf3 19 ♝e3 ②h6 20 ②e4?! and had to struggle for a draw. If Black refrains from taking on e5 immediately White can either revert to e5xf6 or overprotect e5 with his pieces; e.g. 8...♕e7 9 ②d3 ②d7 10 ♝f4. In Ardeleanu-Stefanov, Bucharest 1995, Black tried 8...♔d7!? 9 ②d3 ②a6 10 a3 h5, but after 11 exf6 gxf6 12 g5! ♝d6 13 h4 he had serious problems on the dark squares.

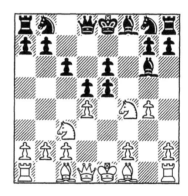

8 ②xg6

Although this damages Black's pawn structure, White has spent time exchanging an active knight for a bishop that might otherwise have had to retreat to f7 (i.e. 8 dxe5 ♝f7).

After 8 dxe5 ♝f7 Korchnoi has assessed 9 ♕e2 as slightly better for White. Jacobs-Johansson, Gausdal 1996, continued 9...♝b4?! 10 ♝d2 ②e7 11 0-0-0 ②d7 12 ②d3 ♝a5 13 f4 with the advantage, but ...♝b4 is a mistake when White still has ②f4-d3. Instead Black should play 9...②d7.

Instead of 9 ♕e2 Al. David-

Korchnoi, Antwerp 1994, saw 9 ♗g2!? ♘d7 10 ♘d3 h5 11 h3 ♘e7 12 ♗g5 ♕a5 13 ♕e2 hxg4 14 hxg4 ♖xh1+ 15 ♗xh1 ♘g6 16 ♗d2 ♕a6 17 f4 ♗e7 18 ♘f2 ♕xe2+ 19 ♘xe2 0-0-0 and Korchnoi gradually outplayed his opponent in the endgame. In general, the problem with these 8 dxe5 ♗f7 positions for White is that, although they look quite nice, it is very difficult to find anything constructive to do; in practice they tend to slowly deteriorate.

The assessment of 8 ♘xe6 has not changed since Nunn-Andersson, London 1982, in which Black made an easy draw after 8...♕e7 9 ♘xf8 exd4+ 10 ♗e2 dxc3 11 ♘xg6 hxg6 12 ♕d3 ♘f6 13 ♕xc3 ♘bd7 14 ♗e3 ♘e4 15 ♕d4 0-0 16 0-0 ♕h4 17 f3 ♘g3! 18 hxg3 ♕xg3+ with perpetual check. As long as Black plays vigorously White will be too preoccupied with defending his weaknesses to be able to reorganise and make anything of the two bishops. It is only Black who can make a serious try for more with 9...♔xf8!? 10 dxe5 ♘d7.

8...hxg6 9 dxe5 ♘d7 10 ♗f4

10...♗b4

In an earlier game against Sax at Tilburg 1989, Korchnoi played 10...♗c5 11 ♗d3 ♘e7 12 ♗g3 ♕c7 13 ♘a4 a5 14 ♕d2 b5 15 ♘xc5 ♘xc5 16 ♕g5 ♖h6 17 ♕e3 ♘xd3+ 18 cxd3 c5 19 ♖c1 ♖c8 20 0-0 ½-½. He also gives 10...♕b6!? 11 ♗d3 0-0-0 as unclear.

11 ♗d3 ♘e7 12 0-0 ♕c7 13 ♘e2 ♘xe5 14 ♘d4 ♗d6 15 ♖e1

If 15 ♘xe6 ♕d7! 16 ♘c5 ♘xd3! 17 ♘xd7 ♘xf4 and the three pieces are better than the queen, and unlike the next note White does not have a forced draw; while if 17 ♘xd3 ♗xf4 18 ♘xf4 White will spend the rest of the game regretting 5 g4.

15...♘xd3 16 ♘xe6 ♕b8

If 16...♘xf4!? 17 ♘xc7+ ♗xc7 18 ♕d4 ♔f7 Korchnoi shows that White has a perpetual: 19 ♖xe7+! ♔xe7 20 ♕xg7+ ♔d6 21 ♕f6+ ♔c5 22 ♕e7+ ♔b6 23 ♕b4+ etc.

17 ♗xd6 ♕xd6 18 ♕xd3 ♕xh2+ 19 ♔f1 ♕d6 20 ♕f3 ♔d7 21 ♖e3 ♖ae8 22 ♖ae1 ♔c8 23 ♘g5 ♕f6 24 ♕xf6

If 24 ♖e5 ♖h4! 25 ♔g2 ♖eg8 26 ♖xe7 ♕xg5 27 ♖e8+ ♖xe8 28 ♖xe8+ ♔c7 29 ♔g3 ♕h6! and the white king is becoming surrounded.

24...gxf6 25 ♖xe7??

In a bad position White blunders the exchange.

25...♖h1+ 0-1

Game 48
Brinck Claussen-Hartvig
Copenhagen 1996

1 e4 c6 2 d4 d5 3 e5 ♗f5 4 ♘c3 e6 5 g4 ♗g6 6 ♘ge2 f6 7 h4

In my second *Trends* booklet I wrote: 'I have always thought that 7 h4 is a little too ambitious as all these early advances leave White with an enormous amount of territory to defend.' Although this may be true, if 7 ♘f4 offers no advantage then White has to try 7 h4, and if some people find the prospect of maintaining a lot of space too frightening perhaps they should not be playing 5 g4 in the first place.

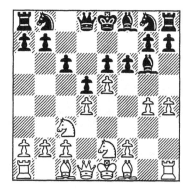

7...fxe5

7...c5!? transposes to Chapter 5, Game 39.

8 h5 ♗f7

Not 8...exd4?? 9 hxg6 dxc3 10 ♖xh7 winning material.

9 dxe5 ♘d7

Black can play 9...c5 10 f4 ♘c6, but this is not really an improvement since the king's knight belongs on c6. Alternatively, 9...♗b4 was tried in Westerinen-Groszpeter, Copenhagen 1988, continuing 10 ♗g2 ♘e7 11 f4 ♘d7 12 ♗d2 ♕c7 13 ♘d4 ♕b6 14 a3 ♗a5 15 ♘xe6 ♗xe6 16 b4 ♕d4 17 bxa5 0-0 18 ♖b1? ♖xf4! 19 ♗xf4 ♕xf4 20 ♘e2 ♕xg4 21 0-0 ♕xh5 22 ♖xb7 ♕xe5 with a clear advantage.

10 f4

This is the critical position in the 6...f6 variation. Both sides have useful looking pawn majorities that are difficult to advance: f4-f5 leaves the e5-pawn en prise, and either ...c5-c4 or ...d5-d4 creates a hole at d4 or e4 respectively. For each player a strike from the flank (b2-b4 or g7-g5) is desirable, and if White has to answer ...g7-g5 with h5xg6 then the bishop will return to g6 to gaze menacingly down the diagonal. For White it is usual to manoeuvre the king's knight to f3 (♘e2-d4-f3) to prevent Black from playing ...g7-g5 without further preparation and also overprotecting e5. Black can in turn try to prevent b2-b4 with ...♕b6, ...c6-c5 and ...♘e7-c6. However, after a2-a3 White can play b2-b4 as a sacrifice, gaining the d4 square and half-open files on the queenside as compensation.

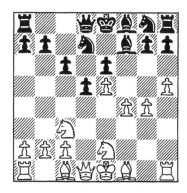

10...♕c7!?

An interesting alternative is 10...♕b6 11 ♘d4 0-0-0 (11...♗c5! transposes to the next game) when the old game, Marjanovic-Campora, Nis 1985, is still the best example of how to play as White: 12 a3! c5 13 ♘f3 ♘e7 14 b4! cxb4 15 axb4 ♘c6 16 ♘a4! ♕xb4+ 17 ♗d2 ♕e4+ 18 ♔f2 ♘dxe5

19 fxe5 ♘xe5 20 ♗d3 ♘xd3+ 21 cxd3 ♕xg4 22 ♕c2+ ♔b8 23 ♖h4 ♕f5 24 ♘c5 ♗xh5 25 ♖xh5 ♕xh5 26 ♘xb7 ♗e7 27 ♘xd8 ♗xd8 28 ♗f4+ ♔b7 29 ♗e3 d4 30 ♗xd4 ♗b6 31 ♕b2 ♕f7 32 ♖xa7+ 1-0. It is clear that White gets ample compensation; his pieces rush into action while Black's are stepping on each other's toes.

It is too soon for 10...g5?! as 11 hxg6 ♗xg6 12 ♘d4! embarrasses the e6-pawn. If the bishop retreats again with 12...♗f7, Kotronias recommends 13 ♘f3! intending ♘g5 with the advantage.

10...♗c5 is considered in the next game.

11 ♘d4 c5?!

The most accurate way to play is 11...a6! (not 11...♘e7?? 12 ♘db5) 12 ♘f3 ♘e7 (allowing the bishop to retreat to g8 after 13 ♘g5) and then ...c6-c5 and ...♘e7-c6.

12 ♘f3 0-0-0 13 ♗d2 ♘h6 14 ♗h3 g6 15 ♘g5!

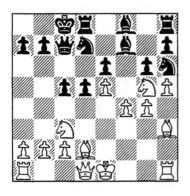

15...♗e7 16 ♕e2 a6 17 0-0-0 ♕c6?!

In overprotecting e6 Black releases the latent pressure on e5, allowing White to make the break.

18 f5! gxf5 19 gxf5 ♗xg5 20 ♗xg5

♘xf5 21 ♗xd8 ♔xd8 22 ♗xf5 exf5 23 ♕f3 d4 24 ♕xf5 ♗e6

Possibly Black was counting on 24...♕h6+? 25 ♔b1 ♗e6 26 ♕f3 dxc3, but then White comes in with 27 ♕xb7.

25 ♕g5+ ♔c8 26 ♘e2 ♗xa2!? 27 b3 ♕b5 28 e6 ♘b6

If 28...♕xe2? 29 exd7+ ♔xd7 30 ♖he1 wins. But now White liquidates to a winning endgame.

29 ♘xd4! cxd4 30 ♕xb5 axb5 31 ♖xd4 ♖e8 32 ♖e1 ♘c4 33 bxc4 ♗xc4 34 ♖d7 1-0

Game 49
Iruzubieta-Izeta
Elgoibar 1994

---

1 e4 c6 2 d4 d5 3 e5 ♗f5 4 ♘c3 e6 5 g4 ♗g6 6 ♘ge2 f6 7 h4 fxe5 8 h5 ♗f7 9 dxe5 ♘d7 10 f4 ♗c5! 11 ♘d4 ♕b6

By making a veiled attack against f2, Black prevents the white knight from completing its manoeuvre to f3.

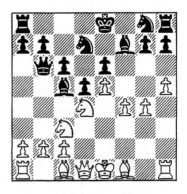

12 ♘a4

12 ♘ce2 is ineffective as White is then unable to prevent ...g7-g5.

12...♕a5+ 13 c3 ♗xd4

If Black withdraws the bishop, he has trouble generating counterplay; e.g. 13...♗e7 14 b4 ♕c7 15 ♗e3 and now if 15...c5? 16 dxc5 ♘xc5 17 ♘b5 ♕c6 18 ♘xc5 ♗xc5 19 ♗xc5 ♕xc5 20 ♘d6+ and 21 ♕d4 with a clear advantage.

14 ♕xd4 c5 15 ♕d1

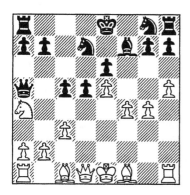

15...♘e7

15...b5? 16 ♘c5 ♘xc5 17 b4 ♕c7 18 bxc5 ♕xc5 19 ♕d4! is dreadful for Black. Van der Wiel-Messa, Graz 1981, was similar: 15...0-0-0? 16 ♗e3 ♘e7 17 ♘xc5! ♘xc5 18 b4 ♕a3 19 ♗xc5 ♕xc3+ 20 ♔f2 ♕b2+ 21 ♔g1 ♘c6 22 ♖h2 ♕a3 23 ♖h3 ♕b2 24 ♖b3 1-0.

16 ♖h3!? 0-0

16...b5? is still answered by ♘xc5 and b2-b4, and 16...d4? 17 b4! cxb4 18 cxb4 ♕xb4? 19 ♗d2 surprisingly wins the queen. While after 16...♕c7 17 b4 cxb4 18 cxb4 ♘xe5? 19 dxe5 ♕xe5+ White now has 20 ♗e3.

17 b4?!

With the knight now able to retreat to c3, Iruzubieta tries b2-b4 as a sacrifice, hoping to achieve something while the black pieces are still disorganised.

17...cxb4 18 cxb4 ♕xb4+ 19 ♘c3 ♘c5!

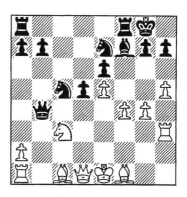

This is the best way to defend the b-pawn. 19...♘b6 and 19...♖ab8 are rather clumsy.

20 ♖b1 ♕a5 21 ♗d2 ♕d8 22 ♘b5 ♘e4 23 ♗d3 ♗e8 24 ♘d4 ♕c8?

This prepares a terrible self-pin. Black should have played 24...♕d7 even though it temporarily obstructs the bishop.

25 ♖c1 ♗c6 26 ♗e3 ♖f7

26...♕xd7?? loses a piece to 27 ♘xc6 and 28 ♗xe4.

27 ♕b3 ♕d8

27...♕d7? is now met by 28 f5!

28 ♗xe4

So as to able to answer ...♕a5+ with ♗d2.

28...dxe4 29 ♘xe6 ♕d5 30 ♘g5 ♖ff8 31 f5 ♕xb3?!

After this final mistake Black is swiftly overrun. 31...h6 32 ♘e6 ♖f7 33 ♗c5! ♕xe5 34 ♗xe7 ♖xe7 35 ♘c7+ ♔h8 36 ♘xa8 ♖e8 offered more drawing chances.

32 axb3 ♗d5 33 ♖c7 ♘c6 34 h6! gxh6 35 ♖xh6 ♘xe5 36 ♖hxh7 ♘f7 37 ♗d4 ♖fc8 38 ♖g7+ ♔f8 39 ♘h7+ 1-0

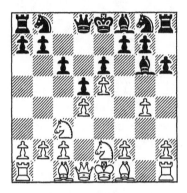

Game 50
Shabalov-Smyslov
Tilburg (rapid) 1993

1 e4 c6 2 d4 d5 3 e5 ♗f5 4 ♘c3 e6 5 g4 ♗g6 6 ♘ge2 h6

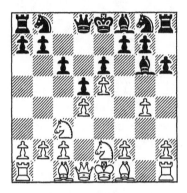

7 h4 is usually recommended here, when Black has the choice of any sixth move variation with 7 h4 h6 thrown in. The drawback of defending against threats in advance is that the opponent may then elect not to make the threat at all. In this case White can either delay h2-h4 or try to do without it altogether.

7 ♗e3! b5!?

7...♕b6 is the only way to justify 6...h6, intending 8 ♕d2 ♕xb2!? 9 ♖b1 ♕xc2 10 ♕xc2 ♗xc2 11 ♖xb7, although White clearly has quite a lot for the pawn.

8 ♗g2 ♘d7 9 0-0 h5!? 10 ♘f4 ♕h4!?

Black's last five moves make a strange impression, especially coming from such a positional master as Smyslov.

11 g5!

If 11 ♘xg6? fxg6 12 g5 ♘e7 it is dif-

ficult to see what White should do next; e.g. 13 ♘e2 ♘f5 14 ♕d3 ♗e7 15 f4 ♘xe3 16 ♕xe3 ♕g4.

11...♘e7?!

If 11...♕xg5? 12 ♘xe6 wins material. 11...♗f5 was better; e.g. 12 ♘ce2 ♘b6 13 b3 ♗a3 14 ♘g3 ♘e7 when Black can prepare ...f7-f6. Instead Black proceeds to help-mate his queen.

12 ♘ce2 ♘f5? 13 ♗d2!

White is able to keep the dark-squared bishop since the knight blocks attack on d4 along the rank. The black queen is now lost. White is ready to play 14 ♘xg6 fxg6 15 f4 when there is no defence to 16 h3 and 17 ♗e1, or if 13...♗h7 14 c3 ♗e7 15 ♘h3 intending 16 f3 and 17 ♗e1.

13...♗e7

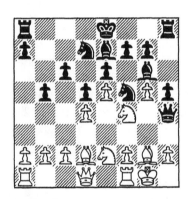

14 ♗f3??

Despite all his accurate moves, in a rapidplay game Shabalov lets the queen escape. 14 ♘xg6 fxg6 15 f4 was winning, as in the previous note.

14...♗xg5 15 ♘g2 ♕h3 16 ♘g3?

Having missed his chance White should be thinking about trying to draw; e.g. 16 ♘ef4 ♗xf4 17 ♘xf4 ♕h4 18 ♘xg6 fxg6 19 c3 with the two bishops, or 16 ♗xd5! and 17 ♗xg5.

16...♗xd2?

16...♘xd4! was much stronger: 17 ♗xg5 ♘xf3+ 18 ♕xf3 ♗e4 and wins, or 17 ♘e1 ♗xc2! 18 ♕c1 ♘xe5.

17 ♕xd2 ♘h4 18 ♘xh4 ♕xh4 19 a4 bxa4 20 ♖xa4

A pawn down, Shabalov tries to open up the position before his opponent can consolidate, but in so doing he allows another little trick.

20...♘xe5! 21 ♗g2 0-0 22 b3 ♘g4 23 h3 ♘h6 24 ♘e2 ♗e4 25 f3 ♗f5 26 ♔h2 ♕e7 27 ♖g1 ♔h8 28 ♘f4 h4 29 ♗f1 ♗h7 30 ♘h5 ♕d6+ 31 ♔h1 ♘f5 32 ♗d3 g6!?

Another weird-looking move. Smyslov's play in this game has been consistent if nothing else.

33 ♕g5 ♕d8 34 ♘f6 ♘g3+ 35 ♖xg3!? hxg3 36 ♖b4 ♖g8 37 ♖b7 ♖g7 38 ♕e5 ♕a5 39 ♔g2 ♕d2+ 40 ♔xg3 ♕c1 41 ♔g2 ♕d2+ 42 ♔g3 ♕c1 43 ♔g2 ♕d2+½-½

> ## Game 51
> ### Ady-Renzi
> *Erevan Olympiad 1996*

1 e4 c6 2 d4 d5 3 e5 ♗f5 4 ♘c3 e6 5 g4 ♗g6 6 ♘ge2 ♘d7

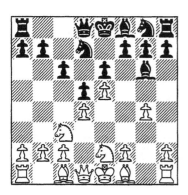

7 h4 h6

This is all rather passive. Black should try 7...h5! and hope that the inclusion of ...♘d7 and h2-h4 makes this a significant improvement on 6...h5. It is then not easy at all to prove an advantage for White. Judewicz-Chaves, Mar del Plata 1987, continued 8 ♘f4 ♘e7 9 ♘xg6 ♘xg6 10 ♗g5 (if 10 gxh5 ♘xh4) 10...♗e7 (or 10...♕b6!? 11 gxh5 ♘e7) 11 gxh5 ♘xh4 12 ♗xh4 ♗xh4 13 ♕g4 g5!? (perhaps 13...♗g5 14 f4 ♗h6) 14 hxg6? ♗xf2+ 15 ♔xf2 ♖xh1 16 g7 ♔e7 17 ♔g2 ♖h7 18 ♗d3 f5 19 exf6+ ♘xf6 20 ♕g5 ♖h5 21 ♕g6 ♕d6 22 ♖g1 and now 22...♕f4 would have won for Black.

8 ♗e3 c5

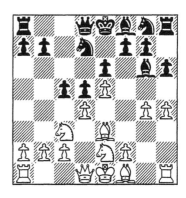

9 f4 ♘e7

Now 10 h5 ♗h7 11 dxc5! ♘c6 12 ♘a4 is a simple way to play, but instead White rushes forward as if nothing has changed.

10 f5!? exf5 11 ♘f4 cxd4 12 ♗xd4 ♘b6

If 12...♕a5 13 ♘xg6 ♘xg6 14 gxf5 ♘gxe5 15 ♗xe5 ♘xe5 16 ♗b5+ ♘c6 17 ♕xd5, or 12...♕b8 13 ♘xg6 ♘xg6 14 gxf5 ♘gxe5 15 ♘xd5 and White is

better; e.g. 15...♗d6 16 ♗b5 0-0 17 f6!
13 ♗b5+ ♘c6 14 ♘xg6 fxg6 15 gxf5 ♗b4 16 ♗xc6+ bxc6 17 ♕g4

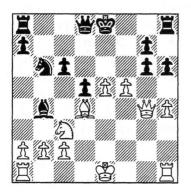

17...♕e7??

This throws two pawns away. 17...0-0 was essential when Black can probably defend; e.g. 18 f6 ♕e8! 19 0-0-0 c5! 20 e6! gxf6 21 e7 ♖f7! 22 ♖hg1 ♕xe7 23 ♕xg6+ ♖g7 23 ♕xg7+ ♕xg7 23 ♗xf6 ♕xg1 24 ♖xg1 ♔f7.
18 ♕xg6+ ♔d7 19 e6+ ♔c7 20 ♗e5+ ♔b7 21 ♕xg7 ♕xg7 22 ♗xg7 ♖h7 23 ♖g1 ♖g8 24 f6 ♖e8 25 0-0-0 ♖xe6 26 f7 ♘d7 27 ♖df1 ♗f8 28 ♗xf8 d4 29 ♘a4 ♘xf8 30 ♘c5+ ♔b6 31 ♘xe6 ♘xe6 32 ♖g6 ♘f8 33 ♖g8 ♘e6 34 ♖e8 1-0

Game 52
Marangunic-Mikac
Austrian Championship 1994

1 e4 c6 2 d4 d5 3 e5 ♗f5 4 ♘c3 e6 5 g4 ♗g6 6 ♘ge2 ♗b4

The original idea of this move was to give the e4 square back to the light-squared bishop, until Black suffered some serious reverses with this plan. So, nowadays, 6...♗b4 is played simply to develop the bishop before play-

ing ...♘e7, answering 7 h4 with 7...h6. However, Black has very little counterplay in this line, and without any specific objective the bishop might as well stay on f8.

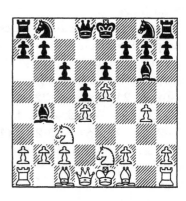

7 h4 ♗e4

If 7...c5 White should reply 8 h5 ♗e4 9 ♖h3, and the loss of tempo over 7...♗e4 is meaningless as Black is no longer able to play ...h7-h5. White has the advantage after 9...h6 10 ♗d2, or 9...cxd4 10 ♘xd4, or 9...♘c6 10 f3 ♗xc2 11 ♕xc2 cxd4 12 a3.

7...h6 is relatively best, but the lack of pressure on the centre allows White a free hand. For example, 8 ♗g2 ♘d7 9 h5 ♗h7 10 ♗e3, intending 0-0 and f2-f4 is straightforward and promising.
8 ♖h3 h5?

8...h6 is the only viable move, reaching positions similar to 7...h6 with the extra move ♖h3 for White; e.g. 9 a3 ♗xc3+ 10 ♘xc3 ♗h7 11 h5 with the advantage.
9 ♘g3 hxg4?!

Vasiukov-Razuvaev, USSR Championship 1980, saw 9...c5 10 ♗g5 f6 11 ♗d2 ♗xc3 12 bxc3 ♘c6 13 exf6 gxf6 14 ♘xe4 dxe4 15 ♕e2, when with two bishops and a lot of weak black pawns to attack White was clearly better.

10 ♕xg4 ♘e7 11 ♘xe4 dxe4 12 ♕xe4 ♘f5 13 ♗g5!

Now 13...♕xd4?? loses to 14 ♕xd4 ♘xd4 15 0-0-0!, while 13...♗e7? 14 0-0-0 ♗xg5+ 15 hxg5 ♖xh3 16 ♗xh3 ♕xg5+ 17 f4 is given by Kotronias. So White is just a pawn up for nothing.

13...♕d5 14 ♕g4! ♘d7 15 0-0-0 ♗xc3 16 ♖xc3 ♘b6

After 16...♕xa2? 17 ♖a3 ♕d5 18 c4 Black would have to give up the knight to save the queen.

17 ♗g2!? ♕xa2 18 ♖a3 ♕c4 19 ♗e4 g6 20 ♔b1 ♘a4?! 21 ♗d3 ♕b4 22 ♖b3 ♕a5 23 d5!

If 23...exd5 24 ♗d2 or 23...cxd5 24 ♗b5+ and White wins the knight, or if 23...♘b6 24 dxe6 fxe6 25 ♗f6 ♖g8 26 h5 etc.

23...♘c5 24 ♖a3 ♕b6 25 dxe6 fxe6 26 ♕c4 ♔f7 27 ♗xf5 1-0

27...gxf5 28 ♗e3 wins a piece.

Game 53
Kupreichik-Kremer
Leeuwarden 1993

---

1 e4 c6 2 d4 d5 3 e5 ♗f5 4 ♘c3 e6 5 g4 ♗g6 6 ♘ge2 ♕h4

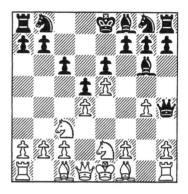

Black utilises the hole created by g2-g4, preventing h2-h4 in radical fashion by occupying the square and attacking the g4-pawn.

7 ♘f4

6...♕h4 was played in one of the first games with 4 ♘c3 e6 5 g4. Blumenfeld-Kasparian, USSR 1931, continued 7 ♗e3 ♘h6?! 8 ♗xh6! gxh6 9 ♘g3 ♗e7 10 f4 f6 11 ♗g2 with a clear advantage.

7 ♖g1!? has the idea that after 7...♕xh2? 8 ♗g5 the queen is trapped and Black only gets one pawn; e.g. 8...h6 9 ♖g2 ♕h3 10 ♖g3 ♕h1 11 ♖h3 ♕xh3 12 ♗xh3 hxg5 13 ♗g2 with a clear advantage in Garside-Brownsord, Correspondence 1990-91. If 7...♘h6 then 8 h3!, threatening g4-g5, while otherwise White plays ♗f4 and rook is not badly placed at g1.

7 h3 has also been suggested by Seirawan, leaving the queen doing nothing on h4. White can then again continue with ♗f4 and ♕d2.

7...♘h6 8 h3 ♗b4 9 a3 ♗xc3+ 10 bxc3 0-0 11 ♗e3

Having gained the two bishops and consolidated his central position, White intends to push the kingside pawns after all by first driving the queen back with ♘g2. The immediate 11 ♘g2 ♕e7 12 h4 fails to 12...f6!, when White cannot play 13 exf6 ♕xf6 14 g5 because of 14...♕xf2 mate. So Kupreichik defends f2 first, and Black cannot in turn play 11...f6? because 12 ♘g2 wins the queen. Kremer finds the only way to guarantee counterplay.

11...c5! 12 ♘g2 ♕e7 13 h4 cxd4! 14 ♗xh6?!

14 cxd4! ♕c7! 15 ♖c1 ♕c3+ 16 ♕d2! ♕xd2+ 17 ♗xd2 ♘xg4 18 f3 ♘h6 19 ♗xh6 gxh6 20 h5 ♗f5 21 ♘e3 is equal.

14...gxh6 15 h5 ♕c7

15...♗e4 16 f3 ♕c7 17 fxe4 ♕xc3+ 18 ♔f2 dxe4 also offers good compensation.

16 hxg6 ♕xc3+ 17 ♔e2 fxg6 18 ♘e1 d3+ 19 ♘xd3 ♘c6

20 ♗g2??

20 f4, giving the king the f2 square, was the only move, and after 20...♘d4+ 21 ♔f2 ♘xc2 White is able to move the rook. If Black sacrifices again with 20...♖xf4! 21 ♘xf4 ♕xe5+ White can probably defend; e.g. 22 ♔f2 ♕xf4+ 23 ♔g2 ♖f8 24 ♖h3 ♕e4+ 25 ♔g1 ♘d4 26 ♗g2 ♘e2+ 27 ♔h1 ♕xg4 28 ♕e1.

20...♘d4+ 21 ♔f1 ♘xc2

Now if White moves the rook he loses the queen to ...♘e3+.

22 ♔e2 ♘xa1 23 ♕xa1 ♕c2+ 24 ♔e3 d4+!

Liquidating into a winning endgame.

25 ♕xd4 ♖ad8 26 ♖c1 ♕xc1+ 27 ♘xc1 ♖xd4 28 ♔xd4 ♖xf2 29 ♗xb7 ♖f4+ 30 ♔c5 ♖xg4 31 ♘e2 ♔f7 32 ♘d4 ♖g3 33 a4 ♖c3+ 34 ♔d6 ♖d3 35 ♔c5 ♖c3+ 36 ♔d6 ♖d3 ½-½

Game 54
Arakhamia-Hort
Women vs. Veterans, London 1996

1 e4 c6 2 d4 d5 3 e5 ♗f5 4 ♘c3 e6 5 g4 ♗g6 6 ♘ge2 ♗e7

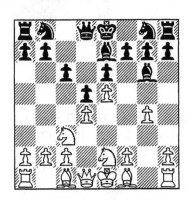

The rather obscure point of this move is to fight for the f5 square with ...h7-h5xg4, while Black intends to defend the kingside with ...♘b8-d7-f8. Apart from vacating f8 for the knight, 6...♗e7 prevents h2-h4 and thus gains the necessary time for Black to carry out his plan. Whether it is a good plan or not is another question.

7 ♗e3!

Kotronias suggests 7 ♗h3!?, intending f4-f5, and if 7...h5 8 ♘f4 hxg4 9 ♗xg4 ♗h7 10 ♘xe6!? fxe6 11 ♗xe6 ♗b4 12 ♕h5+ g6 13 ♕h3 and 'White's attack is more than enough compensation for the missing piece'.

7...♘d7

Varnusz has refined Black's play in this line by 7...♗g5!?, intending 8 ♘f4 ♗xf4 9 ♗xf4 and then 9...h5! having prevented ♘xg6, or if 8 ♕d2 ♗xe3 9 fxe3 ♕h4+ or 9 ♕xe3 ♗xc2. The critical reply is 8 h4! ♗xh4 (8...♗xe3? 9 fxe3 only helps White) 9 ♕d2 intending 0-0-0, f2-f4-f5 with good compensation, while Black must lose more time retreating the bishop.

8 ♕d2 h5 9 ♘f4 ♘f8!?

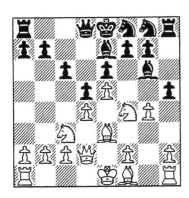

Miles' original idea was to take the g4-pawn and try and defend it; i.e. 9...hxg4 10 ♘xg6 fxg6 11 ♗d3 ♘f8 12 0-0-0 ♖h4 (or 12...♘h6 13 h3! or 12...♕a5 13 ♖dg1 ♖h4 14 ♕d1!) but this artificial plan runs into difficulties after 13 ♘e2! (Minasian) 13...♘h6 (if 13...g5!? 14 ♘g1 intending f2-f3 or h2-h3) 14 ♔b1 ♘f5 (14...♕d7 15 ♗g5) 15 ♘f4 with the advantage. White plans c2-c4, or ♘g2 and ♗e2, while 15...g5 can now be met by 16 ♘xe6!

10 ♘xh5

10 ♘xg6! ♘xg6 11 ♗d3 is more forcing, when 11...hxg4?! 12 ♗xg6 fxg6 13 ♕d3, 11...♘h4 12 0-0-0 hxg4 13 ♕e2 ♘f3 14 h3!, and 11...♘xe5 12 dxe5 d4 and if 13 0-0-0 dxe3 14 ♕xe3 all seem slightly better for White.

10...♗xh5 11 gxh5 ♖xh5 12 ♘e2?

This plan is inappropriate here as Hort gains time to manoeuvre his knights to h4 and h6 and hence to f5. Shabalov-Rogers, Biel 1992, saw 12 0-0-0! ♕a5 13 ♗e2 ♖h8 14 ♖dg1 g6 15 h4!? ♖xh4 16 ♖xh4 ♗xh4 17 ♖h1 ♕d8 18 ♗d3 (intending ♕e2-g4) 18...f5 19 ♘e2 ♕e7 20 ♘f4 g5 21 ♘g2 ♘h7 22 f4 0-0-0 23 ♔d1 ♖d7 24 ♖h3 ♕g7? (24...♕d8) 25 fxg5 ♘xg5 26 ♖h1 f4 27 ♘xf4 ♖f7 28 ♕e2 1-0.

12...♘g6! 13 0-0-0 ♘h4 14 ♘g3 ♖h8 15 c4 ♘h6 16 cxd5 cxd5?!

16...♕xd5 17 ♔b1 ♘6f5 offers more counterplay, intending ...♘f3 and/or ...0-0-0.

17 ♗b5+ ♔f8 18 ♔b1 ♘6f5 19 ♖c1 g6 20 ♗d3 ♕d7

21 ♘xf5 ♘xf5 22 ♗xf5 exf5 23 ♗h6+! ♔g8 24 h4

Now the black kingside does not look so secure.

24...♖c8 25 h5 ♖c6 26 ♖hg1 ♕e6

27 hxg6 fxg6 28 ♗g5 ♔f7 29 ♗xe7 ♕xe7 30 ♕a5

Winning a pawn, so Black seeks refuge in a queen ending.

30...♕d7 31 ♕xa7 ♖hc8 32 ♕a3 ♖xc1+ 33 ♖xc1 ♖xc1+ 34 ♔xc1 ♕b5 35 ♔d2 g5 36 ♕c3 ♕f1 37 ♕e3 ♔e6 38 a3 ♕g2 39 ♕g3 ♕e4 40 ♕c3 f4?

Black had to play 40...♔d7 to prevent the white queen from coming in.

41 f3 ♕b1 42 ♕c8+ ♔f7 43 ♕xb7+ ♔g6 44 e6 ♕g1 45 ♕xd5 ♕e3+ 46 ♔c2 ♕e2+ 47 ♔b3 ♕e3+ 48 ♔a2 ♔f6 49 ♔b1 ♕e1+ 50 ♔c2 ♕e2+ 51 ♔c3 ♕e3+ 52 ♔b4

After a little tour around the b-pawn the king realises it can only hide in the wide open spaces.

52...♕e1+ 53 ♔b5 ♕e2+ 54 ♔c5 ♕xb2 55 ♕e5+ ♔g6 56 e7 ♕xa3+ 57 ♔b6 ♕b4+ 58 ♔c7 1-0

58...♕c4+ 59 ♔d8 and Black has no more checks.

1 e4 c6 2 d4 d5 3 e5 ♗f5 4 ♘c3 e6 5 g4 ♗g6 6 ♘ge2 ♘e7

This is a subtle developing move with a big sting and in Sveshnikov-Dreev, Alusta 1994, White walked straight into Black's idea: 7 h4? h5! 8 ♘f4 hxg4 9 ♘xg6 ♘xg6 10 h5 c5! (since the h-pawn is pinned) 11 ♕xg4 (if 11 ♗g2 ♘h4 or 11...cxd4, or 11 ♗e3 cxd4 12 ♗xd4 ♘c6 13 ♗b5 ♕g5!) 11...cxd4 and now if 12 ♕xd4 ♘c6 13 ♗b5 ♕c7 14 f4 a6 15 ♗xc6 ♕xc6 intending ...♘e7-f5 and Black is clearly

better, so Sveshnikov tried 12 hxg6?! ♖xh1 13 ♕f3 f5 14 ♕xh1 dxc3 15 bxc3 ♕c7 16 ♖b1 ♘d7 17 f4 ♕xc3+ 18 ♗d2 ♕g3+ 19 ♔d1 0-0-0 and Black was winning both materially and strategically.

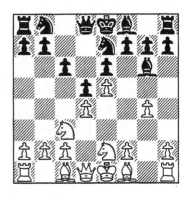

7 ♗e3

This is too simplistic to refute this variation. The only moves which interfere with Black's plans are 7 ♘f4 and 7 ♗g5, for which see the next game. 7 ♗g2 is feeble since the bishop does not belong on the long diagonal. Shabalov-Epishin, Tilburg 1993, continued 7...h5! 8 h3 hxg4 9 hxg4 ♖xh1+ 10 ♗xh1 c5 11 ♗g5 ♘bc6 12 dxc5 ♘xe5 13 ♘d4 ♕a5 14 ♕e2 ♘5c6 15 ♘db5? 0-0-0 16 ♔f1 a6 17 ♘d6+ ♔b8 18 ♗f4 ♔a8 19 a4 ♘c8! and White was busted.

7...h5

Black's alternative plan of 7...♘d7 intending ...c6-c5 and ...♘ec6 is also effective, e.g. 8 ♘f4?! c5! 9 h4 cxd4 10 ♗xd4 ♘c6! and now 11 h5? ♗xc2 12 ♕d2 h6 13 ♕xc2 ♘xd4 14 ♕d1 ♘xe5 and Black was two pawns up in Quillan-Tait, Warrington (rapid) 1991.

8 ♘f4 hxg4 9 ♘xg6 ♘xg6 10 ♗d3

Obviously impressed by Epishin's

play, Shabalov tried 6...♘e7 himself. Valvo-Shabalov, New York 1995, saw 10 ♕xg4? c5! 11 ♗d3 ♕h4! 12 ♕g2?! (if 12 ♕xh4 ♘xh4 White cannot defend his centre) 12...cxd4 13 ♗xg6 dxe3 14 0-0-0 e2 15 ♖xd5! exd5 16 ♗xf7+ ♔xf7 17 ♕xd5+ ♔e8 18 ♕xb7 ♕h6+ 0-1.

10...♘h4

10...♘xe5!? leads to a very messy position after 11 dxe5 d4 12 ♗g6! fxg6 13 ♕xg4.

11 ♕xg4 g6 12 0-0-0 ♗e7 13 ♘e2 ♘d7 14 ♔b1

14 ♘f4?! is inaccurate because it allows Black to castle; i.e. 14...♕a5 15 ♔b1 0-0-0 and Black has no problems. After 14 ♔b1, 14...♕a5 would be met by 15 ♗g5.

14...b5

Nunn-Karpov, Monaco (rapid) 1994 reached this position by transposition, when the FIDE World Champion played 14...♘b6 15 ♘f4 ♘a4 16 ♘e2 b5 and then 17...♘b6, so Black might as well play ...b7-b5 at once. Nunn then put his knight on the queenside: 17 ♘c1 ♘b6 18 ♘b3 ♘c4 19 ♖hg1 a5 20 ♗c1 a4 21 ♘c5 ♗xc5 22 dxc5 ♘xe5, and although the exchange of

knight for bishop left White unopposed on the dark squares, it had cost him a pawn (Nunn later created complications and won).

15 ♘f4 ♘b6 16 ♘h3 a5 17 ♖dg1 ♘c4?

It was necessary now to play ...♘f5, so as to be able to answer ♘g5 with ...♘xe3, or ♗c1 with ...♖h4.

18 ♗c1 ♘f5 19 ♘g5 ♗xg5 20 ♗xg5 ♕b6 21 ♗xf5 gxf5 22 ♕f4 ♔d7

23 ♗f6?

White's major asset is the passed h-pawn so he should advance it at once: 23 h4! ♖h5? 24 ♗f6 c5 25 ♖g5 ♖xg5 26 ♕xg5 cxd4 27 ♕g7 is too fast, or if 23...c5 24 h5 cxd4 25 h6 ♕c5 26 ♗f6 ♕b4 27 ♕c1 ♖h7 28 ♖g7 or 27...d3!? 28 c3! d2 29 cxb4 dxc1♕+ 30 ♔xc1.

23...♖h3! 24 ♖g3 ♖xg3 25 fxg3 ♖g8 26 h3 c5 27 ♖d1 cxd4 28 ♖d3

Or 28 ♖xd4 ♕c5! threatening ...♖xg3 or ...♕b4.

28...♕c5 29 a3

If 29 ♕f2 (intending 29...♕b4 30 c3! dxc3 31 ♕a7+ with a draw) then 29...♔c6! and if 30 c3 dxc3! 31 ♕xc5+ ♔xc5 32 bxc3 ♘b6, intending 33...♘d7, or 32 ♖xc3 ♔d4 and the endgame is dismal for White.

29...a4 30 ♗h4

30 ♕f2 would be met by 30...b4.

30...♖c8 31 ♔a1 ♘xb2! 32 ♖xd4 ♘c4 33 ♖d3 ♘xa3 34 c3 ♘c4 35 ♔b1 ♕a3 36 ♕f2 ♕b3+ 37 ♔a1 ♘a3 0-1

1 e4 c6 2 d4 d5 3 e5 ♗f5 4 ♘c3 e6 5 g4 ♗g6 6 ♘ge2 ♘e7 7 ♘f4!?

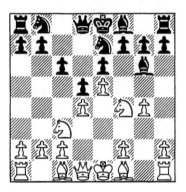

As Black attempted to gain a tempo by prophylactically defending the bishop before ...h7-h5, so White prophylactically attacks the bishop in advance and thus renews the threat of h4-h5. Now 7...h5?! would transpose to 6...h5?! 7 ♘f4 ♘e7.

The only other move to interfere with Black's plan is 7 ♗g5!? and now Black should play 7...♘d7, when Clough-Tait, Correspondence 1994-95, continued 8 ♘f4?! ♕b6! 9 ♖b1 c5 10 dxc5 ♕xc5 11 ♗b5 ♘c6 12 ♘xg6 hxg6 13 ♗e3?! d4 14 ♗xd4 ♘xd4 15 ♗xd7+ ♔e7! 16 ♕d3 ♕xe5+ 17 ♕e4 ♖xh2 18 ♖xh2 ♘f3+ 19 ♔e2 ♕xe4+ 20 ♘xe4 ♘xh2 21 ♗a4 ♘xg4 and

Black emerged two pawns up. If 9 ♘a4 ♕a5+ 10 c3 ♘c8! (intending ...b7-b5) 11 ♘xg6 hxg6 12 b4 ♗xb4! 13 cxb4 ♕xb4+ 14 ♗d2 ♕xd4 is good for Black, so White should look for improvements the move before. 8 h4? allows 8...h6! 9 ♗e3 h5!, but 8 ♕d2 f6!? 9 exf6 gxf6 10 ♗h4 is unclear, or White might try 8 f4!? h5 9 f5! exf5 10 gxf5 ♗xf5 11 ♘g3 with compensation.

7...c5!?

This leads to a forced variation. It is possible to play more quietly with 7...♘d7 8 h4 h6! 9 ♘xg6 ♘xg6 10 h5 ♘e7, and despite White's extra kingside space, essentially this is a French without the bad bishop. In Xie Jun-Brunner, Bern 1995, the players soon agreed a draw: 11 ♗e3 c5 12 f4 ♘c6 13 dxc5 ♗xc5 14 ♗xc5 ♘xc5 15 ♕d2 ♕b6 16 0-0-0 0-0-0 17 ♗g2 ♔b8 18 ♖he1 ♖c8 19 ♔b1 ♖hd8 20 b3 ½-½.

8 h4 cxd4 9 ♘b5 ♘ec6 10 h5 ♗e4 11 f3 ♗xf3 12 ♕xf3 ♘xe5

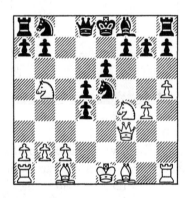

13 ♕e2

13 ♕g3 ♘bc6 14 ♘d3 ♘xd3+ 15 ♗xd3 e5 16 0-0 was tried in Tzoumbas-Kumaran, Chania 1994, and resulted in a convincing victory for Black after 16...♗c5 17 ♗d2 0-0 18 b4

♗e7 19 ♖ab1 a6 20 ♘a3 e4 21 ♗e2 b5 22 ♖b3 ♗d6 23 ♕g2 ♕e7 24 g5 ♘xb4 25 ♗xb4 ♗xb4 26 ♘b1 ♗c5 27 ♔h1 f5 28 gxf6 ♖xf6 29 ♖xf6 ♕xf6 30 ♘d2 ♖f8 31 ♖h3 d3! 32 cxd3 ♕a1+ 33 ♗f1 ♖f2 and wins. In a later game against Tebb at Hastings Masters 1995, Kumaran changed his line for no apparent reason and very quickly got into trouble: 16...♗e7 17 g5 g6?! 18 ♕h3 ♕c8 19 ♕f3 0-0 20 ♕xd5 a6 21 ♘a3 ♕g4+ 22 ♕g2 ♕xh5 23 ♗d2 h6 and now simply 24 gxh6 was strong, and if 24...f5? 25 ♗e2 or 24...♔h7 25 ♖f5 ♕h4 26 ♘c4 and ♘xe5.

13...♘bc6 14 ♗g2 ♗c5 15 c3 dxc3 16 bxc3

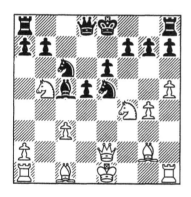

16...0-0

Von Bahr-Engqvist, Stockholm Open 1995, varied here with 16...a6!? 17 h6?? g5 18 ♘xd5 axb5 19 ♗xg5 ♕xg5 20 ♖h5 ♕d8 21 ♖xe5 ♕h4+ 22 ♔d2 0-0-0 23 ♖h5 ♕g3 24 ♖f1 ♕c7 25 ♕xb5 ♘a5 0-1.

17 h6 g6 18 ♖b1 ♕a5 19 ♔f1 ♘c4?!

Seirawan suggested 19...♖fe8, presumably with the idea of defusing the following piece sacrifice; i.e. 20 ♗xd5 exd5 21 ♘xd5 ♘d7 and White has merely given a piece away.

20 ♗xd5! exd5 21 ♘xd5 ♕a4?!

21...♘b6!? covering the d7 square may be better; e.g. 22 ♘f6+ ♔h8 23 ♘c7 ♖ac8 24 ♖b5 ♕a4 25 ♖xc5 ♖xc7 or 22 ♘bc7 ♘xd5 23 ♘xd5 ♕d8 24 ♕e4 f5!? or 24 c4 ♗d4 fighting for control of the long diagonal.

22 ♘f6+ ♔h8 23 ♘d7 ♗b6 24 ♘xf8 ♖xf8 25 ♔g2 ♔g8 26 ♖f1 a6

27 ♘d6 ♘xd6 28 ♖xb6 ♖e8 29 ♕f3 ♘e5 30 ♕f4! ♕xa2+ 31 ♔h3?

The wrong choice. It would have been better to play 31 ♔g1 ♕d5 32 ♕f6 ♕c5+ 33 ♖f2 ♘f3+ 34 ♔g2 ♕xf2+! 35 ♔xf2 ♘e4+ 36 ♔xf3 ♘xf6 37 ♖xf6 and White wins.

31...♕e6?

Better is 31...♕d5! when the apprently strong 32 ♕f6? loses to 32...♕d3+ 33 ♔g2 ♕e4+ 34 ♔g1 ♕xg4+ 35 ♔h2 ♘f5 36 ♖xf5 gxf5.

32 ♖d1 ♖d8 33 ♗a3 ♘ec4 34 ♖bxd6 ♘xd6 35 ♖xd6 ♖xd6 36 ♗xd6 ♕e1 37 ♗e5 ♕h1+ 38 ♔g3 ♕g1+ 39 ♔h4 ♕h1+ 40 ♔g5 ♔f8?!

40...♕d5 is more resilient, and then if 41 ♕f6 ♕d2+.

41 ♗d6+ ♔e8 42 ♕e5+ ♔d7 43 ♕e7+ ♔c6 44 ♕c7+ 1-0

44...♔d5 45 ♕xb7+ wins the queen.

Summary

All the sixth moves considered in this chapter are playable, just so long as Black continues with sufficient vigour, and in particular with a specific plan in mind. If Black plays aimlessly, White will soon have removed all areas for counterplay and Black will then be squashed. Apart from 6...c5, which is the subject of Chapter 5, the two most dangerous moves are 6...♘e7 and 6...f6, both of which set unusual problems for White without excessive risk. With 6...f6 take note that White can virtually force a draw with 7 ♘f4 fxe5 (7...♗f7 is worse) 8 ♘xe6 exd4 9 ♘xf8. If Black is willing to enter these sharp lines at all, it is presumably with the hope of getting more than a draw.

1 e4 c6 2 d4 d5 3 e5 ♗f5 4 ♘c3 e6 5 g4 ♗g6 6 ♘ge2 *(D)*

6...f6
>   6...h6 – *Game 50*
>   6...♘d7 – *Game 51*
>   6...♗b4 – *Game 52*
>   6...♕h4 – *Game 53*
>   6...♗e7 – *Game 54*
>   6...♘e7 *(D)*
>>   7 ♗e3 – *Game 55*
>>   7 ♘f4 – *Game 56*

7 h4
>   7 ♘f4 – *Game 47*

7...fxe5 8 h5 ♗f7 9 dxe5 ♘d7 *(D)* **10 f4 ♕c7**
>   10...♗c5 – *Game 49*

11 ♘d4 – *Game 48*

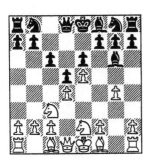

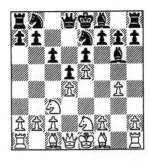

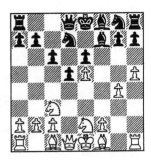

6 ♘ge2   *6...♘e7*   *9...♘d7*

CHAPTER SEVEN

4 ♘c3: Fourth Move Alternatives

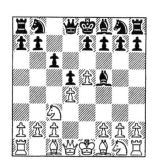

1 e4 c6 2 d4 d5 3 e5 ♝f5 4 ♘c3

Although theoretically there is no reason why Black should avoid the 4...e6 5 g4 ♝g6 6 ♘ge2 main lines, psychologically it may be different. When Black plays a solid defence such as the Caro-Kann it is not always with the aim of participating in a mad hack, and especially not of being on the receiving end. So many players refrain from 4...e6 and look for something a little more sedate. Once again the closed position allows for a lot of leeway. 4...a6, 4...♘d7, 4...h5, and 4...h6 have all been played and the queen has gone to every legal square except d6.

Of these alternatives to 4...e6, by far the most popular is 4...♛b6. The queen often goes to b6 anyway in both the Advance French and the Advance Caro-Kann, so Black hopes to lose nothing by putting it there on move four. The fact that Kasparov once played it has not harmed its reputation either. 4...♛b6 remains solid and dependable. White tends to have the sparkling wins, but points-

wise Black is not far behind.

The first five games in this chapter deal with 4...♛b6. Black's other moves are considered in Games 62 and 63.

Game 57
Votava-Kumaran
World U-18 Ch., Duisburg 1992

1 e4 c6 2 d4 d5 3 e5 ♝f5 4 ♘c3 ♛b6 5 g4

The standard move, but here White can also consider 5 ♘a4, 5 ♘f3 and 5 ♝d3 (Games 59, 60 and 61).

5...♝d7

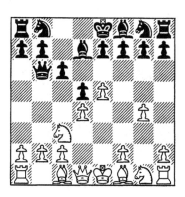

This is the plan adopted once by Kasparov. Black retreats the bishop back into safety and reckons that although White has played g2-g4 'for free', this has only weakened the kingside. White must now contemplate the positional threat of ...h7-h5, without having tactical resources based on exploiting a black bishop at g6.

6 ♘a4!?

Another gratis move and the white knight is on its way to remove the errant bishop. All this is wonderfully anti-positional – it is hard to imagine any sort of French Defence in which White would put so much effort into exchanging Black's light-squared bishop. Still, the position is closed and both sides can take one or two liberties. 6 ♗g2! is considered in the next game.

6...♕c7

6...♕a5?! is met by 7 c3 and 8 b4.

7 ♘c5 e6 8 ♘xd7

8 ♘d3 c5 9 dxc5 ♗b5 is fine for Black.

8...♘xd7

9 c3

The original game Velimirovic-Kasparov, Moscow Interzonal 1982,

saw 9 f4 c5 10 c3 ♘e7 11 ♘f3 h5 and in characteristic fashion Velimirovic tried (and failed) to wipe his opponent out with 12 f5!? hxg4 13 fxe6 gxf3 14 exd7+ ♕xd7 15 ♕xf3. Kasparov preferred 12 gxh5 ♘f5 to which Speelman added 13 ♗d3.

9...h5 10 g5 ♘e7 11 ♗d3 g6 12 ♘e2 c5 13 h4 ♘c6 14 0-0 ♗e7

If 14...♕b6 then 15 ♗c2.

15 ♗e3 a6 16 ♘f4 ♖g8 17 a3 a5?!

17...c4 would have been more prudent, intending 18 ♗c2 ♘a5 and if 19 ♕b1!? ♕b6.

18 ♔g2 ♕b6 19 ♖b1 a4 20 b3 axb3 21 ♖xb3 ♕a7 22 ♕b1 0-0-0!? 23 ♖b5 b6 24 a4 c4?

At last – and at completely the wrong time.

25 ♗xg6! fxg6

25...♖xg6?! 26 ♘xg6 fxg6 27 ♕xg6 ♘f8 28 ♕xh5 and the kingside pawns roll.

26 ♘xe6 ♖de8 27 ♘f4 ♗d8 28 ♘xd5 ♕xa4 29 ♘f4 ♕a8? 30 ♕e4 ♗c7 31 e6 ♘f8 32 d5 ♘e5

33 f3

Planning to attack the knight. 33 ♗xb6! ♗d6 34 ♖a5, planning to attack the king, would have been more effi-

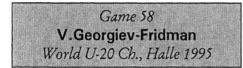

cient.

33...♘d3!? 34 ♕xc4 ♘e5 35 ♕e4 ♕a2+ 36 ♖f2 ♕c4 37 ♗xb6 ♕xb5 38 ♗xc7 ♘c4 39 d6 ♕a6 40 e7 ♘d7 41 ♕d4 ♔b7 42 ♖e2 ♕b5 43 ♘e6 ♘xd6 44 c4 ♘xc4 45 ♕e4+ ♔c8 46 ♖c2 ♘c5 47 ♘xc5 ♕xc5 48 ♖xc4 ♕xc7 49 ♕e6+ ♔b8 50 ♖b4+! ♕b7 51 ♕d6+ 1-0

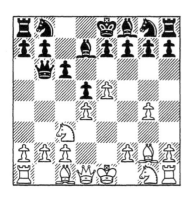

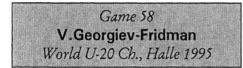

Game 58
V.Georgiev-Fridman
World U-20 Ch., Halle 1995

1 e4 c6 2 d4 d5 3 e5 ♗f5 4 ♘c3 ♕b6 5 g4 ♗d7 6 ♗g2!

White develops rapidly and hopes to exchange a disintegrating centre for the initiative.

6...e6 7 ♘ge2 c5 8 0-0

Karpov's books have repeatedly assessed 8 0-0 as slightly advantageous for White. 8 ♗e3?! should be met by 8...♘c6, as in Bianchi-Kanefsck, Buenos Aires 1995: 9 0-0 cxd4 10 ♘xd4 ♘xd4 11 ♗xd4 ♗c5 12 ♗xc5 ♕xc5 with yet another bad French for White.

8...cxd4

Now if 8...♘c6 9 ♘a4! ♕a6 10

♘xc5 ♗xc5 11 dxc5 ♘xe5 12 ♘d4 and the bishop pair may count for something, or if 8...h5 then 9 g5 is a prudent reply.

9 ♘xd4 ♘c6 10 ♘b3 ♘xe5

Nunn has suggested 10...h5 11 gxh5 (11 g5!?) 11...♕d8!, intending ...♕h4.

11 ♖e1 ♗d6 12 ♗e3

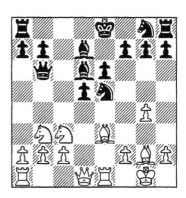

12...♕d8

12...♕c7? is worse as the queen gets hit on this square: 13 f4 ♘g6 14 ♘xd5 ♕c8 15 ♘b6 axb6 16 ♕xd6 ♘h4, Ioseliani-Chiburdanidze, Telavi (m/12) 1988, and now 17 ♗xb6 would have won; e.g. 17...♘xg2 18 ♗c5! ♔d8 (else ♕f8 mate) 19 ♖ed1 with an overwhelming position.

13 ♗d4 ♕g5 14 ♘xd5 ♘xg4

Not 14...exd5 15 ♗xe5 ♗xe5 16 ♕d4 f6 17 f4 ♕xg4 18 fxe5 ♕xd4+ 19 ♘xd4 0-0-0 20 e6 ♗c6 21 ♘f5 with the advantage.

15 h3 ♗h2+!?

If 15...♘4h6 16 ♘c5!, intending ♘e4.

16 ♔h1 h5 17 f3!

17 hxg4!? hxg4 18 ♘e3 may also have been defensible since if 18...♗f4+ 19 ♔g1 ♗h2+ 20 ♔f1 White can block 20...♗b5+ with 21 c4.

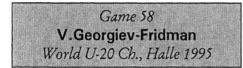

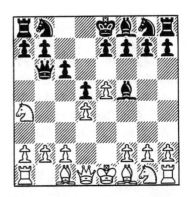

17...♕xd5 18 fxg4 ♕d6 19 ♕e2! hxg4 20 ♕xg4 ♘f6?!

But if 20...♖h7 then 21 ♘c5!, intending ♘xd7 eliminating the dangerous bishop, and White is on top as the remaining black pieces are wholly uncoordinated.

21 ♕xg7 ♖g8 22 ♕xf6 ♗c6

Not 22...♖xg2?? 23 ♕h8+.

23 ♖e2?

White makes a mess of it: 23 ♗e4! wins since White keeps control of the long diagonal; e.g. 23...♕g3 24 ♗xc6+ bxc6 25 ♖e2 or 23...♗g3 24 ♖e2 ♗xe4+ 25 ♖xe4 ♕d5 26 ♕f3.

23...♖xg2! 24 ♖xg2 ♕g3 25 ♕h8+ ♔d7 26 ♘c5+ ♔c7 27 ♘xe6+ fxe6 28 ♕g7+ ♕xg7 29 ♗xg7 ♗d6 30 ♖f1 ♖g8 31 ♖f7+ ♔c8 32 ♔g1 ♗c5+ 33 ♔f1 ♗xg2+ 34 ♔xg2 ♗d4 35 ♖f8+ ♖xf8 36 ♗xf8 ♗xb2 37 ♔f3 ♔d7 38 ♔e4 ♗f6 39 ♗c5 b6 40 ♗d4 ♗h4 ½-½

> ### Game 59
> ### Galdunts-Klamp
> *Wiesbaden Open 1994*

1 e4 c6 2 d4 d5 3 e5 ♗f5 4 ♘c3 ♕b6 5 ♘a4

White again makes use of the queen on b6 to reposition his knight, but reckons that the bishop is best left on f5. The drawback is that the knight is not particularly well-placed at a4 either. Or is it?

5...♕c7 6 c3 e6 7 b4!? a5

This is obviously critical – attacking the pawn chain before White is ready to support it with a2-a3.

8 b5 c5?

8...♘d7 was better and if 9 ♘f3 then 9...♗g4 or even 9...♗e4!? It is surprising how often an early ...c6-c5 gets Black into trouble in these 4...♕b6 lines – even if, as here, White has only one piece out. The reason is that the black queen and bishop, although developed on useful squares, are tactically exposed after the opening of the centre, and White can use them to create a strong initiative.

9 b6! ♕c6 10 dxc5

see following diagram

10...♘d7 11 ♘f3 ♘xc5?

On 11...♗g4 White again plays 12 ♕b3! ♘xc5 13 ♘xc5 ♕xc5 14 ♗e3, or 12...♗xf3 13 ♗b5 ♕c8 14 gxf3. Or if 11...♗xc5 then again 12 ♕b3, intending ♗b5.

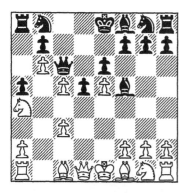

12 ♘d4 ♛c8 13 ♗b5+ ♘d7 14 ♘xf5 exf5 15 0-0 ♘e7 16 ♖e1 ♛d8

A bad move, but then Black didn't have any good ones.

17 e6 fxe6 18 ♘c5 ♘c6 19 ♘xb7 ♛xb6 20 ♖xe6+ 1-0

20...♔f7 21 ♛xd5 winning everything.

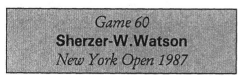

Game 60
Sherzer-W.Watson
New York Open 1987

1 e4 c6 2 d4 d5 3 e5 ♗f5 4 ♘c3 ♛b6 5 ♘f3

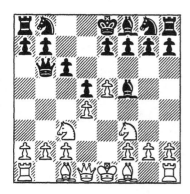

This time White ignores the black queen for the time being, intending first to develop the kingside and castle, and only then commence play on the queenside by ♘a4 and b2-b3, c2-c4. It makes no difference whether White plays first 5 ♘f3 or 5 ♗e2.

5...e6 6 ♗e2 ♗g4 7 0-0 ♗xf3

Ady-Thomson, Scottish Championship 1988, saw 7...♘e7 8 ♘a4 ♛c7 9 b3 b5 10 ♘b2 b4 11 h3 ♗xf3 12 ♗xf3 c5 13 dxc5 ♘ec6 14 ♘d3 ♘d7 (not 14...♘xe5? 15 ♗xd5!) 15 ♗e3 ♘cxe5 16 ♗f4 ♗xc5?! 17 ♗xd5 ♖d8 18 ♗xe6 fxe6 and now instead of 19 ♘xe5?? 0-0 20 ♘d3 ♖xf4 21 ♘xf4 ♛xf4, White should have played 19 ♛h5+ g6 20 ♗xe5 ♘xe5 21 ♛xe5 ♛xe5 22 ♘xe5 and 23 ♘d3 with the advantage. 11 a3 was probably better for White in any case.

8 ♗xf3

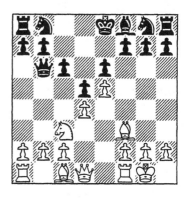

White has a slight lead in development and the two bishops; yet the position is closed and the light-squared bishop is obstructed by the black pawn chain.

8...♘e7 9 ♘a4 ♛a5 10 b3 ♘f5 11 c4?

Too hasty. Black threatened 11...b5 12 ♘b2 ♛c3 attacking the d4-pawn and White should have seen to this first: 11 ♗d2 ♕c7 12 ♗f4 or possibly even 11 ♗g4!?

11...b5!

Not 11...dxc4? 12 bxc4 ♘xd4? 13 ♕xd4 ♕xa4 14 ♖b1!

12 cxb5

If 12 g4 ♘xd4! 13 ♕xd4 bxa4 with a clear advantage.

12...cxb5 13 ♘b2 ♕c3

Or 13...♘c6 14 ♗e3 ♗a3 was also good.

14 a4 b4??

Black sees no hurry and first decides to prevent a4xb5, but this gives White a crucial tempo to defend the centre. Instead 14...♘xd4! 15 axb5 ♘d7 with a clear advantage.

15 ♗e3!

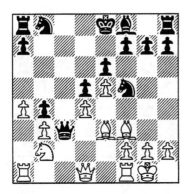

15...♘xe3

The queen gets trapped if she takes the knight: 15...♕xb2 16 ♖e1! ♘c6 17 ♖e2 ♕c3 18 ♖c1 ♘fxd4 (18...♘cxd4? 19 ♖xc3 ♘xe2+ 20 ♕xe2 bxc3 21 ♕b5+) 19 ♖xc3 ♘xe2+ (19...♖xf3+ 20 gxf3 bxc3 21 ♕d3 ♗b4? 22 ♕a6!) 20 ♗xe2 bxc3 21 ♗b5 ♖c8 22 ♗xa7 with the advantage.

16 fxe3 ♕xe3+

16...♕xb2?? 17 ♖c1 ♗e7 18 ♖f2 ♕a3 19 ♖a1 wins the queen again.

17 ♔h1 ♗e7 18 ♖c1 0-0

18...♗d8? 19 ♘c4!

19 ♖c7 ♗g5 20 ♗g4 a5?

Black would also have been in trouble after 20...♘a6 21 ♖cxf7 (21 ♖c6 ♘b8 22 ♖xe6!? ♕c3!) 21...♖xf7 22 ♗xe6 ♖af8 (22...♗f4? 23 ♗xd5) 23 ♕g4! (threatening ♕f5) 23...g6 24 ♗xf7+ ♖xf7 25 ♕e6 ♗f4 26 ♕xa6 ♕xd4 27 e6! or 20...f5 21 exf6 ♗xf6 22 ♘d3! ♕xd4 23 ♗xe6+ ♔h8 24 ♖c5 with a clear advantage.

21 ♖fxf7 ♗h6 22 ♗xe6 ♘d7

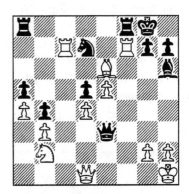

23 ♖xg7+??

Presumably White was in terrible time trouble, since of course 23 ♖f3+ or ♖fxd7+ wins easily.

23...♔xg7 24 ♖xd7+ ♔h8 25 ♗xd5 ♖ac8 26 ♘c4 ♕xb3 27 ♕g1 ♕d3 28 ♘d6 ♖c1 29 ♘f7+ ♖xf7 0-1

> **Game 61**
> **Borge-Berg**
> *Espergarde 1992*

1 e4 c6 2 d4 d5 3 e5 ♗f5 4 ♘c3 ♕b6 5 ♗d3

Offering a kind of transposition by 5...♗xd3 6 ♕xd3 to the 4 ♗d3 line (for which see Chapter 8), when

Kotronias believes the queen to be misplaced on b6. If Black takes the d4-pawn White will gain a lot of time knocking the queen about.

5...♕xd4!? 6 ♘f3

Not 6 ♘ce2?! ♕xe5 7 ♘f3 ♕f6 8 ♗g5 ♕g6! 9 ♘f4 ♕d6 10 ♗xf5 h6 and Black looks likely to consolidate.

6...♕g4 7 h3 ♕h5

Alternatively 7...♕xg2?! 8 ♖g1 ♕xh3 9 ♗f1 ♗xc2 10 ♕e2 ♕d7 (if 10...♕h5 Borge gives 11 ♖g5 ♕h1 12 ♕xc2 ♕xf3? 13 ♗g2 wins the queen) 11 ♕xc2 g6 12 ♗f4 ♗g7 13 0-0-0 and although Black has four pawns for the piece, White's massive lead in development is far more important here.

8 0-0 ♗xd3 9 cxd3 ♕f5

If 9...e6 10 ♘e2 and Black has to waste yet another tempo on 10...h6 to negate the threat of 11 ♘g3 ♕g6 12 ♘h4 winning the queen.

10 ♖e1 ♕c8 11 e6!

Otherwise Black will now play ...e7-e6 himself.

11...fxe6 12 ♘d4 ♘a6 13 ♕f3

After 13 ♕h5+ g6 14 ♕e5 ♘f6 15 ♘xe6 Borge gives 15...♕d7 16 ♗g5 ♔f7 'with counterplay'. Black would play ...♕d6 and ...h7-h6 to drive back

the white pieces.

13...♘f6

If 13...♘c7 14 ♗f4 ♘f6 15 ♗xc7 ♕xc7 16 ♘xe6 ♕d6 White builds up on the e-file with 17 ♖e2 and ♖ae1.

14 g4!? h6 15 ♗f4 g5 16 ♗d6!? ♔f7

16...exd6? loses to 17 ♕xf6, while if 16...♕d8 17 ♗e5! ♘c7 then White builds up again with ♖e2 and ♖ae1.

17 ♖xe6

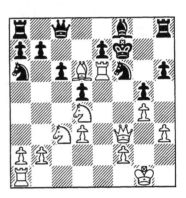

17...♕xe6?

17...c5? loses to both 18 ♘xd5 and 18 ♗xe7. Black had to play 17...♕d8! to overprotect the knight, when Blatny gives 18 ♘xd5! cxd5 19 ♖xf6+ exf6 20 ♕xd5+ ♔g6 21 ♕e4+ ♔f7 and now White can give perpetual with 22 ♕d5+ etc., or try 22 ♕xb7+ ♔g6 23 ♕e4+ ♔f7 24 ♗xf8!? ♕xf8 25 ♕e6+ ♔g6 26 ♕xa6, reestablishing approximate material parity.

18 ♘xe6 exd6 19 ♖e1 ♘c5 20 ♕f5 ♖e8?

20...♘xe6 was essential.

21 ♘xg5+! hxg5 22 ♖xe8 ♔xe8 23 ♕xf6 ♖xh3 24 ♕g6+ ♔d7 25 ♕xg5

Now the passed g-pawn wins the game.

25...♖xd3 26 ♕f5+ ♔e7 27 ♕h7+ ♔d8 28 ♕f7 ♘d7 29 g5 ♖d4 30 f3

♖h4 31 ♘e2 d4 32 ♘f4 ♖xf4 33 ♛xf4 ♗g7 34 ♛f7 ♗h8 35 ♛g8+ 1-0

1 e4 c6 2 d4 d5 3 e5 ♗f5 4 ♘c3 a6!?

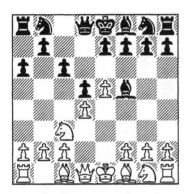

As with 4...♛b6 Black holds back ...e7-e6 and will retreat the bishop back to d7 if White plays g2-g4. The lack of pressure on b2 allows White to develop the queen's bishop, but apart from that there are no useful waiting moves that would both allow and fit in with the sharp 4...e6 5 g4 ♗g6 system. Black could also play 4...♛c7 first.

5 ♗e3 ♛b6?!

5...♛c7! was Speelman's idea, envisaging the later ...c6-c5. For Black to support the pawn break with the queen on c7, ...a7-a6 is also required to prevent White's ♘b5, so Black's fourth and fifth moves fit together logically while waiting to see what White does. In Timman-Speelman, Reykjavik 1991, White went astray: 6 ♘ge2?! e6 7 ♘g3 ♘e7 8 ♘xf5?! ♘xf5 9

♗d3 ♘xe3 10 fxe3 c5 and Black already had a very satisfactory position.

6 ♗d3!?

Offering a 4 ♗d3 line with ...♛b6 – plus ♗e3 and ...a7-a6 thrown in. Instead 6 ♘a4 is similar to 4...♛b6 5 ♘a4 (see Game 59). Or White might try 6 ♖b1!?, intending 6...e6 7 g4 ♗g6 8 ♘ge2 etc. It is worth noting that this idea does not work against 4...♛b6, as 5 ♖b1 e6 6 g4 is refuted 6...♗b4!

6...♛xb2?

Black should acquiesce with 6...♗xd3 7 ♛xd3 e6.

7 ♘a4 ♛a3 8 c3

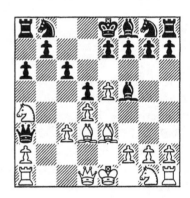

8...b5

Forced. 8...♗xd3? loses to 9 ♗c1, or if 8...e6? 9 ♗c1 ♛e7 10 ♗xf5 exf5 11 ♘b6 ♖a7 12 ♘c8 forks the rook and queen.

9 ♗xf5 e6 10 ♗c2?!

10 ♘b6! ♖a7 11 ♘c8 is stronger. Black can get three pawns for the piece but surely they aren't enough.

10...bxa4 11 ♘e2 g6 12 ♛b1?!

This is less effective now that Black has blocked the b1-h7 diagonal. 12 ♗xa4 looks better.

12...♛e7 13 ♛b6 ♛a7 14 ♖b1 ♛xb6 15 ♖xb6 ♘d7!

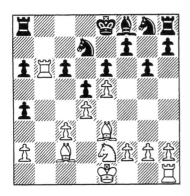

Mestel conducts an exemplary defence, giving up the c-pawn for four tempi on the rook.

16 ♖xc6 ♘e7 17 ♖c7 ♔d8 18 ♖b7 ♔c8 19 ♖b1 a3 20 ♗a4 ♔c7 21 ♗xd7 ♔xd7 22 ♔d2 ♘c6 23 ♖b7+ ♔c8!

And again, giving up the f-pawn to push the rook off on the kingside.

24 ♖xf7 ♘d8 25 ♖f3 ♖b8 26 ♔d3 ♗e7 27 h4

If 27 c4 ♘c6! and ...♘b4+.

27...♖b2 28 ♘c1 ♔d7 29 h5 g5 30 h6 ♖g8 31 g4 ♔e8 32 c4 ½-½

1 e4 c6 2 d4 d5 3 e5 ♗f5 4 ♘c3 ♕d7

Black prevents g2-g4 temporarily and gains time to play ...h7-h6 when, after g2-g4, Black can retreat the bishop back to the less exposed h7 square. The queen will probably have to move again from d7, but if White has prepared g2-g4 with h2-h3, then the time gained for ...h7-h6 may have been usefully spent.

Why not play 4...h6 straightaway? Because after 5 g4 ♗h7 White has the very strong move 6 e6!, paralysing the black kingside (as in Nunn-Bellon, Thessaloniki Olympiad 1984). Whereas after 4...♕d7 5 h3 h6 6 g4 ♗h7 the queen defends the e6 square.

4...♕c8 has similar intentions to ...♕d7 and may be the better move. It fulfills all the requirements of ...♕d7 while also leaving d7 for the knight and supporting ...c6-c5 in the case of an early break. And if Black moves the queen again it makes little difference whether it was on c8 or d7.

Finally, 4...h5 was popular for a while but after 5 ♗d3 ♗xd3 6 ♕xd3 e6 7 ♘f3, Black's position proved fragile in Nunn-Dlugy, London 1986, after 7...♘h6 (7...♕b6 8 0-0 ♕a6 9 ♕d1! maintained White's advantage in Short-Seirawan, Rotterdam 1989) 8 0-0 ♘f5 9 ♘e2 ♘d7 10 ♘g3! ♘h4 11 ♘xh4 ♕xh4 12 ♗e3 ♕d8 13 ♖fd1 and now Black forgot that his plan was to play solid for a draw and opened up the centre on his own king: 13...♖c8 14 b3 c5? 15 c4 cxd4 16 cxd5! ♘xe5 17 ♕xd4 ♕xd5? 18 ♕a4+ 1-0, since 18...♕c6 19 ♖ac1 wins the rook. If Black had tried 16...dxe3 17 fxe6 exf2+ 18 ♔f1 ♖d6 19 exf7+ ♔xf7 20 e6+ ♔g8 then 21 ♕d5! with too many threats.

5 ♘f3

5 ♗e3 h6 has been played several times, and then:

a) 6 h3 e6 7 g4 ♗h7 8 f4 ♗b4 9 ♘e2 ♘e7 10 a3 ♗xc3+ 11 ♘xc3 ♕c7 12 ♗d3 ♘d7 13 ♗xh7 ♖xh7 14 ♕d3 g6 15 ♗f2 ♖g7! (to meet ♗h4 with ...g6-g5) and Black was fine in Van der Wiel-Hort, Wijk aan Zee 1986.

b) Kotronias suggests, as usual, 6 ♗d3 ♗xd3 7 ♕xd3 e6 and then 8 ♘ge2 c5 9 dxc5 ♘a6 10 c6! ♕xc6 11 ♘d4 or 8...♘e7 9 0-0 ♘f5 10 ♘g3 with a slight advantage.

The whole of this chapter shows the worth for White of studying all the various Advance systems. Rather than continue with the plan of g2-g4 in all positions it is often best to play another variation – e.g. 4 ♗d3, 4 h4 or 4 ♘e2 – aiming to show that Black's alternative fourth move (after 4 ♘c3) was not the best in a particular system.
5...e6

6 ♘h4!? ♗g6 7 ♗e3 ♕c7 8 f4 a6

Kotronias gives this a dubious mark and writes, 'Black should not have allowed 9 f5 (thus 8...♘e7)'. However, after 8...♘e7 White can prepare f4-f5 with g2-g4, and as the knight on h4 keeps the h-file closed, White can answer ...h7-h5 with h2-h3; e.g. 9 ♕d2 ♘d7 10 0-0-0 0-0-0 11 g4 ♘b6 12 ♕f2 intending f4-f5. Blatny also suggested 6...♘e7 but a later g2-g4 and f2-f4 will reach a similar position. It would perhaps have been better to play 7...♗e7

and put the question to the knight.
9 f5!?

Again 9 g4 was possible.
9...♗xf5

Or 9...exf5 10 ♗d3.
10 ♘xf5 exf5 11 ♗d3 g6 12 g4!

By opening the kingside White gets excellent compensation for the pawn.

12...fxg4 13 ♕xg4 ♕d7 14 ♕f3 ♗h6 15 0-0-0 ♗xe3+ 16 ♕xe3 ♕e7 17 h4 ♘d7

If 17...h5 then 18 ♖dg1 and e5-e6, and if 18...♕e6 19 ♘e2 and ♘f4.
18 h5 gxh5?!

18...g5 was better, and if 19 h6 f6!
19 ♖xh5 0-0-0 20 ♗f5!

Intending 21 ♘a4 ♔b8 22 ♕g3.
20...b5 21 ♕g3 f6

White threatened ♕g3-g7, or if 21...♕f8 then 22 ♖f1 is strong.
22 ♖e1 ♕f7 23 ♗g4 fxe5 24 dxe5 ♕e7 25 ♘e2 ♔b7 26 ♘f4 ♘f8 27 ♘d3

After 27...♖e8 Black is still no nearer to developing his pieces, but now he blunders instead.
27...♘h6?? 28 ♖xh6 ♕g5+ 29 ♕f4 1-0

Summary

While none of Black's fourth moves in this chapter is quite as strong as 4...e6, they all are playable and do have psychological value. With 4 ♘c3 White intimates a desire for a sharp game, and by refraining from 4...e6 Black spoils the fun. Theoretically these variations are inferior if Black needs to win, but they are mostly good enough for a draw. And if White has to win then playing solidly as Black, and waiting for the opponent to overextend, can be an effective way of scoring points.

1 e4 c6 2 d4 d5 3 e5 ♗f5 4 ♘c3

4...♕b6 *(D)*
    4...a6 – *Game 62*
    4...♕d7 – *Game 63*
5 g4 *(D)*
    5 ♘a4 – *Game 59*
    5 ♗d3 – *Game 60*
    5 ♘f3 – *Game 61*
5...♗d7 *(D)* **6 ♗g2**
    6 ♘a4 – *Game 57*
6...e6 – *Game 58*

4...♕b6   *5 g4*   *5...♗d7*

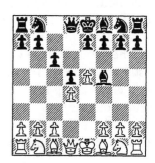

CHAPTER EIGHT

Fourth Move Alternatives for White

1 e4 c6 2 d4 d5 3 e5 ♗f5

Of the alternatives to 4 ♘c3 and 4 ♘f3 the most important is 4 h4. This sets the simple but useful trap of 4...e6?? 5 g4 ♗g6 6 h5 winning the bishop, which Black has to answer before developing the kingside with ...e7-e6. After 4...h6 White can continue with 5 g4 and if the bishop retreats to d7 White can prevent the further thrust ...h6-h5 by putting his own h-pawn on that square (Game 67); while if the light-squared bishop leaves the c8-h3 diagonal Black has to reckon with the disruptive e5-e6. So Black most often elects to prevent g2-g4 altogether by playing 4...h5, and then White gets on with the game hoping that the slight weaknesses created at h5 and g5 have improved his chances. The usual choice is 5 c4 (Games 64-66) aiming for a favourable version of the quieter 4 c4 (Game 68).

4 ♗d3 (Game 69) is not dangerous. In closed French positions Black will often go to extraordinary lengths to exchange the light-squared bishops.

Here White obligingly offers the exchange himself, and in the absence of any weaknesses Black should have no problems. Nevertheless, it is always possible to lose by playing badly.

> *Game 64*
> **Shirov-Lobron**
> *Munich 1993*

1 e4 c6 2 d4 d5 3 e5 ♗f5 4 h4 h5

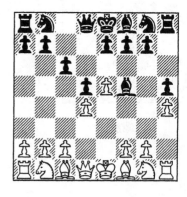

5 c4

The alternative 5 ♘e2 e6 6 ♘g3 ♗g6, transposing to 4 ♘e2 e6 5 ♘g3 ♗g6 6 h4 h5 (while avoiding 6...h6), is harmless. The main line is 7 ♗e2 c5! and Black has no problems; e.g. 8 ♗g5 ♗e7 9 ♗xe7 ♘xe7 10 c3 ♕b6 11 ♗xh5 ♕xb2 12 ♗xg6 ♘xg6 13 h5 ♕xa1 14 ♕b3 ♘e7 15 0-0 cxd4 and the queen gets out, Kovalev-Adams, Tilburg 1992. Or 8 ♗xh5 ♗xh5 9 ♘xh5 ♘c6 10 dxc5 ♘xe5 11 ♗g5 ♕a5+ 12 ♘d2 ♕xc5 and White was worse in Langner-Mikh.Tseitlin, Ostrava 1991, or 9...g6 10 ♗g5 ♗e7 11 ♗xe7 ♕xe7 12 ♘g3 ♖xh4. If 8 ♘xh5 ♗xh5 9 ♗xh5 g6 and ...♖xh4 and again Black is better. With the centre disintegrating White should forget about the h5-pawn and try to equalise; e.g. 8 c3 ♘c6 9 ♗e3 ♕b6 10 dxc5 ♕xb2 11 0-0 0-0-0 12 ♕b3 ♕xb3 13 axb3 a6 ½-½ Spassky-Dzindzichashvili, Tilburg 1978, or 8 dxc5! ♗xc5 9 ♘d2 ♘c6 10 ♘b3 ♗b6 11 ♗xh5 ♘xe5 12 ♗xg6 ♘xg6 13 ♗g5 ♕d6 14 ♕e2 ♕e5 15 ♕xe5 ♘xe5 with equality, as in Bronstein-Botvinnik, USSR 1966.

5...e6

The most accurate move, although others are sometimes seen:

a) 5...♗xb1?! 6 ♖xb1 ♕a5+? 7 ♗d2 ♕xa2? loses the queen after 8 ♖h3, and 6...e6 is too passive: 7 c5! (Vasiukov) shuts Black down completely; i.e. 7...b6 8 b4 a5 9 a3. Note that this is only possible because, thanks to 5...♗xb1 6 ♖xb1, the rooks are no longer in opposition on the a-file.

b) 5...dxc4 6 ♗xc4 e6 7 ♘c3 is also often seen, transposing to positions with a later ...d5xc4. By delaying the capture White is prevented from playing an early ♘e2-g3, attacking the bishop and the h-pawn (unless White is willing to sacrifice the c-pawn). If

Black delays too long White may suddenly throw in c4xd5 when the black pieces may not be on the correct squares.

6 ♘c3 dxc4

6...♘e7 is seen in the next game and 6...♗e7 in Game 66.

Against 6...♘d7 White can try 7 ♗g5 when Timman-Karpov, Linares 1992, went 7...f6?! (too soon) 8 exf6 gxf6 9 ♗e3 dxc4 10 ♗xc4 ♘b6 11 ♗e2 ♗g6 12 ♘h3 and Black's position was loose. Better is 7...♕b6 aiming for ...f7-f6 later.

7 ♗xc4 ♘d7 8 ♗g5 ♗e7

8...♘e7 transposes to 6...♘e7 7 ♗g5 dxc4 8 ♗xc4 ♘d7 (see the notes to the next game).

9 ♕d2 ♘b6 10 ♗b3 a5?!

This is a dubious continuation. A better way to play would have been 10...♕d7 11 ♘ge2 ♗b4 12 a3 ♗a5 13 ♗a2 ♘d5 14 b4 ♘xc3! 15 ♕xc3 ♗b6 16 ♕g3 ♘e7 17 0-0 ♘d5 and Black was fine in Blatny-Plachetka, Namestovo 1987.

11 a3 a4 12 ♗a2 ♗xg5 13 hxg5 ♘e7 14 ♘ge2 ♘ed5 15 ♘g3 ♗g6

If instead 15...♘xc3 16 ♘xf5 ♘xa2 17 ♘d6+ ♔f8 18 ♕f4 ♕d7 19 g6 f5 20 exf6! with a strong attack; e.g. 20...♘d5 21 fxg7+ ♔xg7 22 ♕e5+ ♔xg6 23 ♖h3 h4 24 ♕e4+ ♔g7 25 ♕g4+ ♔f8 and now instead of 26 ♖f3+ ♔e7 27 ♖f7+ ♔xd6 28 ♖xd7+ ♔xd7 29 ♖xa2 ♖ag8 with counterplay, Shirov prefers to attack by 26 ♘c4!

16 ♘ge4 ♘c8 17 g4?

White should have played 17 ♗xd5 cxd5 18 ♘c5 b6 19 ♘5xa4 (Shirov) when Black has insufficient compensation for the pawn, or if 18...b5 White has full control over the dark squares, with ideas such as ♘a2-b4, ♖ac1, ♕f4 or possibly e5-e6.

17...♘xc3 18 ♘xc3 ♔d7 19 0-0-0 ♔c7?

Black returns the favour. Black should have played 19...♘e7!, consolidating his position with a slight advantage to Black according to Shirov. 19...hxg4? loses to 20 d5! exd5 21 ♘xd5.

20 ♗b1 ♘e7 21 ♗xg6 fxg6 22 ♕c2 hxg4 23 ♖xh8 ♕xh8 24 ♘xa4 ♘d5 25 ♘c5 ♕e8 26 ♕e2 b6 27 ♘e4 ♕f7 28 ♕xg4 ♕f5?

It would have been more prudent to play 28...♖h8 and try to hold the endgame after 29 ♘d6 ♕f4+ 30 ♕xf4 ♘xf4 31 ♔d2 (Shirov).

29 ♕e2 ♖h8 30 ♘d6 ♕xg5+ 31 ♔b1 ♕h5 32 ♕c2 ♖a8 33 ♖c1 ♘e7 34 ♕b3 ♕g4 35 f3! ♕h3 36 ♕b4 ♕h4?

36...♘d5? loses to 37 ♘e8+, intending ♕d6, or if 36...♘c8 Shirov had intended 37 ♖c3 and ♖b3.

37 ♘c4 ♘c8 38 d5 c5

38...exd5 39 ♘xb6! ♕xb4 40 ♘xa8+ winning material.

39 ♘xb6 1-0

Game 65
Adams-Karpov
Tilburg 1996

1 e4 c6 2 d4 d5 3 e5 ♗f5 4 h4 h5 5 c4 e6 6 ♘c3 ♘e7

7 ♘ge2!?

White has not been able to prove any advantage with other moves; e.g. 7 ♗g5 dxc4 8 ♗xc4 ♘d7 9 ♘ge2 ♘b6 10 ♗b3 ♕d7 11 ♘g3 ♗g6 12 ♘ge4 ♗xe4 13 ♘xe4 ♘f5 14 0-0 ♗e7 15 ♘c5 ♗xc5 16 dxc5 ♕xd1 17 ♖fxd1 ♘d7 with the knight pair, Minasian-Meduna, Cappelle la Grande 1995.

7...dxc4

The critical reply, although Black could still play 7...♘d7 8 ♘g3 ♗g6.

8 ♘g3 ♗g6 9 ♗g5

White makes it a true gambit, since if 9 ♗xc4 ♘f5! and Black has solved all his problems.

9...♕b6 10 ♕d2 ♕b4 11 a3 ♕b3 12 ♖c1 ♘d5 13 ♘ce4 b5 14 ♗e2 ♘d7 15 0-0

If 15 ♖h3 Karpov intended to hide the queen at a2.

15...♘7b6 16 ♘c3

On 16 ♗d1 Karpov intended again

16...♕a2 and then 17 f4 ♗xe4 18 ♘xe4 b4 with counterplay.

16...b4 17 axb4 ♕xb4 18 f4 f5 19 exf6 gxf6 20 f5 ♗xf5

20...exf5 is met by 21 ♗xf6! (Karpov), since if 21...♘xf6 22 ♕g5 ♔f7 23 ♘xf5 ♗xf5 24 ♖xf5 and White piles up on f6.

21 ♘xf5 exf5 22 ♘xd5

Not 22 ♗xf6? ♘xf6 23 ♕g5 ♗e7! with a clear advantage to Black (Karpov).

22...♘xd5 23 ♖xc4 ♕xd2 24 ♗xd2 ♖b8 25 ♗c1 ♔d7 26 ♗d3 ♗h6 27 ♗xf5+

Adams finally regains his pawn, but Karpov holds the draw.

27...♔d6 28 ♖e1 ♘c7 29 ♖c2 ♗xc1 30 ♖exc1 ♖b6 31 ♗e4 ♘d5 32 ♖f2 ♖f8 33 ♗f3 ♖b4 34 ♖d1 f5 35 ♗xh5 ♖h8 36 ♖xf5 ♖xb2 37 ♖e1 a5 38 g3 a4 39 ♗f3 ♖g8 40 ♗xd5 ♖xg3+ 41 ♔f1 cxd5 42 ♖f6+ ♔d7 43 ♖f7+ ♔d8 44 ♖f8+ ♔d7 45 ♖f7+ ½-½

> *Game 66*
> **Gulko-Karpov**
> *Dos Hermanas 1994*

1 e4 c6 2 d4 d5 3 e5 ♗f5 4 h4 h5 5 c4 e6 6 ♘c3 ♗e7

An insolent idea: Black decides that it is White's h-pawn which is weak. If now 7 ♘f3 ♗g4 8 ♗e3 ♘h6 9 cxd5 cxd5 10 ♕b3 ♕d7 11 ♗d3 ♘f5 12 ♘h2 ♘xe3 13 fxe3 ♘c6 14 ♘xg4 hxg4 15 ♕d1 ♖xh4 16 ♖xh4 ♗xh4+ 17 ♔d2 ♕e7 18 ♕xg4 ♗g5 19 ♖f1 0-0-0 20 a3 f6 and Black was clearly better in Nunn-Miles, Amsterdam 1985. So White instead resolves the position in the centre while the e7-bishop is hampering Black's natural development.

7 cxd5 cxd5

7...exd5?! weakens the f5 square, and Blatny recommends 8 g3 ♘d7 9 ♗d3 with a slight advantage.

8 ♗d3

White has nothing much after 8 ♗g5 ♘c6 9 ♕d2 ♕b6 10 ♗b5; e.g. 10...♗b4 11 ♘ge2 ♘ge7 12 a3 ♗xc3 13 ♘xc3 0-0 14 ♖d1 ♗h7 15 ♗xe7 ♘xe7 16 ♗e2 f6! and Black had generated sufficient counterplay to draw in Malaniuk-Giorgadze, Simferopol 1988: 17 exf6 ♖xf6 18 ♗xh5 ♖af8 19 0-0 ♖h6 20 ♗g4 ♖xh4 21 ♕g5 ♘g6 22 ♘a4 ♕d6 23 g3 ♖h6 24 ♘c5 ♖f6 25 ♘xb7 ♕e7 26 ♘c5 ♘f4 27 ♕e5 ♗f5 28 f3 ♖hg6 ½-½. Black might also consider playing ...f7-f6 earlier, while the bishop is still on e7.

8...♗xd3 9 ♕xd3 ♘c6 10 ♘f3 ♘b4?!

An odd move for Karpov to make as it doesn't achieve anything. Instead 10...♘h6 is met by 11 ♗xh6! ♖xh6 12 g3 with the advantage since the black pieces are strangely placed. Blatny suggested the logical development 10...♗b4 intending ...♘e7-f5. In Yudasin-Rogers, Tilburg 1994, Black took this a stage further by 10...a6!, the idea being that 10...♗b4 is met by 11 0-0, whereas now if White wants to castle he has first to defend the h-pawn with g2-g3. If White prevents ...♗b4 with 11 a3 Black can come in on the light squares with 11...♘a5 and ...♘c4. The game continued 11 g3 ♗b4 12 0-0 ♘ge7 13 ♘e2 ♘f5 and now, having developed the kingside, the bishop was free to return to e7 with equality according to Yudasin.

11 ♕e2 ♖c8 12 0-0 ♘c6 13 g3 ♕d7 14 ♗d2

Preparing to meet 14...♗b4? by 15 ♘b5!

14...♘h6 15 ♗xh6 ♖xh6 16 ♖ac1 ♔f8

If 16...♖g6!? 17 a3 ♖g4 18 ♖fd1 g5 (Blatny) 19 hxg5 then Black has to contend with ♘c3-b5-d6 if or when he recaptures on g5.

17 ♘a4 ♖c7!

To answer 18 ♕b5? with 18...♘xe5!

18 ♖c3 ♖g6 19 ♖fc1 ♖g4 20 ♕d3 ♔g8 21 a3 f6 22 ♘c5 ♗xc5 23 ♖xc5 ♕f7! 24 b4 a6 25 ♕c3 ♖d7?

After finding imaginative counterplay, Karpov slips up by not carrying it through consistently. The threat to

the pinned knight could be ignored, and Gulko gives 25...♕g6! 26 a4 b6! 27 ♖xc6 ♖xc6 28 ♕xc6 ♖xg3+ with perpetual check. Instead White is given the time to make his breakthrough.

26 a4 ♘e7 27 ♘h2!

Now if 27...♖e4? 28 f3 ♖e2 29 ♕d3 ♖a2 30 ♖c8+ and wins (Gulko), so the black rook has to go away again and White then has a clear advantage.

27...♖g6 28 ♕d3 ♘f5 29 ♖c8+ ♔h7 30 ♔h1 ♘h6? 31 ♖1c2?

It would have been better to play 31 g4! intending 31...hxg4 32 h5, or if 31...f5 32 g5 and the rook is buried at g6 (Gulko). White is then completely winning.

31...♘f5 32 b5 axb5 33 axb5 ♕e7 34 ♖2c5 b6 35 ♖5c6 ♖a7 36 ♘f3 ♖a3 37 ♕d1 ♖g4? 38 exf6

White should have played 38 ♖6c7! and if 36...♕b4 39 exf6 ♕b2 40 ♘g5+ ♔g6 41 f7 ♕xf2 White has a pretty mate with 42 f8♘+ ♔h6 43 ♘f7 (Gulko).

38...♕xf6 39 ♘g5+ ♖xg5 40 hxg5 ♕xg5 41 ♖xe6 h4 42 ♖ee8 hxg3 43 ♖h8+ ♔g6 44 f4 ♘e3 45 ♖c6+ ♔f7 46 fxg5 ♘xd1 47 g6+ ♔e7 48 ♔g2 ♘e3+ 49 ♔xg3 ♘f5+ 50 ♔f4 ♘xd4

51 Ξxb6 ⚘e6+ 52 ⚔e5 Ξe3+ 53 ⚔xd5 Ξe1 54 Ξxe6+ 1-0

1 e4 c6 2 d4 d5 3 e5 ⚭f5 4 h4

It is appropriate to note here that 4 g4 does not offer any advantage; e.g. 4...⚭e4 (to block the d1-h5 diagonal) 5 f3 ⚭g6 6 h4 h5 7 e6 ⚖d6 8 exf7+ ⚭xf7 (Alekhine) or 7 ⚭d3 ⚭xd3 8 ⚖xd3 e6 and Black has no problems. Kochiev-Bahrah, St Petersburg 1995, saw instead 6 ⚘e2 e6 7 h4 ⚭b4+ 8 c3 ⚭e7 9 h5 ⚭h4+ 10 ⚔d2 ⚭g5+ 11 ⚔e1 ⚭h4+ 12 ⚔d2 ⚭g5+ 13 ⚔e1 ⚭h4+ ½-½; White outgraded his opponent in this game by 415 Elo points!

4...h6

4...c5?! 5 dxc5 is significantly worse for Black than 3...c5 since ...e7-e6 cannot be achieved easily because of the latent threat to the bishop; i.e. 5...⚘c6 6 ⚭b5 e6? 7 ⚭xc6+ bxc6 8 g4 wins.

4...⚖b6 has the same idea as after 4 ⚘c3, in that the bishop can still retreat down the h3-c8 diagonal, while Black has not (yet) weakened the kingside;

e.g. 5 g4 ⚭d7 6 h5 e6 and Black has gained a tempo by not playing ...h7-h6. If White plays slowly Black can play ...h7-h5 or ...h7-h6 after all.

5 g4 ⚭e4

5...⚭h7 6 e6 ⚖d6! 7 exf7+ ⚔xf7 is similar and will in fact transpose if White plays f2-f4.

Practice has shown White to have the better chances after 5...⚭d7 6 h5 c5 7 c3 e6 8 f4 ⚘c6 9 ⚘f3 ⚖b6. Essentially this is an Advance French with a kingside clamp thrown in for nothing. White now usually plays 10 ⚔f2! – it is not yet clear where to put the pieces, so White first 'castles' by hand; i.e. without moving the rook at all. Okhotnik-Berezhnoi, USSR 1981, continued 10...0-0-0 11 ⚔g3 ⚘ge7 12 a3 c4 13 ⚘bd2 ⚘a5 14 Ξb1 ⚘b3 15 ⚭xc4! ⚘xd2 16 ⚘xd2 dxc4 17 ⚘xc4 ⚖c7 18 ⚘d6+ ⚔b8 19 ⚘xf7 Ξg8 20 ⚘xd8 ⚖xd8 with a clear advantage to White. Adams-Khalifman, New York 1994, saw instead 10...cxd4 11 cxd4 ⚘ge7 12 ⚔g2 a5 13 ⚘c3 ⚘a7 14 ⚭d3 ⚘ec6 15 ⚭b1 and again Black struggled to find something to do while White slowly built up his position.

6 f3 ⚭h7 7 e6 ⚖d6 8 exf7+ ⚔xf7 9 ⚭d3?!

White has had better results with other moves; e.g. 9 ⚘e2 ⚘d7 10 ⚘bc3 e5 11 ⚭h3 Ξe8 12 ⚭e3 ⚘gf6 13 g5 exd4 14 ⚖xd4 ⚘e5 15 0-0-0 ⚘c4 16 ⚭d2 ⚖b4 17 ⚘xd5 ⚖a4 18 ⚘b4 ⚘xd2 19 Ξxd2 ⚭xb4 20 ⚘c3 ⚖a4 21 gxf6 gxf6 22 ⚖c4+ ⚔f8 23 ⚖f4 with a clear advantage to White in Gubanov-Orlov, St Petersburg 1995. Or 9 f4!? transposing to Romero-Magem, Spanish Team Championship 1995, which continued 9...♕e6+ 10 ♔d2 ♘f6 11 f5 ♕d6 12 ♕f3 ♕g3 13 ♗h3 ♕xh4 14 ♔e2 ♘bd7 15 ♗f4 ♘e4 16 ♘d2 ♘xd2 17 ♔xd2 ♕f6 18 ♘e2 g5 19 fxg6+ ♕xg6 20 ♕b3 ♘f6 21 ♖af1 ♗g7 22 ♘g3 ♖he8 23 ♘f5 ♗f8 24 ♕xb7 and again White was better.

9...e5!

According to Korchnoi Black already has an advantage.

10 ♗xh7 ♖xh7 11 dxe5 ♕xe5+ 12 ♘e2 ♘d7 13 ♘bc3 ♖e8 14 ♕d3 ♘gf6 15 h5

To give the queen the g6 square in the event of ...♘c5. If 15 ♗d2 ♘c5 White would have to play 16 ♕f5 ♕xf5 17 gxf5.

15...d4! 16 ♕c4+ ♖e6 17 ♘e4 ♘xe4 18 fxe4 ♔e8 19 0-0 g5!

Black prevents anything from coming to f4, and intends to attack with ...♗d6 and ...♕xe4.

20 ♖f5 ♕d6

20...♕xe4?! 21 ♘g3 ♕e1+ 22 ♔g2 is now not so clear.

21 ♕d3

If 21 ♕xd4? ♕xd4 22 ♘xd4 ♖xe4 and everything drops off.

21...♘c5 22 ♕f3 ♘xe4 23 b3 ♖d7 24 ♗b2 ♗g7 25 ♖d1 c5 26 b4 ♕b6

27 ♕b3 c4 28 ♕xc4 d3+ 29 ♔h2 ♗xb2 30 cxd3 ♘f6 31 ♘g3 ♗e5 32 ♖xe5 ♖xe5 33 d4 ♕e6 34 ♕c8+ ♖d8 35 ♕xd8+ ♔xd8 36 dxe5+ ♘d7 0-1

Game 68
Morozevich-Meduna
European Cup, Lubniewice 1994

1 e4 c6 2 d4 d5 3 e5 ♗f5 4 c4

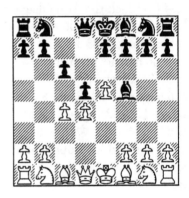

After ...d5xc4 the position will resemble a Queen's Gambit Accepted: 1 d4 d5 2 c4 dxc4 3 e4 ♘f6 4 e5 ♘d5 5 ♗xc4. With active piece play White hopes to exploit Black's dark-squared weaknesses, particularly d6, while the backward pawn on d4 is not easily attacked. However, despite the inclusion of...c7-c6, Black has gained time, since in the QGA Black is not ready to support a knight on d5 and has to move it back to b6. In this Caro-Kann the queen's knight can go to b6 and after...e7-e6 the king's knight will develop to e7 and d5 (or f5).

4...e6 5 ♘c3 ♘e7

Black often captures straightaway: 5...dxc4 6 ♗xc4 ♘d7 7 ♘ge2 ♘b6 8 ♗b3 ♘e7 9 0-0, and now the game Morozevich-Adianto, London Lloyds

Bank Masters 1994, continued 9...h5?!
10 ♗g5 h4 11 f3 ♕d7 12 ♕e1 ♘ed5 13
♖d1 ♗e7 14 ♗xe7 ♕xe7 15 ♕d2 0-0-0
16 ♘e4 and White was better. Moro-
zevich-Korchnoi, London PCA
(rapid) 1994, saw instead 9...♗g6 10
♘f4 ♕d7 11 ♗e3 ♘ed5 12 ♘fxd5
♘xd5 13 ♘xd5 exd5 14 f4 ♗f5 and
Black had no problems. White is not
yet ready to conduct the minority attack on the queenside, so Black has
plenty of time to prepare for it.

6 a3!?

Morozevich wants to play the
QGA position, so by threatening c4-
c5 he encourages Black to capture on
c4. If 6 c5 immediately then 6...b6! 7
b4 a5 and White cannot support his
pawn chain.

**6...dxc4 7 ♗xc4 ♘d5 8 ♘ge2 ♘d7 9
0-0 h5?!**

No QGA player would ever make
this move, but Black is clearly still
thinking in terms of a Caro-Kann.
9...♘7b6 10 ♗b3 ♕d7 would be more
logical, and if 11 ♘g3 ♗g6 12 f4 0-0-0.

10 ♘g3!? g6

If 10...♗g6 Morozevich intended to
advance f4-f5; i.e. 11 f4 h4 12 f5! hxg3
13 fxg6 or 11...♘e7 12 f5!? (anyway)
12...♘xf5 13 ♘xf5 ♗xf5 14 ♖xf5! exf5
15 ♕b3 ♕b6 16 ♗xf7+ ♔d8 17 ♗g5+
with an attack; e.g. 17...♗e7 18 ♗xe7+
♔xe7 19 ♕e6+ ♔d8 20 ♖d1 ♕xb2? 21
♕d6, intending e5-e6.

11 ♗e2 h4 12 ♘xf5 gxf5

Now the black king will be uncomfortable on either side of the board.

**13 ♗f3 ♗e7 14 ♕c2 ♘7b6 15 ♘e2
♕d7 16 ♗d2 0-0-0 17 b4 ♔b8 18
♖fb1? f6!**

And White realised he had put the

wrong rook on b1. If 19 a4 fxe5 20 a5
♘c8 21 dxe5 a6 then the rook is doing
nothing on a1, while after 19 exf6
Black gains time by hitting the rook
on the long diagonal.

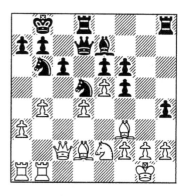

**19 exf6 ♗xf6 20 a4 e5 21 dxe5
♗xe5 22 ♖a2 h3 23 g3 f4 24 a5
♘c8 25 a6 b5?!**

Morozevich gives 25...fxg3 26 ♘xg3
b5 as better.

**26 gxf4! ♗f6 27 ♖c1 ♖he8 28 ♘g3
♘cb6 29 ♕xc6 ♕xc6 30 ♖xc6 ♘c4!**

Black has found some counterplay:
if 31 ♘e4? ♖xe4 32 ♗xe4 ♘c3 33 ♖xf6
♘xe4. So White sets a trap by prophylactically defending the back rank.

31 ♘f1! ♘xd2??

Losing a piece; instead 31...♗d4!
and then Black can take on d2 and b4.
Morozevich had planned 32 ♖h6!, intending ♖xh3 or ♖h7, with a slight
advantage.

**32 ♖xd2 ♖e1 33 ♗xd5 ♖d7 34 ♖d3
♗d4 35 ♖g3 1-0**

> ## Game 69
> ## Van der Werf-Khalifman
> *Wijk aan Zee 1995*

1 e4 c6 2 d4 d5 3 e5 ♗f5 4 ♗d3

♗xd3 5 ♕xd3 e6

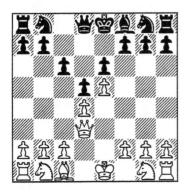

6 ♘e2

6 ♘c3 can be played first, and then Hellers-Ivanchuk, Biel 1989, continued 6...♘e7 7 ♘ge2 ♘d7 8 0-0 a6 9 ♘d1 c5 10 c3 ♖c8 11 ♘e3 h5 12 ♗d2 g6 and Black was fine.

6 ♘c3 ♕b6 has some importance as it can arise from 4 ♘c3 ♕b6 5 ♗d3 ♗xd3 6 ♕xd3 e6. The manoeuvre ...♕b6-a6 used to be regarded as a simple way to equalise for Black, but Kotronias believes that Black has played ...♕b6 too soon. After 7 ♘ge2 ♕a6 8 ♕h3 White will castle short and play a2-a4, deterring an early ...c6-c5 by enabling ♘c3-b5, and White can consider exchanging his own bad bishop with b2-b3 and ♗a3. Meanwhile the queen is not doing much on a6, and she also sets Black up for some tricks; e.g. 8...c5? 9 ♘xd5! exd5 10 ♕c8+ with a strong attack.

Instead of 7...♕a6, 7...c5?! 8 dxc5 ♗xc5 9 0-0 ♘e7 10 ♘a4 ♕c6 11 ♘xc5 ♕xc5 12 ♗e3 ♕c7 13 f4 ♘f5 was the well-known game, Nimzowitsch-Capablanca, New York 1927.

6...♕a5+ 7 ♘bc3 ♘e7 8 0-0 ♘d7

8...♕a6?! 9 ♕h3 ♘d7 10 a4! would

have transposed to Kotronias-Khalifman, Moscow 1987, when Black admitted his mistake by returning the queen with 10...♕b6.

9 a4 c5 10 ♗d2 ♕d8 11 ♗g5!?

If 11 ♘b5 ♘f5 12 c3 a6 13 ♘a3 the knight is misplaced.

11...a6 12 f4 g6 13 ♘g3 ♕c7 14 f5!? cxd4!

If 14...gxf5 15 ♗xe7 ♗xe7 16 ♘xf5 exf5 17 ♘xd5 ♕c6 18 ♘xe7 ♔xe7 19 d5 White has good compensation according to Khalifman.

15 fxe6 fxe6 16 ♕xd4

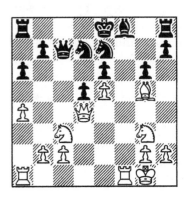

Or 16 ♘ce2 ♘xe5 17 ♕xd4 ♘f5! 18 ♘xf5 gxf5 (Khalifman) and the threat of ...♗c5 gives Black the necessary time to consolidate.

16...♕c5! 17 ♕xc5 ♘xc5 18 ♖f6?

White cannot force b2-b4 so this move is just a waste of time.

18...♘c6 19 ♗e3?! ♗e7 20 ♗xc5 ♗xc5+ 21 ♔h1 ♔e7 22 ♖af1 ♖hf8 23 ♖xf8 ♖xf8 24 ♖xf8 ♔xf8

And the e5-pawn drops off.

25 ♘ce2 ♘xe5 26 ♘f4 ♔e7 27 ♘ge2 ♘c4 28 b3 ♘e3 29 c3 ♔f6 30 h4 e5 31 ♘d3 ♗d6 32 ♔g1 e4 33 ♘df4 ♗xf4 34 ♘xf4 ♔e5 35 g3 ♘f5 36 ♘e2 d4 0-1

Summary

All White's fourth move alternatives have their adherents, and they are all certainly playable if White is willing to forgo an opening advantage. Apart from 4 ♘c3 and 4 ♘f3 which form the bulk of this book, 4 h4 is the only alternative system with any pedigree. The theoretical assessment is okay for Black, yet there is enough play in the position to make the game interesting. The fact that Karpov has lost more than once to 4 h4 shows that it cannot be such a simple matter for Black to draw.

1 e4 c6 2 d4 d5 3 e5 ♗f5

4 h4 *(D)*
> 4 c4 – *Game 68*
> 4 ♗d3 – *Game 69*

4...h5 *(D)*
> 4...h6 – *Game 67*

5 c4 e6 6 ♘c3 *(D)* **dxc4**
> 6...♘e7 – *Game 65*
> 6...♗e7 – *Game 66*

7 ♗xc4 – *Game 64*

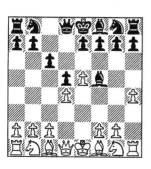

4 h4

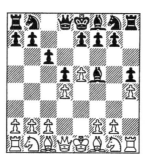

4...h5

6 ♘c3

CHAPTER NINE

Third Move Alternatives

1 e4 c6 2 d4 d5 3 e5

The lack of immediate conflict after 3 e5 allows for a great deal of choice and Black has tried virtually every non-suicidal third move; e.g. 3...a6, 3...b6, 3...e6, 3...f6 and 3...h5.

3...c5 is an important alternative to 3...♗f5. Previous books have without exception regarded it as dubious, reciting some old analysis by Boleslavsky. The point is that although Black usually assaults the pawn base with ...c6-c5 in the Advance variation, to do so immediately allows 4 dxc5 when Black is unready to recapture, not having yet played ...e7-e6. White can then make it very difficult (sometimes impossible) for Black to regain the pawn or, alternatively, can use it to accomplish the exchange of dark-squared bishops, aiming for a Classical French with full control of the d4 square; i.e. a typical good knight vs. bad bishop scenario.

Undeterred, GMs Khenkin, Arkell and L.B.Hansen, and IM S.Lalic have been scoring extremely well with this line for years. And now the big boys –

Karpov and Korchnoi included – are starting to take notice. The major benefit of 3...c5 – if Black can get away with it – is that then all White's alternative systems after 3...♗f5 become irrelevant and Black eliminates a lot of learning without having to indulge in illogical moves.

Apart from 3...♗f5 and 3...c5, the only two moves to be seen regularly are 3...g6 and 3...♘a6, and these are considered in Games 74 and 75.

Game 70
Galdunts-Arkell
Gelsenkirchen 1994

1 e4 c6 2 d4 d5 3 e5 c5 4 dxc5 ♘c6

Korchnoi has experimented with 4...e6 here – see Game 73.

5 ♗b5 e6 6 ♗e3

The offbeat 6 ♕g4 is discussed in Game 72.

6...♗d7

6...♘e7 is considered in the next game. Checking on a5 with the queen is almost always a bad idea in this variation and this position is no exception, e.g. 6...♕a5+?! 7 ♘c3 ♗d7 8 ♘f3 ♘ge7 9 a3 ♕c7 10 b4 ♘g6 11 ♗xc6 bxc6 12 ♗d4 f6? 13 exf6 gxf6 14 ♗xf6 and White was well on top in Kotronias-Chiburdanidze, Karditsa 1995.

7 ♗xc6 ♗xc6 8 ♘f3 ♘e7 9 c3 ♘f5 10 ♗d4 ♘xd4

The plan is to answer 11 cxd4?! with 11...b6!, when after 12 cxb6 ♕xb6 Black's queenside pressure and the two bishops provide excellent compensation for the pawn.

11 ♕xd4 a5 12 a4!?

If 12 b4 Almasi suggests 12...♕c7!?, aiming simply to develop while restraining the white pawns by keeping control of the a4 square. Instead Almasi-De la Villa Garcia, Pamplona 1997, ended abruptly with 12...axb4?! 13 cxb4 b6 14 cxb6 ♖a4 15 a3 ♗b5? 16 ♘fd2 ♕a8 17 ♘c3 ♖xb4 18 b7 1-0. On 15...♕a8 Almasi analyses 16 0-0 ♗xb4 17 ♘c3! ♖xa3 18 b7! ♕xb7 (not 18...♗xb7? 19 ♘b5) 19 ♖ab1 ♗xc3 20 ♖xb7 ♗xd4 21 ♖b8+ winning.

12...♕e7 13 b4 axb4 14 cxb4 b6 15 cxb6

In Chabanon-Arkell, French League 1995, White tried 15 b5!? bxc5 16 ♕b2 ♕b7 17 0-0 d4 18 ♘bd2 ♗e7 19 ♕b3 ♗d5 20 ♘c4 0-0 21 a5 ♖fb8 22 ♖fd1 and slowly advanced his connected pawns: 22...♗d8 23 ♘fd2 ♕e7 24 ♕g3 ♕d7 25 b6 ♕c6 26 ♕b3 ♗g5 27 ♕d3 h5 28 f3 ♗f4 29 ♘e4 h4 30 g3 hxg3 31 hxg3 ♗xc4 32 ♕xc4 ♗xe5 33 ♖b5 ♗d6 34 ♔g2 ♗e7 35 ♖c1 ♖d8 36 ♘xc5 d3 37 b7 ♖ab8 38 a6 d2 39 ♖d1 ♖d4 40 ♕xd4 ♕xb5 41 a7 ♕e2+ and now just as his pawns were ready to queen he blundered it all away: 42 ♕f2?? (42 ♔h3! wins) 42...♕xf2+ 43 ♔h3 ♗d6 0-1. Thus Keith Arkell gained his third and final GM norm.

15...♕xb4+ 16 ♘bd2

16...♖a6?

On 16...♗c5 Galdunts gives 17 ♕xb4 ♗xb4 18 ♔e2 ♔d7 19 ♖hb1 ♗a5 20 b7 ♖ab8 21 ♘b3 ♗b4 22 ♘bd4 ♖xb7 23 ♘xc6 ♔xc6 24 ♘d4+ ♔d7 25 ♖b3 ♖c8 26 ♖ab1 and White wins by advancing the a-pawn. However, 25...♖hb8 26 ♖ab1 ♖b6, intending 27....♗a5, is fine for Black.

17 ♖b1 ♕xd4 18 ♘xd4 ♗b7 19 0-0 ♗c5?!

This loses by force. It would have been better to play 19...♖xa4 20 ♘b5 ♗b4 21 ♖fc1! 0-0 22 ♘f3, intending

罝c7, ♘d6 forcing through the b-pawn (Galdunts).

20 ♘b5 ♚d7 21 ♘b3 ♗xb6 22 a5 ♗a7 23 ♘xa7 罝xa7 24 ♘c5+ ♚c7

25 罝b6?!

Galdunts slowly fritters his win away. He listed all his missed wins in *Informator 60*: 25 罝fc1! ♗c6 26 ♘xe6+ fxe6 27 罝b6 罝xa5 28 罝bxc6+ ♚b7 29 罝xe6 with a winning endgame.

25...罝c8 26 罝d6! ♗c6 27 罝c1 ♚b8 28 ♘xe6 罝xa5 29 ♘xg7 d4 30 ♘f5 罝xe5 31 ♘xd4 ♗b7 32 罝b1 罝g5 33 f3?!

33 罝d7 罝c7 34 ♘c6+ 罝xc6 35 罝bxb7 and with the rooks on the seventh White wins easily.

33...♚c7 34 罝f6 ♗d5 35 ♘b5+?

35 罝c1+ ♚d7 36 罝xc8 ♚xc8 37 罝h6 winning another pawn.

35...♚d7 36 h4 罝g6 37 罝f5 ♗e6 38 罝f4 罝c2 39 g4 罝d2 40 ♘c3 f5 41 罝b7+ ♚c8 42 罝a7 ♗d7 43 罝a2 ½-½

1 e4 c6 2 d4 d5 3 e5 c5 4 dxc5 ♘c6 5 ♗b5 e6 6 ♗e3 ♘e7 7 c3!

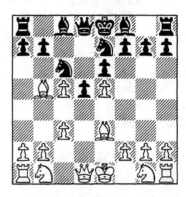

This both supports b2-b4 and protects d4 so that White can put the bishop there after 7...♘f5.

7 ♘f3 is inaccurate as 7...♘f5! 8 ♗d4 ♘xd4 9 ♕xd4 ♕a5+! 10 ♘c3 ♕xb5 11 ♘xb5 ♘xd4 12 ♘bxd4 ♗xc5 is a dead drawn position. In Shirov-Karpov, Monaco (rapid) 1996, Black went for more with 7...♗d7!? 8 0-0!? (8 ♗xc6 ♘xc6 9 c3 ♕c7 transposes below) 8...♘xe5 9 ♘xe5 ♗xb5 10 c4!? ♗c6 11 ♘c3 dxc4 12 ♕g4 ♘f5 13 罝ad1 ♕h4 14 ♕xh4 ♘xh4 15 ♘xc6 bxc6 16 罝d4 ♗e7 17 罝xc4 0-0 18 b4 a6 19 a4 ♘g6 20 b5 axb5 21 axb5 cxb5 22 ♘xb5 ♘e5 23 罝c2 罝fc8. Karpov eventually won the c5-pawn and then the endgame with his kingside pawn majority.

7...♗d7 8 ♗xc6

Xie Jun-S.Lalic, Erevan Women's Olympiad 1996, saw 8 ♘f3?! ♘xe5 9 ♘xe5 ♗xb5 10 ♘a3 ♗d7 11 ♕b3 ♘c6 12 ♘xd7 ♕xd7 13 0-0-0 ♗e7 with the desired structural advantage.

8...♘xc6

8...♗xc6 9 ♘f3 would transpose to 6...♗d7 (Game 70). The point of 8...♘xc6 is that the light-squared bishop is not now blocking the c-file, so after 9 ♘f3 ♛c7! 10 ♗d4 ♘xd4 White is prevented from recapturing with the queen since the c5-pawn is en prise.

The drawback is that, as opposed to after ...♘e7-f5, the lack of pressure on the ♗e3 allows White to support the centre with 9 f4!, e.g. 9...g5!? (9...♛c7, intending ...♘e7-f5 or ...♘b8-a6, is possible, e.g. 10 ♘f3 ♘a5 11 b4 ♘c4 12 ♗f2 b6!? 13 cxb6 axb6 when both White's a- and c-pawns are backward) 10 ♘f3 (10 fxg5! ♘xe5 11 ♘f3 makes more sense, e.g. 11...♛c7 12 ♘xe5 ♛xe5 13 ♛d4! ♛xd4 14 cxd4 b6!? 15 cxb6 axb6 16 0-0 and Black did not have enough for the pawn in Bosch-Van der Werf, Enschede 1996) 10...gxf4 11 ♗xf4 ♗xc5 12 ♘bd2 ♛b6 13 ♘b3 ♗f2+ 14 ♔e2 ♘a5 with unclear play, Ad.David-Khenkin, Geneva 1996.

9 ♘f3 ♛c7!

10 ♗d4 ♘xd4 11 cxd4

This is the point. 11 ♛xd4? would now be answered by 11...♗xc5.

11...b6! 12 cxb6 ♛xb6 13 ♛b3 ♛a6

Now White cannot castle, and Black's two bishops and queenside pressure offer good compensation for the pawn.

14 ♘c3 ♗e7 15 ♛c2 ♖b8 16 ♖b1 ♗b4 17 a3 ♗a4 18 ♛c1 ♗xc3+ 19 bxc3 0-0 20 ♔d2 ♛c4 21 ♖b4 ♖xb4 22 cxb4 ♛a2+ 23 ♔e3 f6 24 exf6 ♖xf6

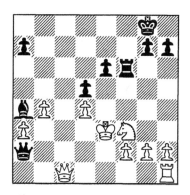

25 ♛c8+?! ♖f8 26 ♛c3 e5 27 dxe5 d4+ 28 ♛xd4 ♗b5 29 ♖e1 ♛b3+ 30 ♔d2 ♛a2+ 31 ♔e3 ♛xa3+ 32 ♔d2 ♛a2+ 33 ♔e3 ♛b3+ 34 ♔d2 ♛a2+ 35 ♔e3 ♛b3+

After making a few checks to approach the time control, Black plays the winning move.

36 ♔d2 ♖c8 37 ♖c1 ♛a2+ 38 ♔e3 ♖xc1 39 ♛d8+ ♔f7 40 e6+ ♛xe6+ 41 ♔d2 ♛c8

41...♛h6+ 42 ♘g5 ♔g6 was a simpler way to win.

42 ♘g5+ ♔g6 43 ♛d6+ ♔h5 44 g4+ ♛xg4 45 ♔xc1 ♛xg5+ 46 f4 ♛g1+ 47 ♔b2 ♛xh2+ 48 ♔a3 ♛g3+ 0-1

> *Game 72*
> ## Smirin-Khenkin
> *Ischia 1996*

1 e4 c6 2 d4 d5 3 e5 c5 4 dxc5 ♘c6 5 ♗b5

Since White has been struggling to

achieve an advantage after 5 ♗b5 e6 6 ♗e3, several other ideas have been tried recently. 5 ♗f4!? aims for the Advance French 4 dxc5 with the extra move ♗f4, but White has not demonstrated anything here either. The other way of defending the e5-pawn is 5 ♘f3 ♗g4 6 ♗b5 and possibly this maligned system deserves further investigation, since after 6...e6 7 ♗e3 Black has no other plan than 7...♕a5+ 8 ♘c3, and White can then continue with a2-a3 and b2-b4; e.g. 8...♘e7 9 a3 ♘f5 10 b4 ♕c7 11 ♗f4 or 8...a6 9 ♗xc6+ bxc6 10 a3 ♗xf3 11 gxf3 and 12 b4.

5...e6 6 ♕g4!?

Alternatively, if 6 ♗xc6+ bxc6 7 ♕g4!? then 7...♕a5+ 8 b4 ♕a4 9 c3 ♕c2 10 ♕f4 ♗a6 with good play on the light squares. In Lane-Arkell, London Lloyds Bank Masters 1993, White played 7 ♗e3 ♖b8 8 b3 ♘e7 9 ♗d4 ♘f5 10 c3 a5!? 11 ♘e2 ♗a6, but Black again had good play on the light squares. Black could also have won back his pawn immediately with 10...♕g5 11 g3 ♘xd4 12 cxd4 ♗xc5!

6 b4?! is premature: 6...♗d7 8 ♗xc6 ♗xc6 8 ♘f3 a5 9 c3 axb4 10 cxb4 b6! 11 0-0 bxc5 12 bxc5 ♗xc5 and Black has regained the pawn, maintaining a superior structure.

6...♕a5+

Alternatively, on 6...♗d7 7 ♗xc6 ♗xc6 8 ♘f3 h5 9 ♕f4 ♗xc5 Yudasin suggests 10 ♗e3! ♗xe3 11 ♕xe3; 10...♗e7 11 ♘bd2 intending ♘b3-d4 or 10...♕b6 11 ♗xc5 ♕xc5 12 ♘c3 with a slight advantage to White in all cases.

7 ♘c3 h5

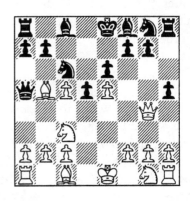

8 ♗xc6+!

Improving on Mark Tseitlin-Khenkin, Israel 1996: 8 ♕f4 ♗xc5 9 ♘f3 ♘e7 10 0-0 ♘g6 11 ♕g5 ♗d7 12 ♗d3 ♗e7 13 ♕e3 d4 14 ♘xd4 ♘cxe5 with a messy position. The immediate 8 ♕a4?! ♕xa4 9 ♘xa4 ♗d7! (intending ...♘xe5!) is good for Black.

8...bxc6 9 ♕a4 ♕c7

9...♕xc5 10 ♗e3 forces 10...♕c4 11 ♕xc4 dxc4 12 ♘e4 with a clear advantage.

10 ♗e3 ♖b8 11 0-0-0 ♘h6 12 f4 ♘f5 13 ♗f2 a5 14 ♘ge2

Not 14 a3?! ♗a6, intending ...♗b5.

14...♖b4 15 ♕a3 ♕a7 16 ♘a4 ♗a6 17 ♘d4 ♗b5 18 ♘b6 ♗xc5 19 ♘c8?

19 ♘xb5! ♕xb6 20 ♗xc5 ♕xc5 21 ♘c7+ and ♘a6 wins the exchange.

19...♕c7 20 ♘xf5 ♗xf2 21 ♘cd6+ ♔d7 22 ♘xb5 cxb5 23 ♕f3 ♕b6 24 ♔b1?

24 ♘xg7? ♖xf4! 25 ♕h3 ♕e3+ 26 ♕xe3 ♗xe3+ and 27...♖g4 traps the knight. So Greenfeld suggested 24 ♖hf1!, and then if 24...♗d4 25 ♘xd4 ♖xd4 26 f5 or 24...♗c5 25 ♘xg7 ♖xf4 26 ♕e2 ♖f2 27 ♖xf2 ♗xf2 28 ♔b1! with a clear advantage.

24...exf5 25 ♕xd5+ ♔c7 26 ♕xf7+

♔b8 27 e6 ♗d4 28 b3 ♕c6?

28...♗f6, intending ...♕c6-c3, was stronger.

29 ♕xf5 ♕c3 30 ♖xd4 ♖xd4 31 e7 ♖d2 32 ♕xb5+♔c7 33 ♖c1 ♕e3 34 ♕xa5+ ♔d7 35 ♕g5 ♖e8 36 ♕xh5 ♖xe7 37 g3

Consolidating his five pawns for a rook.

37...♕e2 38 ♕a5 ♖d1 39 ♖xd1+ ♕xd1+ 40 ♔b2 ♕d6 41 ♕b5+ ♔e6 42 ♕c4+ ♕d5 43 ♕c8+ ♔f7 44 ♕c3 ♖e4 45 a4 ♕d4 46 ♕xd4 ♖xd4 47 ♔c3 ♖d1 48 ♔b4 ♔e6 49 ♔c5 ♖d5+ 50 ♔b6 ♖d2 51 a5 ♔d7 52 b4 ♖xc2 53 a6 ♖c6+ 54 ♔b5 ♖c7 55 ♔b6 ♖c6+ ½-½

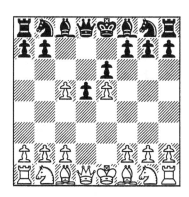

Game 73
Kindermann-Korchnoi
Ptuj Zonal 1995

1 e4 c6 2 d4 d5 3 e5 c5 4 dxc5 e6!?

This is 1 e4 e6 2 d4 d5 3 e5 c5 4 dxc5!? with White to play. Basically Black is saying that this version of the Advance French is unattractive even with an extra move.

5 ♗e3!

Boleslavsky's move, after which he analysed 5...♘e7 6 c3 ♘f5 7 ♗d4 to a clear advantage to White – which tells us only that 5...♘e7 is not very good. Against other moves (5 ♘f3 or 5 ♗d3) Guliev favours 5...♘d7, intending to recapture on c5 with the knight, rather than debate the question as to whether White can make constructive use of the extra tempo after 5...♗xc5 or 5...♘c6.

5...♘d7! 6 ♗b5

White wants the bishop on f8 to make the capture on c5 so that he can exchange and reach a more favourable French position.

6...♕c7 7 ♘f3 ♗xc5 8 ♗xc5 ♕xc5 9 ♘c3

9...♘e7 10 0-0

The strategically desirable 10 ♕d4 ♕xd4 11 ♘xd4 is too slow; i.e. 11...♘g6! 12 ♘f3 ♔e7 13 ♗xd7 ♗xd7 and White is nowhere near ready to exploit the bad bishop.

10...a6

Lutz-Campora, Biel 1996, saw 10...0-0 11 ♖e1 ♘g6 12 ♗d3 a6 13 ♘g5! ♕e7 (13...♘cxe5? loses to 14 ♖xe5! ♘xe5 15 ♗xh7+ etc.) 14 ♕h5 h6 15 ♘h3 d4 16 ♘d1 ♕c5 17 f4 with a slight advantage to White.

11 ♗d3 h6 12 ♖e1 ♘c6 13 ♕d2 g5

Just as White is threatening to consolidate, Korchnoi finds some improbable counterplay.

14 h3 ♖g8 15 a3

To prevent 15...g4 16 hxg4 ♕b4! So Korchnoi goes round another way.

15...♕f8! 16 g4 h5 17 ♕e3 ♕h6 18 ♗f1 hxg4 19 hxg4 b6 20 ♗g2 ♗b7 21 ♘a4 ♖h8 22 ♘xb6 ♘cxe5! 23 ♘xd7

23 ♘xa8?? loses to 23...d4! intending 24...♘xf3+ 25 ♗xf3 ♕h1+ etc.

23...♘xd7 24 ♖ad1 ♖c8 25 ♕a7 ♖c7 26 ♖d3

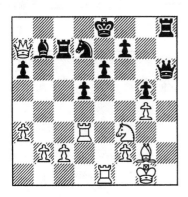

And now in mutual time trouble the players agreed a draw.

½-½

Or did they? Actually, at this point Korchnoi castled his king into safety (26...0-0) and the players continued to blitz out their moves as if nothing out of the ordinary had happened. Both flags fell at move 47 and it was only then when the arbiter tried to reconstruct the game with the help of a computer that they discovered the mistake. Korchnoi's 26...0-0 was illegal as he had already moved his rook! In such a case the rules require that the players restart from the position in which the illegal move occurred, with the clock set back to the times at that point, and here with Korchnoi obliged to move his king. But the players could not face the prospect of negotiating another time scramble, so they retrospectively agreed a draw!

Game 74
Murshed-Sollars
London Lloyds Bank 1988

1 e4 c6 2 d4 d5 3 e5 g6

Black tries for a type of Gurgenidze system. The normal move order is 1 e4 c6 2 d4 d5 3 ♘c3 g6 and then if 4 f4 ♗g7 5 e5 h5; Black clamps down on the kingside light squares, and follows up with ...♘h6, ...♗g4, ...e7-e6 and ...c6-c5. White has a space advantage, but Black's position is difficult to break down.

4 c4!?

A troublesome move. The point is that Black would normally answer c2-c4 with ...e7-e6, ...♘e7, ...d5xc4 and ...♘d5, but to continue in this fashion given the inclusion of ...g7-g6 would weaken the dark squares, especially with a white knight coming to e4.

4 h4!? is another approach. White threatens h4-h5, so Black stops this with 4...h5. Now both players should be happy: Black generally wants to play ...h7-h5 anyway. White, on the other hand, no longer has to fear ...f7-f6 as this would leave the black kingside hanging; therefore, with no need to play f2-f4, White can use f4 and g5 for pieces, and if necessary can contest the light squares with f2-f3 and g2-g4. Beshukov-Vlad.Sergeev, Berlin 1995, continued 5 ♘h3 ♗xh3?! 6 ♖xh3 e6 7 ♗g5 ♗e7 8 ♕d2 ♘d7 9 ♕f4 ♕a5+ 10 ♘d2 ♖h7 11 0-0-0 ♗xg5 12 hxg5 ♘f8 13 ♔b1 ♘e7 14 f3 ♕c7 15 g4 hxg4 16 ♖xh7 ♘xh7 17 fxg4 ♘c8 18 ♗d3 ♕e7 19 ♘f3 ♘b6 20 ♖h1 ♘f8 21 ♕f6 ♘bd7 22 ♕g7 a6 23 ♕g8 c5? (Black should have castled) 24 ♖h7 (threatening 25 ♗xg6) 24...0-0-0 (too late) 25 ♖xf7 ♕e8 26 ♕g7 c4 27 ♗e2 c3 28 ♖e7 1-0.

4...♗e6

ECO recommends 4 c4 on the basis of 4...♗g7 5 ♘c3, transposing to Hort-Cardoso, Las Palmas 1975: 1 d4 g6 2 c4 c6 3 ♘c3 ♗g7 4 e4 d5 5 e5 dxc4 6 ♗xc4 ♘h6 7 h3 ♘f5 8 ♘f3 b5 9 ♗b3 h5 10 ♘e4 ♘a6 11 ♘eg5 e6 12 a4 b4 13 ♘e4 ♕a5 14 ♗g5 c5 15 ♘f6+ ♔f8 16 d5 ♗h6 17 ♗xh6+ ♖xh6 18 0-0 ♕d8 19 ♕c1 ♔g7 20 ♖d1 ♕e7 21 d6 ♕d8 22 ♘g5 ♗d7 23 ♗c2 ♖h8 24 ♗xf5 gxf5 25 h4 ♗c6 26 ♖d3 ♖h6 27 ♖g3 ♖g6 28 ♘xe6+! fxe6 29 ♖xg6+ 1-0. In the Advance Caro-Kann there is no need to put the bishop on g7 just yet as White has already volunteered e4-e5. Murshed-Sollars actually started 1 d4 c6 2 e4 g6 3 c4 d5 4 e5.

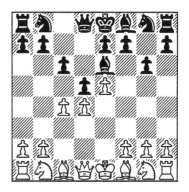

5 cxd5 ♗xd5 6 ♘c3 ♗e6?!

It would have been better to leave the bishop to his fate as now Black goes rapidly backwards.

7 ♘f3 ♘h6 8 ♘g5 ♗g4 9 f3 ♗c8 10 ♗c4 ♗g7 11 ♗f4 ♘d7?!

After 11...0-0 12 ♕d2 White would have had a ready-made attack, and of course Black did not want to play 11...e6 creating lots of holes, but what else can he do? If left alone White may throw in e5-e6 himself at some point.

12 ♗xf7+!

12 e6 also looks good; 12...♘b6 13 exf7+ ♔f8 14 ♗e6 or 12...♘f6 13 exf7+ ♔f8 14 ♕b3 threatening ♕xb7.

12...♘xf7 13 ♘e6 ♕b6 14 ♘xg7+ ♔f8 15 ♘e6+ ♔e8?!

Or 15...⌾g8 16 ♕e2 with an enormous position.

16 ♕e2?!

The last two moves are marked dubious only because 16 ♘a4! ♕b4+ 17 ♗d2 ♕c4 18 ♘c7+ ⌾d8 19 b3 ♕d3 20 ♘b2 ♕f5 21 g4 would have won the queen.

16...♘b8 17 ♘c5 a5 18 0-0 ♘a6 19 e6 ♘d8 20 ♕e5 ♖g8 21 ♘3e4 ♘xc5 22 ♘xc5 ♕b4 23 ♖ad1 ♕c4 24 ♘d7 ♖a6

If 24...♗xd7 25 exd7+ ⌾xd7 26 d5, or 24...♕xe6 25 ♘b6 ♖a6 26 ♘xc8 ♕xc8 27 ♖fe1 with a winning attack in both cases.

25 ♕c7 ♕xe6 26 ♘c5 ♕f5 27 g4 ♕c2

Or 27...♕f7 28 ♕xc8 ♕xf4 29 ♘xb7 wins the knight.

28 ♕xc8 ♖b6 29 ♖fe1 ♖xb2 30 ♕d7+ 1-0

> ## Game 75
> ## Vajda-Mikh.Tseitlin
> ### *Budapest 1996*

1 e4 c6 2 d4 d5 3 e5 ♘a6

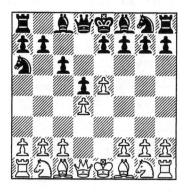

Kotronias gives this a dubious mark and asks 'what is the idea?' I think the idea is to play a non-committal move (or not very committal anyway) and wait to see what White does next. Black, on the other hand, might now do anything: play ...♗f5 after all, or wait for ♘f3 and play ...♗g4, or play ...g7-g6, or even ...e7-e6.

3...♕b6!? has a similar purpose. 4 ♘c3 can be met either by 4...♗f5, transposing to a normal line, or more interestingly by 4...e6!? (which is 1 e4 e6 2 d4 d5 3 ♘c3 ♘f6 4 e5 ♘g8!? with the extra moves ...c7-c6 and ...♕b6 for Black), while on 4 ♘f3 Black again plays 4...♗g4.

Against both moves White can choose a Short set-up with ♘f3 and ♗e2, hoping to show that ...♕b6 and ...♘a6 are not the best. So perhaps Black should select opponents with care. If White wants to play a Short system anyway then it may not be a good idea to offer these favourable versions. But if White is aiming for one of the sharp systems (e.g. 3...♗f5 4 ♘c3 e6 5 g4) then a move such as 3...♘a6 may be a little perturbing.

4 c3

Kotronias suggests 4 ♘d2 ♕b6 5 c3 (intending b2-b4) 5...c5 6 dxc5 ♘xc5 7 ♘b3 ♘xb3 8 axb3 'and White is clearly better'. Or if 5...♗f5 6 b4 e6 7 a3! (Black threatened 7...♗xb4 8 cxb4 ♘xb4) 7...♘c7 (threatening ...a7-a5) 8 ♘b3 and Black's pieces are completely misplaced. So Black should try 4...♗f5 instead and not worry about 5 ♗xa6 bxa6.

4...♗f5

No-one has ever taken the knight on a6 so it seems there is no need to move it just yet. Tseitlin has also played both ...♘a6 and ...♕b6 together: 4...♕b6 5 f4 ♗f5 6 ♗d3 ♗xd3 7 ♕xd3 e6 8 a3 c5 9 ♘f3 ♘h6 10 ♘bd2 cxd4 11 cxd4 ♖c8 12 0-0 ♗e7 13 ♘b3 0-0 14 ♗d2 ♘b8! 15 ♖ac1 a6 with equality in Schotten-Tseitlin, Crailsheim 1996. For White 5 ♘d2! is better, transposing to the previous note.

5 ♘f3 e6 6 ♗e2 ♘e7 7 ♘h4 ♗e4!? 8 ♘d2 ♘f5! 9 ♘xe4

9 ♘xf5 would have eased the cramp in Black's position. Tseitlin suggests calmly returning the knight to f3.

9...♘xh4 10 ♗g5 ♘xg2+! 11 ♔f1 ♕b6 12 ♘c5

If 12 ♘d6+ ♗xd6 13 exd6 h6! (Tseitlin) or 12 ♘g3 h6! similarly. So White should have played 12 ♔xg2 dxe4 13 ♕c2.

12...h6 13 ♗xa6 hxg5?!

13...♗xc5 14 ♗d3 ♗f8! was stronger, and if 15 ♕h5? hxg5! 16 ♕xh8 ♘f4 17 ♖d1 ♕xb2 (Tseitlin) intending 18...♘xd3 19 ♖xd3 ♕b1+ and wins.

14 ♗xb7

14...♘f4!

Not 14...♗xc5? 15 ♕b3 ♖b8 16 ♕xb6 ♗xb6 17 ♗xc6+ ♔e7 18 ♔xg2

with a clear advantage (Tseitlin).

15 ♗xa8 ♗xc5 16 ♕b3?!

Tseitlin gives 16 dxc5 ♕b5+ 17 ♔e1 ♖h3 18 ♗c6 ♕c6 19 ♕b3 f6 20 ef6 d4 'winning', or 17 ♔g1 ♖h4 'with a clear advantage'. Although that is hardly conclusive analysis Black does have a strong attack; e.g. 17 ♔e1 ♖h3 18 ♕c2 ♘d3+ 19 ♔f1 ♖f3 20 ♔g1 g4 intending ...♘f4-h3+; or 17 ♔g1 ♖h4 18 h3 ♘e2+ 19 ♔h2 ♘f4 20 ♔g3 ♕a6 intending ...♕c8xa8, and meanwhile it is not obvious how White gets out of the bind.

16...♕a6+ 17 c4 dxc4

Or 17...♗xd4 18 ♕b8+ ♔d7 19 ♕d6+ ♔c8 20 ♕xc6+ ♕xc6 21 ♗xc6 ♗xb2 22 ♖b1 ♗e5; while 18 ♖d1 ♗xe5 19 ♗b7 ♕xc4+ 20 ♕xc4 dxc4 21 ♗xc6+ ♔e7 transposes to the game.

18 ♕b7

18 ♕b8+? ♔d7 19 ♕xh8 allows 19...c3+ 20 ♔g1 cxb2 21 ♖b1 ♕d3 winning either the rook or the king, probably both in fact.

18...♕xb7 19 ♗xb7 ♗xd4 20 ♗xc6+ ♔e7 21 ♖d1 ♗xe5 22 ♗b5 ♖b8 23 ♗xc4 ♖xb2

Black has two pawns and a monstrous knight for the useless rook on h1.

24 h3 ♗d4!

Using the back rank weakness to improve the position of his pieces even more.

25 ♖h2 f5 26 ♗b3 e5 27 ♖c1 ♔d6 28 ♗c2 e4 29 a4 ♔e5 30 ♔e1 ♗c3+ 31 ♔d1 ♖b4 32 ♗b1 ♔d4 33 f3 ♘d5 34 fxe4 ♘e3+ 35 ♔e2 ♖b2+ 36 ♗c2 ♘xc2 37 ♔f3 ♘e1+ 38 ♖xe1 ♖xh2 39 ♖d1+ ♖d2 0-1

Summary

The theoretical verdict on 3...c5 is not yet clear. In the 4 dxc5 ♘c6 5 ♗b5 e6 6 ♗e3 main line White has more-or-less whittled the defences down to 6...♘e7 7 c3 ♗d7 8 ♗xc6 ♘xc6!, but in this Black is fighting with all the ferocity of a cornered rat. Without substantial improvements in this line White may have to forgo material ambitions altogether and aim merely for a favourable French.

None of the other third move alternatives can be regarded as 'best'. Nevertheless, there is a lot of scope for experiment, and in these days of endless theory, presenting the opponent with unusual and unexpected problems early in the opening does have something to be said for it.

1 e4 c6 2 d4 d5 3 e5

3...c5
>   3...g6 – *Game 74*
>   3...♘a6 – *Game 75*
4 dxc5 *(D)* ♘c6
>   4...e6 – *Game 73*
5 ♗b5 e6 *(D)* 6 ♗e3
>   6 ♕g4 – *Game 72*
6...♗d7 *(D)*
>   6...♘e7 – *Game 71*
7 ♗xc6 – *Game 70*

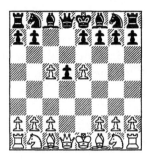

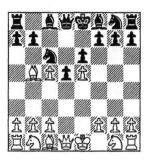

4 dxc5   *5...e6*   *6...♗d7*

INDEX OF GAMES

CPSIA information can be obtained
at www.ICGtesting.com
Printed in the USA
BVHW042307270221
600953BV00004B/49